MW01225180

COTTAGE COVE

A Chechako in Alaska

by

Royal LaPlante

Black Forest Press
San Diego, California
May, 1998

First Edition

COTTAGE COVE

A Chechako in Alaska

by

Royal LaPlante

PUBLISHED IN THE UNITED STATES OF AMERICA

BY

BLACK FOREST PRESS

539 TELEGRAPH CANYON ROAD

BOX 521

CHULA VISTA, CA 91910

Cover Design by Raul Espinoza

Printed in the United States of America
Library of Congress
Cataloging-in-Publication

ISBN: 1-881116-92-1

ACKNOWLEDGEMENTS

The author acknowledges the inestimable contribution of his wife, Joanne LaPlante, for editing and preparing the manuscript of *Cottage Cove, A Checkako in Alaska.* Back-up editing and story suggestions by his mother, Margaret LaPlante, were critical in developing this novel.

Special thanks were earned by Robert Corfman in graphics works, Mary Inbody for editing the final draft, and Keith Pearson and Dahk Knox of Black Forest Press for their excellent advice and assistance in shaping this published book.

I owe a debt of gratitude to Captain Warren Larson, retired towboat skipper from Tacoma, whose appearance in this story, as a genuine historical figure, is permitted. Many of his tales are incorporated into the plot, including his prize-winning entry *"Nightmare Deluxe"*, which took honors as a tall tale in the 1952 Seattle Towboaters' contest.

PROLOGUE

The silvery-bearded old man squatted awkwardly at his net spread over the small purse seiner's deck, carefully arranging its folds for the next sweep. A dark wool stocking cap was perched atop his curly tangle of equally gray hair, age not diminishing its thick mat. His light blue eyes were in sharp contrast to swarthy Russian features, aged by the years and weathered by the rugged Alaskan terrain. As he came erect to stretch his tired muscles, yet did he remain stooped and twisted, a deformity of the spine his companion from birth.

Gregori Zohkov's gaze took in the ethereal beauty of his adopted home, in his mind a heaven on earth. He spotted a tug and barge sailing toward him and called to his friend Tsimchuck in their private version of Chinook, a cross between Tsimshian and English. Though both spoke the tribal dialect fluently, their partnership of forty years had created a bond transcending the spoken word. However, their form of pidgin shorthand was useful and required no further enumeration. His hand waved indifferently in the direction of the visitors as he wondered what they were doing so close to Duke Island.

His Indian partner was more direct in contemplating the noisy intruders, muttering vindictives at the white men aboard the vessels approaching Ray Anchorage, a scant mile beyond the inlet where his line of cork buoys bobbed in the tug's wake. The seine stretched across a familiar channel where the salmon ran every summer.

Whereas Gregori was obviously old, Tsimchuck appeared ancient in comparison, wrinkles dominating his face, neck, hands and even the forearms exposed to view below rolled up red flannel sleeves. His greasy hair was plastered to his broad skull, grayness hidden by the oily mixture which protected his head from the sun and wind. Bushy eyebrows all but hid his lively dark eyes which studied the world about him with an air of concern for his people and their island home.

The Tsimshians had followed Father William Duncan to Annette Island in 1887, the same year that Tsimchuck, an eleven–year old boy, had rowed with his father and brothers in a great war canoe from Canada across the wide waters to their new village at Metlakatla. He had passed this very spot forty years before anyone lived here and wondered anew what had happened to the Tlingit halfbreed who had built a cabin on the cove for his Tsimshian bride. After she died in childbirth, the lonely widower had became a recluse, disappearing when the white man's draft board came looking for soldiers to fight in the great war.

The old Indian knew all about the war against the Japs because his grandson had been a true Tsimshian hero at Okinawa, a story the grandfather relished telling whenever the occasion arose. Of all ten children and twenty-eight grandchildren, Malcolm Angias was his favorite, love and pride mutually shared in their consanguine relationship.

Spitting out an unearned epithet at the men on the tug disappearing around Duchess Island, the gnarled old Indian began collecting the seine and its catch of king salmon, declaring an end to their fishing trip. They would not stay in the cabin tonight after all, wanting no part of the white men anchored in the cove.

It seemed the white man's incursion into the Tsimshian domain was steadily increasing since the end of the great war, those sailors on the boat being a disturbance to the quiet life of the Indian fishermen. His friend Gregori was not a white man in his mind, since Ivan Zohkov had been born in Sitka when the Russians ruled there. Because the Tsar sold out his Alaskan countrymen, the father had left Sitka to find work, Gregori being born in Seattle. As a young man he ventured north to his father's old home and later moved to Metlakatla to live with the hospitable tribe where people accepted him as a person — not an ugly freak. His partner often thought Gregori avoided rejection by remaining a lifelong bachelor and by adopting the personality of a hermit.

When the sound of distant engines disappeared and a primal still settled over the fishing boat, Tsimchuck and Gregori expressed mixed feelings with almost identical gloomy smiles, happy with the return of solitude but cognizant of its temporal nature. Performing rote tasks as the purse seiner headed home, both men's thoughts turned to the cabin by the cove and the hope it would welcome them on their next trip.

Chapter One

The tall young man stood alertly at the wheel of the powerful tugboat, glorying in the feel of control as he steered a firm course toward Seymour Narrows and its ever-dangerous navigational hazard known as Ripple Rock. White puffy clouds skittered across the otherwise clear blue skies, an occasional shadow deepening the verdant green color of the forests ashore or dimming the sheen of brilliant whitecaps ruffling the narrowing channel. Such a panorama of frontier beauty had become the hallmark of Canada's western isles as the *MacDonald* plied north through the inland passage toward Ketchikan.

Bill was standing his third watch as quartermaster since the ship had sailed from Dupont on Friday morning. The *MacDonald* was towing a huge barge shaped like a coastal steamer or, more simply, like a large wooden canoe, the trailing vessel laden with two hundred tons of dynamite and munitions bound for the port of Valdez and eventually Fort Richardson or Fort Wainright.

'I wonder if those crates on our barge's deck are really grenades, like that longshoreman told me,' his smile broadened to a grin at such barracks gossip. He had learned to take whispered confidences with a grain of salt while serving in the Marines, but never entirely discounted such stories. In silent conclusion he mentally shrugged his shoulders, *'Oh heck, it's just another cargo at the end of a long steel cable.'*

π   π   π

Peering into the bright seas before him creased his tanned face into wrinkles around steady blue eyes, his brown hair bleached light by the July sun. Bill's glance moved to the compass automatically, and he slowly rotated the wheel counterclockwise three spokes. As the bow swung to port just a notch, he spun the wheel to its original position and checked the *MacDonald's* compass reading.

"Steady as she goes," he muttered under his breath, remembering to look over his right shoulder at their trailing barge before relaxing.

"Well done, Slim," came the skipper's deep voice from over his other shoulder. "You're getting the hang of this job, aren't you? Isn't it better than working as an oiler or a cook's helper?"

"Ha! Ha! You bet, Captain Hairston. Give me fresh air and sunshine anytime," the new deckhand replied, quite happy to be topside after two trips below deck.

"Hrmph!" grunted the burly second mate, ever-ready to grumble at his deckhand on watch. The three men were of equal height and yet quite different in appearance, the skipper was athletically built with rugged good looks and curly dark hair flecked with gray, while Jack Anderson was thick and muscular with a jowly face covered by a five o'clock shadow and topped by thinning hair. Bill had a lanky basketballer's frame with long legs, thus nicknamed Slim by his friends aboard ship.

The mate brushed Bill aside with his broad hip as he ordered, "I'm taking the wheel, Slim. We're coming to Ripple Rock and a tricky bit of navigating." He changed course and rang the engine room for more power.

Twin Fairbanks-Morse diesel engines responded immediately with the shuddering force of fifteen hundred horsepower, wheelhouse windows rattling as the tugboat surged forward. The shortened tow cable snapped clear of the sea momentarily as the barge's inertia changed, slowly settling under the surface as the tandem rushed into Seymour Narrows.

"Look ahead, Slim," Elmer Hairston gestured toward the narrows. "The flood tide has almost reached its peak. We're running through that gut while the currents around Ripple Rock are relatively quiet. That's why we circled in the bay just as you came on watch. We had to kill an hour or so to pass through here at the right time."

Bill nodded in appreciation for the skipper's explanation, wondering why Jack never took time to teach him anything.

Scanning the open water ahead, the young man asked, 'Where is Ripple Rock, Captain?"

Pointing to roiling eddies off the port bow, Elmer answered, "See those ripples on the west side of the narrows? Well, Ripple Rock is well-named, and now it's lying six or eight feet below the surface, just about right to tear the bottom out of our barge if it's allowed to wander over there. As a matter of fact, several ships have suffered such a fate over the years. I always come through here on the daylight tide. You know, an ebb tide is much worse because the rock is above water and currents even more treacherous."

Captain Hairston inspected the *MacDonald's* course and its barge's movement for several moments before relaxing, praising the mate, "Steady as she goes, Jack. You're right on course."

To Bill he ordered, "Go below and tell the cook to bring us coffee. It'll be a quarter of an hour before this proud old towboat is clear of Seymour Narrows."

ᴨ ᴨ ᴨ

As the tug's bow slapped into the quartering seas of Millbanke Sound, white salty foam sprayed over Bill's head as high as the wheelhouse. A groan escaped his lips as he looked up at the brine-covered windows, and he muttered in mock alarm, "I'll be washing windows on tomorrow's watch!"

Soon the *MacDonald* sailed alee of a large island, calmer seas allowing Bill to stand on the deck with hands in pockets and ruminate on his good fortune in finding this job.

Three months ago he had been a carefree junior at the College of Puget Sound in Tacoma when the Bursar sent him a bill for almost a hundred dollars. His G.I. Bill benefits had run out, which was a shock though not a surprise. His heavy load of mathematics and science classes made finding a job before summer break impractical.

'Well', he thought with some pride, *'I've paid off my debt to the college and my folks, got the old Buick fixed and settled my fraternity account. I'm solvent again and can save for fall tuition.'*

The familiar sound of a country school bell tolled clearly, reminding Bill of the evening poker game. No one knew where the cook had found the hand bell, but everybody on the crew recognized its call. Of the fourteen men sailing together this summer, only the second engineer skipped the daily event.

The new oiler hadn't considered the effect of comradeship when he sat in his first game. With eighteen dollars to his name and feeling a need to make friends with his shipmates, he joined in the fun, hoping to last a couple of hours. His conservative betting was accompanied by a run of good luck, which proved to be a winning combination. By the time they returned to Tacoma on that first trip, Bill was over eighty dollars ahead and a popular crew member.

Laughing silently at the memory of a conversation which he overheard as the *MacDonald* crossed Commencement Bay to berth at Baker Dock, he recalled his bruised pride when the chief engineer described him as a lousy oiler and suggested the Captain replace him on the next voyage. It was small consolation to hear both men agreeing that he was a "good guy" as they drifted out of earshot discussing his future on the *MacDonald*.

Bill was greatly relieved when the cook asked him to be his helper on the next trip north. The older man slapped him on the back good-naturedly, parroting the officers' comment, "You're a 'good guy,' Slim. The skipper suggested you take over for Tony while he's on vacation."

Nodding gratefully in acceptance, Bill had to use his poker face to cover that wounded pride when the cook inadvertently spouted, "We can't let you leave the ship with our money, can we? You know, being cook's helper is easier for a newcomer than working in the engine room."

A cryptic smile creased his countenance once again as he thought of his new status as deckhand. *'Was I promoted or couldn't the crew stand my cooking? Heck, feeding everyone pork chops in the middle of the gulf storm was a typical cook's joke. I got seasick, too. Well, at least the skipper has a sense of humor - I got another chance.'*

An impatient hand rang the school bell again, and Bill hurried to the mess cabin, knowing his friends were waiting for him.

ᵀᵀ ᵀᵀ ᵀᵀ

Awakening as a hand rocked his shoulder, Bill muttered, "Okay!" and rolled out of his bunk in the forecastle. Still dressed in a plaid wool shirt and denim trousers, he slid on his waterproof boots, not sure whether he would be sent on deck or not. He wished Jack would talk to him more often - like the captain did with his deckhand.

Bill stepped into the wheelhouse and moved to one side, feeling his way along the side of the cabin, his eyes slow to adjust to the green-tinged darkness, a combination of radar and compass lights illuminating the bridge. Discordant electronic noises echoed from the radio, the sheer mountains surrounding them blocking regular radio traffic.

Peering through the salt-stained glass, he saw only blackness until finally a thinly disparate, deep blue V notch appeared dead ahead, the waterway assuming the appearance of a giant trough in the mountains. As he watched the skyline, a subtle glow of light appeared behind the V five miles ahead, as if mother nature were slowly turning on a rheostat switch. He knew they were in Grenville Channel, and he surmised another ship was up ahead.

The captain confirmed his unspoken guess, telling the mate, "Jack, the helm is yours. That light should be the *Princess Louise* cruising south if I heard the radio correctly - the static is terrible."

As Bill relieved the deckhand going off watch, the skipper suggested, "You'd better watch the radar closely as we pass the *Princess*. This channel narrows to four hundred yards pretty soon, and while these cliffs are sheer to the bottom, there are plenty of rocky outcroppings near shore. Call me when the *Princess* is in sight."

The two men on watch shared a silent vigil for several minutes, the glow ahead soon becoming the mass of individual lights characteristic of a passenger liner.

The mate struck the bulkhead sharply with his hand and shouted, "Elmer! The *Princess* is less than a mile ahead."

Captain Hairston appeared immediately, observing the situation without comment.

The cruise ship was running along the east side of the channel at fifteen knots or so, and at a distance of several hundred yards her steam horn sounded authoritatively.

Jack breathed a sigh of relief as he returned the signal and announced, "A starboard to starboard pass makes sense. There's a fine Canadian officer on the bridge. Hold her steady, Slim."

The skipper explained the applicable rule of navigation to the new deckhand, "Port to port passing is normal at sea. Good seamanship requires signaling your intentions whenever two ships are in close quarters, and passenger ships have priority. Well, good night gentlemen, I'm turning in."

After a few moments the mate moved Bill aside in his usual brusque manner, ordering, "Slim, I have the wheel. Go aft and check our barge and tow line, and bring some coffee back with you."

The deckhand hustled to the stern, first looking over their perennial shadow with its distinctive running lights and then inspecting the steel cable and dogged-down winch. Everything was shipshape, so he proceeded to the galley for coffee, carrying two cups up to the wheelhouse. Wordlessly he relieved the mate at the wheel.

Checking the radar routinely, the mate ordered slight course changes to accommodate their position in the channel, maintaining a distance of one hundred yards from the western shore. As Grenville Channel narrowed, even greater darkness closed about them, and the eastern mountainside appeared very close in the reflection of the *MacDonald's* running lights.

Bill asked nervously, "How close is the other side? I can almost see the shoreline."

"Ha! Ha! Kind of eerie, isn't it? I guess we're about three hundred yards away, but don't worry. There's no wind or tide to speak of," the mate replied in seemingly good humor, actually humming to himself off and on during the ensuing hour.

π π π

A gentle glow once again emerged, creating the familiar V in the distance. Soon a craggy mass on the eastern shore was outlined. Bill and the mate exchanging knowing glances at the phenomenon.

Jack muttered the obvious, "Must be a ship coming south behind that point of land ahead."

Abruptly the concentrated beam of a powerful spotlight flashed over the dark tor, playing along the shoreline on both sides of the channel. As its source came into view, a tugboat's running lights appeared from the shadows, followed seconds later by those of its trailing barge.

"Steady as she goes, Slim. That tug should pass on our starboard, just like the *Princess Louise*. The channel is narrow here, but there's plenty of room for both of us."

As the oncoming vessel approached to within a mile, her spotlight jumped as if in alarm, its rays reaching out to the *MacDonald*. A subtle shift in the tug's running lights indicated a change in her course.

"Holy mackerel! Has that skipper just spotted us? What's he doing, anyway?" the mate cried anxiously.

The oncoming tug's horn split the night shrilly, a sense of urgency accompanying its strident tones as Bill recognized the signal for port to port passing.

Jack shouted a hurried order, "Hard astarboard, Slim!" and responded with a blast of the horn acknowledging the southbound ship's signal.

The *MacDonald* heeled sharply in the water, closing inexorably with the other tug as the *Mac* turned toward the eastern wall of granite. Looking aft, the mate muttered in distress, "Oh my God! Our barge is right on our stern. It's likely to run right past us into the other tug."

Bill cringed in confusion, asking, "The wheel's hard astarboard, Jack. What do I do?"

The mate moaned but acted, ordering, "Hard aport, Slim. We're in an outhouse of trouble. Bring her back to our old course," and then promptly sounded the horn for a starboard to starboard pass. He rang the engine room for more power and whomped the bulkhead with his clenched fist.

"Elmer! Emergency in the wheelhouse," he yelled in alarm.

To Bill he directed, "Keep her steady, or we'll be on the rocks."

The young deckhand gulped and watched with dread as the hapless tugboat crossed before the *MacDonald*, lights from both ships illuminating the name atop her wheelhouse, *Amanda Jackson*. As his adrenaline took hold, Bill queried the mate in an unnaturally mild voice, "What do we do, Jack?"

Leaping into the wheelhouse with a bang and grasping the problem instantly, Captain Hairston barked an answer to his question, "Hard aport!" and rang full astern.

In the seconds that the thundering splash of twin screws took control of the *Mac's* momentum, the luckless green and white tug came under the lifting bow of the *MacDonald*. The *Amanda Jackson's* captain was in plain sight as he fought her wheel, attempting a one-hundred-eighty degree turn in the confinement of Grenville Channel. The *MacDonald's* horn sounded intermittently in warning to both crews as the *Mac's* bow struck the Jackson with a knifing thrust just astern of the wheelhouse. In spite of the warning and his clear view of the impending collision, Bill was slammed against the wheel with bruising force.

The skipper reversed engines to slow ahead even before the *MacDonald* broke free of her victim, a massive hole in her super-structure reaching well below the waterline and seawater flowing into her engine room.

"Jack, take the wheel! Bring us alongside the *Amanda Jackson*. Slim, get to the first mate and tell him to start rescue operations," the skipper ordered.

Even as the words left his lips, the listing tug's engine died and her lights went out. Over the void between the closing ships came that dreaded seaman's cry, "All hands on deck! Prepare to abandon ship!"

Captain Hairston leaned out the starboard window and shouted, "We're coming alongside, Jerry. Get your crew aboard the *MacDonald* now, your ship's going down by the stern."

"Right, Elmer! All hands abandon ship! Hurry men, let's move before our bottom falls out," came the captain's reply.

Meanwhile Bill had joined his crewmates at the starboard rail and quickly offered his hand to a scrambling old Scandinavian leaving his ship unceremoniously.

"Thanks, Sonny! Now help me with my partner. He's got a banged up leg."

Together they lifted a half-dressed and bedraggled young sailor over the rail, all three men pausing to watch as the *Amanda Jackson* slid stern first below the surface, doomed to a six hundred foot grave at the bottom of the Grenville Channel.

One of the survivors yelled in astonishment, "Look! The barges have collided. By golly, the *Amanda Jackson's* tow cable is still attached, and her dead weight is pulling the barge down."

Another voice added in awe, "Look at the hole in our steel barge. It must be two feet wide, and that wooden barge is hardly scratched."

Captain Jerry Ross was counting his survivors for the third time, finally calling out, "We're missing a man. . .my God, where's the cook? Has anyone seen Daniel Huggins?"

Crew members exchanged looks, all shaking their heads in the negative, Jerry finally looking up to the wheelhouse and asking, "Can you see anyone in the water, Elmer? Daniel's one-legged and may have been caught below deck."

The *MacDonald's* searchlight played along the listing steel barge, then over the water where the *Amanda Jackson* had been and finally along the shoreline a scant seventy yards away.

"We'll search the channel as soon as I put a couple of men on our barge. I see a crack in the bow at her waterline. We'll need to get her pump working. Do you want to look over your barge, Jerry? What are you carrying?"

The *Jackson's* skipper shook his head sadly, "No, she's filled with gold concentrate and is obviously done for. Being well–lighted she's not a navigational hazard. Can you leave your barge to search for Dan?"

"Yes, but it's loaded with high explosives and does represent a potential danger to shipping. What say we search for an hour or until your barge sinks and then consider our options," Captain Hairston observed, adding nervously, "I need to get my tow into a safe berth for repairs."

π   π   π

A gray dawn was brushing the overcast sky as Bill spoke to the limping seaman who was walking beside him along the port deck searching the rocks ashore, "Do those shoes fit, Dave?"

"Yes, thanks. Your sweater is warm, too. I'll return them as soon as we hit port."

"Nah, they're yours to keep. I'm glad you feel okay."

Dave grabbed his new friend's arm, pointing his finger over the bow,

"Look, Bill! Our barge is going down. Wow! That's over one-hundred thousand dollars in gold going to the bottom."

The *MacDonald's* searchlight swung over to the munitions barge, the chief engineer and first mate standing at her rail with hands on hips. As the *Mac* eased alongside the now drifting barge, Bill could hear the sounds of a gas-driven pump and splashing water.

"Slim!" Jack Anderson yelled to get his attention and then ordered, "Go aft and help the first mate secure our tow."

Bill ran along the port deck, two survivors stepping aside to clear a path for him. Grabbing a pair of leather-palmed gloves from the winch mounting, the deckhand grasped the rough and heavy cable to straighten a loop, his hands feeling the barbs of broken steel threads as they snagged the leather. The crew's other two deckhands joined him, Ray at his side lifting the cable, and a gloveless big Harry taking the steel coupling across the rail to the mate. Ray grunted as the two men carried the steel cable across the deck and over the rail, giving the mate slack enough to fasten the barge to its tug.

Bill's playful chuckle brought a quick response from the old man as Ray groaned, "This cable must weigh at least three or four pounds a foot, and we're holding up sixty or seventy feet of it."

With a grin and a nod the younger man agreed, giving one last heave to put the cable into the bracketed steel roller. As the mate ordered, "All clear," Bill released the cable and stepped back, but Ray remained in place, hunched over his gloved hand caught by a pocket of frayed steel wires. The *Mac* moved slowly up channel, and the cable shifted under its own weight.

"Look out, Ray!" Bill shouted anxiously as the tow cable snapped taut, the old seaman's glove sliding over the roller as he belatedly jumped clear, his right hand scant inches from being entrapped.

"Damn!" muttered the fortunate sailor, showing his crewmate a lacerated palm as he stated calmly, "That one barb went right through the leather."

Inspecting the bleeding cut briefly, Bill suggested, "You'd better have the cook clean and bandage it, Ray. I'll handle the tow work."

The older seaman chuckled, pain mixed with humor at his own fate, "Heh! Heh! I guess it's light duty for me on the rest of this trip. You and Harry will have to handle the heavy work."

π   π   π

A long swell rolled under the keel, upsetting Bill's tenuous seat against the bulkhead and dumping him on the deck beside the tow winch. Looking up at his laughing partner, he grinned unabashedly as he struggled to his feet.

"Hmm! Must have dozed off," he muttered as he stretched his tired muscles, asking groggily, "Harry, where are we anyway?"

The amused deckhand replied, "We're in Dixon Entrance and picking up a Pacific swell. The skipper called down to let out another hundred feet of tow cable. Are you awake enough to handle the winch?"

"Sure! You check the cable as I release it," Bill said, and as he moved to the controls, he asked, "Are we out of Canadian waters yet?"

"Not for another half hour, Slim. The skipper radioed the U.S. Coast Guard in Ketchikan as soon as we cleared Grenville Channel, reporting the sinking of the *Amanda Jackson* with Daniel Huggins missing. Captain Ross is still shaken and mourning the loss of his cook as well as his boat."

Bill thought for several moments as he released cable slowly, finally dogging the winch before asking, "Ross isn't unhappy with our search, is he? That fellow was nowhere to be seen, either by searchlight or by daylight."

"No, all his crewmates figured he was trapped below deck when the tug sank. And there's no blame being discussed by either crew. Those *Jackson* guys are a good bunch. I wouldn't mind sailing with them."

Feeling his stomach rumbling, Bill asked, "Can you watch our tow while I get a bite?"

At a nod from Harry, the young seaman headed forward to enter the crowded mess, taking a seat offered by Swede and helping himself to hot rolls and coffee.

Swede braced his backside against the cabin wall beside Bill and commented tongue-in-cheek, "Dave was bushed and headed for the nearest bunk. I hope you aren't planning to turn in since that bunk is yours."

"Ha! Ha! No, more power to him. Harry and I have the duty until our barge is in a safe haven. Captain Hairston is pulling into the first protected spot in U.S. waters to make necessary repairs. Actually she's trailing us without any visible problem."

"Well, I sure am glad all that dynamite didn't blow, or we'd all be at the bottom of the Grenville Channel...or splattered on the mountainside," Swede remarked, asking, "Say, didn't we just pass Dundas Island?

Nodding with his mouth full, Bill swallowed twice before replying, "Yes, we'll cross the international boundary line anytime now. I'd better get back to work."

ᴨ   ᴨ   ᴨ

Bill lounged beside the capstan at the bow, no longer needing to brace himself as the *MacDonald* plied the calmer waters of Revillagigedo Channel. He had been eyeing Duke Island off their port side for the better part of an hour, and the distance had closed enough to make out a fishing boat and two figures tending their nets near a small offshore islet. '*I wonder where they live, I can't see any cabins on the shore.'* Unknowingly he muttered his next thought, "Real wilderness - but beautiful this summer day."

From overhead came the skipper's jovial chuckle, followed by a comradely endorsement, "You're a hundred percent correct, Slim. But try sailing this channel in the winter, and you'll have a different view - still beautiful in a stark and stormy way."

Slim glanced up to meet Captain Hairston's eyes as he stood at the wheelhouse window, his grin still in place. The young man posed a question which had been on his mind for some time, "Does anyone live on these islands? Who owns all this land and timber?"

"Indians mainly, and an occasional hermit or homesteader. They're the only year–round residents until we reach Ketchikan about fifty miles north. I hear there's a salmon cannery in Boca de Quadra Inlet up thataway," Elmer pointed northeast, adding, "It's a busy place this time of year, but dead in the winter."

The skipper looked over his shoulder at the barge, his face sober when he turned back to order Bill, "Slim, tell Jack to shorten our towline to fifty feet and prepare to go alongside. We're going into Ray Anchorage for repairs."

At Bill's puzzled frown Captain Hairston's lips twitched, and he enumerated with good humor, "About three miles off our port bow behind Duke Point. Now move out, Slim."

Relaying the order to the first mate resting in the mess brought the *Jackson's* crew members on deck to view the action, the veteran seamen instinctively staying clear of the work area as Harry winched in the cable, engine bells sounding as the *MacDonald* slowed perceptibly, her barge closing under a taut line.

Ten minutes later the tow cable was snubbed to the stern, and hawsers were run out to secure the barge alongside the tug. The coupling was released and pulled aboard the stern deck as the *MacDonald* resumed the course around Duke Point.

Glancing at his wristwatch, Bill confirmed that it was past noon and gladly hurried to the bridge and his afternoon watch. Jack had just relieved Ray at the wheel and was firmly entrenched, grasping its spokes tightly as he muttered gruffly, "I'll take her into the anchorage, Slim. Shouldn't you be helping Harry?"

Disappointment mixed with irritation to cloud Bill's features, the mate's rudeness not unusual, but the loss of a good view of Duke Island a likely blow to his active curiosity.

"We're shipshape below, Jack. Harry won't need help until we drop anchor," he replied quickly.

"Better keep Slim with you for an extra pair of eyes, Jack. I'm going to make the rounds before we anchor," Captain Hairston said, bringing an expected smile to Bill's face.

Observing the open water before the *MacDonald* from first one side of the wheelhouse and then the other, Bill stole several looks at the navigational chart, seeing their destination written in bold letters and noting a long inlet stretching westward from the anchorage. Pointing to the gap in the shoreline, he asked Jack, "Are we going into Morse Cove?"

"No, it's much too shallow for the *MacDonald*. We'll moor in Cottage Cove - over there," he answered curtly, frowning as he pointed casually to the south side of the snug harbor.

At that moment Elmer returned to add with a friendly smile, "You asked for a house, Slim, and there it is. Cottage Cove is aptly named. Now go below and help Harry with our anchor, we still have a full day's work before us."

ᵾ   ᵾ   ᵾ

A sudden quiet fell over Cottage Cove as the *Mac's* engines were stilled, the skipper's voice resounding eerily off the nearby shore. Before leaving the capstan, Bill studied the cottage, a simple one-room clapboard shack whose sides had been bleached white by sun, wind and rain. It sat snugly ten feet above the high tide mark, a small meadow of three or four acres between the cabin and the forest, dissected by a rill of fresh water flowing from the hill to the south. Sitka spruce was his first thought, quickly followed by another, fresh water in the summertime. What a beautiful spot - one in a million.

Hearing his name called from the barge, Bill scurried over the rail onto its deck. The skipper was all business as he spoke to the full crew, "I talked to the owners this morning and told them we're fit to cross the Gulf of Alaska as long as the good weather holds. We'll drop off the *Amanda Jackson's* crew in Ketchikan and pick up our San Francisco lawyer on Tuesday. In the meantime we have two tasks, caulking the crack behind the bowstem and raising the barge's prow by at least a foot."

A puzzled mumble in the ranks interrupted Captain Hairston's spiel, but he smiled, a bit grimly perhaps, and explained further, "We have twenty tons of dynamite in the forward hold over the split. I figure if we shift part of that cargo twenty feet aft, the hole will be above water. Now, the first mate and the engineers will take care of the patchwork, and everyone else will help the second mate move the dynamite. Jack, can you explain what is to be done?"

"Yes, sir! We will shift a thousand wooden crates of dynamite to the back of that hold. It's a confined space where only six of you men can work, so I excused Cookie and Ray. Is there anyone else who can't handle a fifty-pound crate?"

Harry laughed nervously, speaking for all six seamen, "A fifty-pound crate is easy, Jack, but what if someone drops one?"

Jack's seldom seen humor came forth, "Ha! Ha! You won't have to move the rest of the crates, my friend."

The skipper shook his head in consternation at the pitiful joke, finally joining the apprehensive giggles of the crew in adding, "Don't! I say don't find out the hard way. Dynamite can take a lot of jostling without exploding. Be careful, and you can enjoy your day's wages. The insurance company has authorized eight hours overtime today. You all get regular overtime, Sunday pay and explosives handling rates, which figures out to a bonus of a couple of hundred dollars each. I'll add a night in your own bunk and a day off tomorrow for fishing. Now let's get to work."

After wrestling several boxes from one pile to another in the restricted storage space, Bill concluded the emergency lighting was sufficient. *'Who wants to see what he's doing?'* he laughed to himself, literally tossing a crate to the cook's helper atop the stack. He glanced about to find everyone being as casual with the dynamite although their actions were deliberate and careful, too. *'Quite a scene,'* he thought, *'Something to tell my grandchildren.'*

Harry stumbled on the planked decking, his crate falling into Bill's lap as the younger man hit the deck, absorbing its shock unceremoniously. The two men grinned at each other in fatigue, saying, "Thanks" simultaneously.

When most of the forward stacks had been moved, Jack went topside to view the bowstem. The completed patchwork was well above the waterline, good news which he quickly shared with his companions, "Guys, it's working. Another hour and we can tie this dynamite down."

As the last pile of crates was dwindling, Harry called out a pseudo-complaint in bantering tones, "Hey, Jack! We've only moved seven hundred cases of dynamite. Where are the others you promised?"

Everyone in the hold laughed good–naturedly, relieved that the end was in sight. Casually, Harry tripped over the last row of wooden crates, appearing momentarily to be clowning, but six pairs of eyes looked on in horror as his crate flew through the narrow space, striking the bulkhead with a crash. The men cringed for what seemed an eternity, a silent prayer on each man's lips. Harry muttered, "God, what...?" as he rushed to the fractured crate and gently lifted it to view. A one by four slat was splintered, and each man caught a glimpse of its contents, sticks of dynamite packed in sawdust.

"Easy does it, men. You all tote the rest of the crates aft while Harry and I put this one back together," Jack stated in a shaking voice.

It was a very sober crew which returned topside after finishing the task, exhausted by the tension as much as the physical exertion. Bill found a spot at the *Mac's* bow to meditate on the day's events, enjoying the setting sun while counting his blessings, too drained to crave a meal and his bunk. He knew they were needed, but time remained at a standstill as the last rays of sunlight left his contemplative face.

TT   TT   TT

Fishing line wrapped around his left hand, Bill leaned over the rail and thought about the shimmering reflection of Cottage Cove on the gently undulating surface of the water. *'It's amazing,'* he thought in his reverie, *'that the sea can be a mirror today and probably seem like a washboard tomorrow. Maybe that's why all we can catch our bottom fish.'*

Harry had been fishing beside him for over an hour and was muttering under his breath, the vindictives escaping his lips marking him as a serious fisherman. He had talked all morning of working in a nearby cannery in forty-seven and on a commercial boat the following summer. Having so stated his expertise to all who would listen, he was determined to nab a king salmon, disdaining the lingcod Ray had brought in and the halibut Bill had landed. He dangled his bait at twenty feet while the other two deckhands mooched the bottom a hundred feet deeper.

Suddenly Harry's hand-held line slid through his fingers, both hands needed to slow the running fish.

"I've got a good one," came an exuberant shout as he pulled his line up hand over hand.

"Ha! Ha! Some king you have there, Harry. Ha! Ha!" Ray guffawed loudly as his friend's catch came into sight - a sizable dogfish on his hook.

Muffling his own laughter as Harry's face turned a bright pink, Bill gazed instead at the white clapboard cottage ashore, wondering anew who had built it and why anyone would leave such a lovely site. He ignored the ribald argument raging next to him and visualized in his mind a boat ramp near the mouth of the stream. "I bet a fellow could make a living in this place," he muttered aloud.

"Winters are a might wet and cold, Bill," came Dave's voice from behind him, adding, "But lots of veterans are settling up here. Didn't you tell me you served in the Marines during the war?"

Turning his head, Bill smiled as he retorted, "That's right, my friend. Was I dreaming out loud or talking in my sleep?"

"Ha! Ha! No, I overheard you this morning at breakfast saying you were a G. I. Bill student. I can't figure out what a college graduate sees in this desolate place."

"Well, Dave, I have the same concern. I've been offered an insurance actuary's job because I'm a math major, and an oil company wants to talk to me when I get my degree. But next summer I may try commercial fishing even with my B. A. in hand," Bill mused with more than a half serious tone.

Dave shook his head and said, "If I had a degree I'd take one of your soft jobs. In the meantime, how about letting me fish for awhile. Your poker buddies are waiting for you."

π   π   π

Their quiet sojourn in Ray Anchorage was interrupted as they got underway Tuesday morning. First an oil tanker heading north kicked up waves just as the *MacDonald* separated from her barge and let out the towline, and then a small fishing boat hailed the *Mac*.

"Ahoy, Elmer! Do you need any assistance? I heard your call on Sunday," shouted the skipper of the seiner as they paralleled the tug's course.

"No thanks, Ralph, we're headed into Ketchikan under our own power. However, your old buddy Harry wants to trade a halibut for a salmon. Didn't you teach him properly when he was on your boat?"

"Ha! Ha! Hi there, Harry. Still can't catch a salmon, eh?" came his former captain's joshing reply.

An abashed grin covered the quartermaster's face as he waved back from the wheelhouse, knowing no explanation would let him off the hook. The two captains would have their fun at his expense as they traded news and fish.

They soon parted as the fishing boat cast off and moved clear of the tugboat's trailing barge, the *MacDonald* following the distant tanker to Ketchikan.

ᴛᴛ   ᴛᴛ   ᴛᴛ

Bill bid good-by to Dave and Swede at the mess table before the skipper eased the *MacDonald* and her barge into the pier. He had worked the lines, securing the two craft side-by-side as they lay in Tongass Narrows off the port of Ketchikan. Now he climbed to the wheelhouse to stand watch with Jack while Captain Hairston reported to the U.S. Coast Guard Office.

After polishing brass and rubbing a bright sheen into the varnished wood surfaces, the seaman tackled the windows - washing glass always a tedious chore. At one point the view through the clear glass windows provided an unblemished panorama of the gateway city, its dominant wood-frame buildings lining a narrow street along the waterfront. Fishing boats were moored southeast of their pier, a small cove marking the outlet of a creek. Sitting on bleached creosote pilings on the far shore of the cove were a string of one– and two–story houses, the hillside rising steeply behind the structures.

"Hey, Jack! Does Ketchikan only have one street?"

The mate nodded somberly, replying, "Almost, Slim, the business district over there has a half dozen cross streets, and a rough road follows the creek up to a few old prospectors' cabins. Otherwise the waterfront street is all there is."

"Who lives in those houses across the cove?" Bill asked naively.

Jack's lips twisted in a playful leer as he answered, "That's Creek Street where some of Ketchikan's most famous citizens live. See that nice two–story at the far end? That's Dolly Arthur's."

The door clicked open, allowing a smattering of voices from below to accompany the skipper's footsteps as he entered with a quip. "Infamous is a better word for our college senior, mate," he laughed as he addressed Bill, "Ha! Ha! Creek Street is Ketchikan's red light district, and Dolly was a freeswinging and prosperous madam until she retired a few years ago."

Elmer turned to introduce a well-dressed, middle-aged man with a primly professional manner, who was dutifully smiling at the skipper's remark, "Meet Philo Severn, our attorney from San Francisco. He wants to talk to all of us about the accident in Grenville Channel. We have to testify at a Coast Guard hearing in Seattle - probably sometime in September. Philo will represent the company and each of us."

The lawyer fingered his bow tie and then slipped pince-nez reading spectacles onto his nose. Taking a notepad from his briefcase, he stated, "Just a few questions, gentlemen, and you can proceed to Valdez. Our two insurance companies are dealing with each other, and the Canadian authorities have agreed to defer investigatory authority to the Coast Guard since everyone involved is American."

Philo Severn paused and cleared his throat as he glanced at Elmer and Jack, "However, since a life was lost in the collision, the Coast Guard will ask same sticky questions about your competence with the possibility of suspending your licenses."

Jack interrupted anxiously, "You mean they might suspend my 'ticket'? I have a family to feed."

Holding up a palm and gesturing calm, the lawyer answered with assurance, "I hope not. That's why I'm here to get the facts. I'll do my best to protect the company and its employees," and with a touch of smugness in his voice concluded, "and I haven't lost a case in some time. Trust me."

π   π   π

Bill was physically jarred out of a deep sleep by a hand roughly shaking his left shoulder.

"Wha. . .?" he mumbled into the bulkhead before he twisted toward his disturber.

"Slim! Wake up, Slim! Captain Hairston needs help, and I've got the runs," Ray moaned.

Rubbing his eyes, Bill rolled out of his bunk and began dressing, asking several questions in blurred tones, "What time is it? Where are we? Where does Elmer need me, wheelhouse or afterdeck? Cheez! Why are we crossways to the swells?"

"Dress warm for the afterdeck. The sun's shining, but there's a stout breeze in Cross Sound. We've just left Icy Strait and changed heading for Cape Spencer. Your watch starts in a couple of hours. I'll stand two hours of your midnight shift if I feel okay."

Bill lurched as the towboat reeled broadside in the southwesterly swell. Abandoning any further conversation, he shuffled to the stairs and climbed tentatively onto the deck. Working his way aft with one hand or the other always grasping a handhold, he noted the *MacDonald's* decks were awash with seawater as the boat came about to meet their wallowing barge now off the starboard bow.

"Wow!" he shouted as he slid up to Harry on the wet surface, "Isn't the barge down by the head? And she's taking water, too."

"Yes! Her pump must have conked out. Lay out lines, we're coming alongside. Some time for Ray to get sick - he'll miss all the fun. Ha! Ha!" Harry joked as he winched in the long steel cable, pulling the two craft ever closer together.

Bill quickly laid out the hawsers and stood holding a spring line at ready. The first mate stood beside him poised to grab a cleat on the barge as Harry moved over to position a tire bumper between the two jostling vessels. The mate deftly sprang aboard the barge, turning to catch the leader rope Bill threw to him, and then pulled the hawser aboard the barge and secured it.

Harry helped the engineer cross over, handing him his tool kit as the mate and Bill secured two more lines, whereupon the skipper rang full ahead. The twin mickey-micks reverberated throughout the boat as the paired vessels came smartly about on an easterly heading back into the calmer waters of Icy Strait.

Bill went forward to relieve Jack at the wheel, the skipper praising his job, "Nice work, Slim. I appreciate your filling in for Ray. You can eat after Jack gets a bite. How is our sick friend doing?"

"Terrible, Elmer, but he figures to handle his evening watch okay. Where are we going now?"

"We'll go into Hoonah and spend the night. The weather report calls for calmer seas in the gulf by morning. That's Glacier Bay aport, but I prefer running before the wind. Our barge can't take any more water," the skipper answered in conversational tones.

Bill nodded agreeably, commenting in pseudo-disappointment, "But I wanted to see all those glaciers. Is it true that the whole bay is one big glacier?"

"Ha! Ha! No, my friend, but it seems like it when you sail the northern reaches, particularly when the glaciers are calving. It's a spectacular sight but not meant for sailing. The town of Hoonah is a calm anchorage, and the Tlingit Indians are friendly people. We'll enjoy a good night's sleep before we cross the Gulf of Alaska," the skipper concluded as he bent over his charts and began calculating their new course to the southeast.

They were entering Port Frederick, a fiord-like bay, when Jack returned from the mess and took the wheel in his naturally brusque manner, ordering without preface, "Eat fast, Slim, I'll need you before we anchor in Hoonah."

Bill returned in ten minutes, munching a roast beef sandwich as he surveyed the town on their port side. Fishing boats clustered about the long pier, several boats unloading their morning catch. A Union Oil sign provided a patch of orange color against a backdrop of whitewash and bleached clapboard buildings, the dark pilings and moss covered rocks on the shoreline giving a grayness to the overall picture. His first study of Hoonah struck the deckhand as pristine but beautiful in its purely Alaskan setting.

Bill estimated the town's population at three hundred people or so. As he looked around the bay, he concluded everyone lived in the village, and most of the people were Indians. He saw nary a shack, a boat or any smoke in the surrounding area.

He said as much aloud, "I can't see any houses except in town. Everyone must live here."

Elmer replied with a nod, "There are Tlingits all through these islands, but you're probably right about Hoonah. It's the only town for thirty miles and the biggest for a hundred miles. They even became an incorporated city a couple of years ago."

To both men he added, "How about fresh salmon for dinner? I'll have Cookie buy a few fish from the Indians."

He rang slow ahead to the engine room as he ordered, "Bring her about, Jack."

To Bill he instructed, "Go below and stand by the capstan. Can you drop anchor by yourself?"

"Sure, Captain Hairston. Just yell when you're ready."

π   π   π

Blue skies had turned an ominous gray overnight, but contrary to his meteorological guesstimate, the seas in Cross Sound were calmer as the *MacDonald* headed westerly into the Gulf of Alaska. Massive headlands were visible to the north, but Bill couldn't decide which point of land was Cape Spencer, and his downright surly mate was impossible to talk to. It wasn't until the next watch came on duty at four o'clock that his curiosity was satisfied, Harry pointing out the promontory in question aft of their barge.

Bill slid into an empty seat in the mess to join the poker game in progress, but everyone was edgy and distracted by their makeshift repairs on the barge. *'Crossing the gulf with a crippled tow would make anyone absentminded,'* Bill thought as the gamblers drifted away one by one.

π   π   π

Soon Cookie was his only company, and when he suggested that his former helper cook pork chops for the crew, Bill just laughed and went below to his bunk, never quite sure when his friend was poking fun at him.

Nature smiled on the towboat during the ensuing watches, and by sunset the following day they entered Prince William Sound. The tow cable was shortened to a hundred yards, and the officers looked over the repaired bow, finally pronouncing it still seaworthy as the light disappeared. The skipper proceeded at reduced power across the open waters to Valdez Arm, entering the waterway after dawn.

Hearing the maneuvering of the *Mac* as she came alongside the barge, Bill realized they had successfully reached their destination. However, when he hurried onto deck to help with mooring lines, the first mate was lowering the barge's anchor, and Valdez was in view two miles across the water.

"What's going on, Cookie?" he asked curiously.

"Heh! Heh! The Port Captain refuses to let all of these explosives on the pier. The company freight agent came over to handle the un-loading - by lighter, I expect. Everyone ashore is afraid our damaged cargo might go 'boom'," Cookie replied, adding in a complaining voice, "And I'm missing good drinking time. Want to join me at Mabel's when we dock?"

"No thanks, Cookie. I want to look the town over, and besides, I can't keep up with you."

"You younguns, no staying-power when good liquor is available," the older man joshed.

Ⴈ   Ⴈ   Ⴈ

Valdez had the rundown look of a coastal shanty town, its long, broad wharf appearing to be the stoutest construction in the gathering of clapboard buildings. *'Of course,'* thought Bill, *'Why would you build a permanent structure under that monstrous glacier a mile away?'*

The young seaman strolled past the dilapidated two–story hotel built alongside the pier, its original shape twisted by age until no two windows were aligned nor joints perpendicular. Elmer had told him that the hotel had sold for sixty thousand dollars last year, and the new owners were making big money. Its decrepit and unstable appearance evidently didn't stop people from staying there.

Across the timbered pier stood Mabel's Tavern, a honkytonk fixture of Valdez run by two "ladies" who used to work in their Seattle office. They were getting rich, too. Everyone in Alaska was making a bundle although Bill was aware that prices were often double those charged for identical items down below.

He hesitated in the first intersection, no automobile threatening his well-being in the middle of Main Street, and finally chose to enter the corner drug store, emerging a few minutes later chewing a bar of candy and carrying a magazine under his arm - the monthly copy of *Argosy*. Muffled curses could be heard from the sidewalk, Bill's searching eyes spotting an altercation in the barber shop across the street.

Suddenly there was a bang synchronized with shattering glass, and a disheveled old man whose face wore the wrinkled tribulation of a local Indian stumbled out the broken window waving a pistol and shouting incoherent obscenities into the air. Bill shrank back into the alcove of a grocery store, but the old fellow was oblivious to everything except his path to a small skiff tied to a piling on the gravelly beach. He rowed away still cursing like a trooper.

Bill walked over to the barber shop, not surprised to find a sprawled body in the barber's chair, but was startled when a bald-headed man jumped up, exclaiming, "Did you see that damn drunken Indian smash my window?"

Not waiting for an answer, the barber stepped to the opening and shouted, "Marshal Fedders! Indian Jake shot out my window, and he'll have to pay for repairs."

The officer smilingly replied as he walked by the shop, "You bet, Curly Bob. I'll tell him the next time he visits town."

"Isn't he going to arrest that Indian?" Bill asked.

Curly Bob smiled knowingly as he replied, "Nah, you must be a chechako. The marshal only chases real criminals, and Jake doesn't have a mean bone in his carcass - except when he's drinking. He'll be ashamed of himself when he sobers up."

He paused as he looked Bill over, conjecturing, "Say, aren't you off the *MacDonald*? What happened down below?"

Abiding by Philo's legal counsel, Bill chatted with the barber about their mutual friend Swede, the engineer, without discussing the collision itself.

π π π

Sitting with Ray on the boat's rail, Bill watched Harry and the cook's helper walk across the gangplank onto the *MacDonald's* deck, the old seaman commenting, "Everyone's aboard now except for Cookie. He's probably still at Mabel's drinking."

Captain Hairston overheard the remark as he stepped on deck in the gathering dusk of an Alaskan summer day, irritation sounding in his tones as he said, "I told everyone to be aboard by eleven o'clock. Is Cookie the only late crew member?"

"That's right, Elmer," Ray replied easily, "I'd go fetch him, but you know he won't pay me no mind nohow."

The skipper called into the mess, "Hey, Jack! Go round up Cookie and march him back here."

Jack grunted his displeasure as he stepped on deck, but he was nodding in compliance as he left the boat. Within minutes he returned, ushering the befuddled cook down the pier and before the *Mac*, he disdainfully ignored the drunken man as he called out, "Skipper, here's your cook."

Cookie staggered to a halt and pulled himself erect with a be-atific smile lighting his face, and raising his hand gingerly in the parody of a salute, he proclaimed loudly, "I'm here. . . hic. . . ready to sail. . .hic. . .Captain Hairston, sir." Whereupon the inebriated cook shuffled his feet tentatively and with militant forthrightness strode toward the waiting captain.

Bill and Ray cried with unintended unison, "No, Cookie, use. . .", as the ill-fated drunk missed the gangplank and stepped into the glacial waters of the bay. Stunned crew members rushed en masse to the rescue, all laughing spontaneously, albeit shakily, as a blue-skinned and big-eyed cook was lifted onto the dock.

With a blink of his eyes, Cookie muttered, "Damn it, I'm sober. Don't sail without me, fellas," and marched purposefully back to Mabel's Tavern.

The crew looked meaningfully at the laughing Elmer, who shook his head and conceded, "Ha! Ha! I guess we'll sail at midnight, men."

In the quiet and uneventful trip south with an empty barge and little out of the ordinary, Bill created an analogy in his mind. Considering his view of Alaska a bit like a coin, he relished the side which was full of action, challenges and adventures, but chafed at the monotony and hard work of the other side. 'I wonder if I'm cut out for this kind of life?' he thought repeatedly in the days to come, 'This country certainly does things on a grand scale - it keeps you on your toes.'

Chapter Two

The dimly lit courtroom in Seattle's Federal Building seemed spacious and perhaps a tad intimidating to the sailors seated behind two tables facing the judge's bench. Empty seats filled the jury box and the victors' gallery for the Coast Guard hearing scheduled at ten o'clock on this rainy September day.

A door to the judge's chambers opened, the bailiff emerging to flick a light switch as a prelude to his sonorous announcement, "All please rise, the court is now in session. The Honorable Clarence Atkins presiding."

Judge Atkins walked briskly to his place and seated himself, speaking somewhat tersely, "Gentlemen, please be seated."

Studying a paper before him, the judge continued more deliberately, "This session is an official United States Coast Guard hearing into the collision between the *MacDonald* and the *Amanda Jackson* in Canadian waters on August 9, 1949."

Looking up, he studied the six men before him, finally addressing the lawyers, "Good morning, Mister Severn, Mister Quillen. Would you please introduce yourselves, your client firms and your colleagues for the record."

The other attorney rose and addressed the court, "John Quillen, counsel for the Jackson Towing Company of Seattle, and my associate, Captain Gerald Ross of the *Amanda Jackson*."

As he concluded, Philo rose and stated, "Philo Severn, counsel for the Alaska Tug Company of Tacoma and my associates, Captain Elmer Hairston, Second Mate Jack Anderson and Deckhand William Pardue of the *MacDonald*."

"Thank you, gentlemen. The Coast Guard report before me shows the aforementioned tugboats with their barges collided in Grenville Channel, British Columbia, Canada, at two o'clock on the morning of August 9, 1949. The *Amanda Jackson* sank immediately, and her barge sank two hours later. The *Amanda Jackson's* cook, Daniel Huggins, was lost, and rescue efforts were not successful."

Pausing briefly to study the report further, the judge asked in a curious tone, "How is it that the Canadian authorities turned jurisdiction over to this court?"

Philo Severn rose to explain, "Your honor, the *MacDonald's* barge was laden with explosives and posed a serious navigational hazard to ship traffic in its damaged condition. Grenville Channel is surrounded by mountains which inhibit radio communication, so Captain Hairston chose to seek refuge in Ray Anchorage on Duke Island, promptly reporting the accident and repairing the barge. His formal report was submitted two days later to the Coast Guard Commander in Ketchikan."

"Do you agree with this account, Mister Quillen?" the judge inquired.

Standing briefly to answer, the lawyer stated, "Yes, your Honor. Captain Ross concurs with Captain Hairston's actions following the collision."

"Very well, counselors. This court has two duties, first to ascertain the validity of the Coast Guard report, and second to review the actions of the responsible officers as regards to their maritime licenses. The court has depositions from Captain Ross and Captain Hairston, but Second Mate Anderson and Deckhand Pardue will need to testify. Mister Severn, are your associates prepared to do so? Have you advised them of their legal rights?"

"Yes, your Honor. They have agreed to my representing them in court..." Philo began.

Judge Atkins interrupted to query, "Mister Anderson, Mister Pardue, do you concur?"

Following a clear "yes" from each man, Philo resumed, "Your Honor, since a man died in the accident, I've advised both Mister Anderson and Mister Pardue to refuse to testify on the grounds they may incriminate themselves should wrongful death be a finding of the court."

The judge responded thoughtfully. "I see the problem. Mister Severn, and agree to accept their refusal. Do you have a suggestion for the court to resolve this dispute?"

"Your Honor, I don't believe there is a dispute as such. Our insurance carriers have reached a tentative settlement, and a simple finding of accidental sinking will conclude this hearing."

John Quillen rose to concur, and Judge Atkins pronounced, "So be it. A maritime accident is declared with no fault assigned. Court is adjourned." A clap of the gavel concluded the hearing.

Bill breathed a sigh of relief as he declared, "Whew! Is that all there is to it?"

Elmer relaxed visibly as he chuckled aloud, "Ha! Ha! That's the way it should go. Philo knows what he's doing."

The lawyer's expression remained somber as he elucidated, "Your refusal to testify was crucial, Bill. Elmer and Jack could have had their tickets pulled for a year if enough questions were answered."

Jack muttered in irritation, "Oh, for crying out loud, no one was at fault. It was just an accident."

Philo put a hand on Jack's shoulder, agreeing, "That's what the ruling is, but a man died as a result. If the accident had been in territorial waters, the judge might have been tougher on us. Well,

gentlemen, I have to catch an afternoon flight to San Francisco.
Smooth sailing!"

As they parted, Elmer stated his gratitude, "Thanks, Slim. You're
a good guy. Anytime you need a berth, give me a call. Good luck in
finishing your degree."

ᚭ   ᚭ   ᚭ

Driving back to Tacoma in his 1942 Buick coupe, Bill mentally reviewed his class schedule which had commenced the previous week.
He was enrolled in Northwest history as well as fifteen hours of
calculus, physics, ethics and health. With such an academic load, he
would not be able to work this semester. He knew his limitations, and
he was determined to graduate in June.

'Well, the check in my pocket will pay my expenses this semester,' he thought. Smiling ruefully as he recalled his dad's advice,
he muttered aloud, "Maybe the folks are right, 'Old Buick', I should sell
you. Why, I could ride a Harley like Ralph for a lot less gas money."

In his amused state of mind, he recalled last week's ride around
campus. His roommate at the Theta Chi House had loaned him his
motorcycle to practice his driving skills, and after ten blocks of maneuvering between cars and pedestrians he was feeling like a veteran
cyclist. Relaxing a bit too much with his success, he failed to round
the last corner before his fraternity house, hitting the curb as he
slammed on the brakes too late. He sailed over the handlebars, the
left handle striking him at an awkward angle, catching in his trousers
fly with zipper and cloth tearing loose from the pants.

A gray-haired lady working in her rose garden hurried forward in
concern, asking, "Are you hurt, young man? Don't get up, your friends
are running to. . .oh my!"

Her last expression caused Bill to blush in embarrassment as he
stood and tried to pull the shreds of cloth together. He had luckily
escaped any physical injury in the spill, but his modesty was inexorably breached. Red-faced and stammering, he thanked the kind

lady and curtained by a circle of his fraternity brothers, shuffled up the sidewalk to the house under scrutiny from bystanders.

'I guess I won't buy a cycle,' he admitted to himself, *'But I will have to sell my Buick by Christmas. And I'll need to find a job after finals in January.'* Since second semester classes were going to be an easier load, he figured it would be easy enough to earn a few dollars.

As he drove past Federal Way High School, he realized the time was short to rehearse his oral report on George Vancouver for an afternoon history class. This professor had a knack for knowing when you weren't prepared.

᛭   ᛭   ᛭

Bill rose from his seat and walked to the podium up front, aware that he had been chosen as the first presenter because he had entered as the bell finished ringing. Everyone in the classroom was smiling at his dilemma, being out of breath and first to report. Even the professor was amused and offered a respite, "Would you like to make your presentation at the end of the period, Mister Pardue?"

Shaking his head vigorously while taking a deep breath, Bill faced the class, apologizing, "I'm sorry to be tardy, but I'm ready to talk about Captain George Vancouver and his explorations in this state, Canada and the Territory of Alaska."

Pausing for another deep breath, he talked for twice as long as allotted, but no one interrupted his engaging report. Realizing he was over his time limit, Bill wondered whether his classmates were interested in the subject matter or just glad he was using up more of their class hour.

Glancing out into the hallway later during a boring report, Bill saw a blonde girl waiting by the door and smiled at her when she waved, almost returning the gesture until he remembered Charley Blakely was seated behind him near the window. Babs was a popular and exciting young woman whom Bill had dated last fall. She liked basketball and basketball players, but when Bill was cut from the squad, Babs accepted his handsome rival's fraternity pin. Of course, Charley had made the team, and his folks had money, still Bill's feelings were hurt. He still had a yen for the pretty coed.

Clearing the mental cobwebs from his reverie at the bell's sound, he rose to receive a comradely slap on the back and a friendly, "You did well, Bill. Thanks for taking so much time. Ha! Ha! But I did like hearing about Canada and Alaska. I'm working for my uncle in Ketchikan next summer. See you at the fraternity meeting tonight."

Bill rejoined lamely, "Sure thing, Charley."

A hand brushed his arm hesitantly to claim his attention. A short round-faced girl with Indian features stood beside him, her dark eyes looking as if she expected rejection by the august senior. He recalled with a tinge of guilt that he had ignored her presence in class because she was quiet and a bit homely.

"I liked your report, especially when you spoke of my people and the Alaskan Islands. You like my country, I could tell by the tone of your voice," the shy girl said. With subdued and diminishing volume, she concluded, "I'm Helen Duncan, but my family is no relation to our famous minister."

Out of the corner of his eye, Bill observed Charley and Babs watching them and whispering to each other and heard quiet laughter as they disappeared down the hallway.

He felt a blush in his cheek and a tinge of impatience with the girl standing beside him. Suddenly a thought popped into mind, *'My re - action is all wrong. Helen is a shy girl trying to be friendly. Why should I care about Charley and Babs?'*

A smile creased his face as he suggested, "Do you have time for a Coke at the S.U.B.? I'd like to hear more about Alaska and the Tsimshians. Did I pronounce that right?"

"Yes, you did. Thank you, I'm hungry for hot chocolate. I skipped breakfast this morning to practice my report, but the professor didn't call on me," she complained in a matter-of-fact voice.

Laughing aloud as they strolled out of Jones Hall, he replied, "Ha! Ha! I should be so lucky, Helen. I didn't have time to do much studying, and he had my number. Tell me about your family home."

Bill and Helen developed a sincere friendship over the ensuing weeks, more comradely than romantic. He drove her to Cushman Indian Hospital the day her brother was discharged from the tuberculosis ward, dropping him off at the ferry in Seattle to begin his trip home. On another occasion he escorted her to a performance of the Adelphian Choir when her date stood her up.

She, in turn, attended several intramural basketball games to cheer him on. Helen knew his fraternity team celebrated, or commiserated, as a group after the game, and she always left the stands as the game ended.

One stormy morning in January she missed their history class, meeting him in the doorway of Jones Hall and presenting him with a knitted scarf, a Tsimshian talisman for good luck.

His pleased but puzzled expression elicited a brief explanation mixed with a pair of moist eyes, "I'm going home today. Mother is very ill, and my family needs me. The scarf is a thank you for being my friend. Maybe you will remember me when you wear it."

"Gee, Helen! I'll miss you. Thanks for the scarf. Didn't you tell me swapping good luck charms was customary?" Bill detached a rabbit's foot from his car keys and handed it to her, adding, "I'm sorry I don't have something nicer to give you."

Helen beamed with pleasure at his small gesture, sighing, "It's your thoughtfulness that I'll always remember, Bill. Good-by, my friend."

Impulsively she reached out, and they embraced briefly. Helen skipped down the brick stairway to the waiting taxi cab, a fleeting wave of her hand through glass was her final good-by.

From behind Bill came one of Charley's insensitive jokes, "Bill, aren't you the romantic lover. Where is your Indian girlfriend going?"

Babs' laughter joined her boyfriend's as Bill ignored their crude teasing, restraining his irritation. Without embarrassment he thought, *'Maybe I've grown up a little since September,'* and calmly walked away.

Accepting a receipt from the motherly clerk behind the Bursar's counter, Bill fell into deep reverie, mentally subtracting yet another debit from the sale of his Buick. With a slipping clutch and a tired battery, his automobile hadn't brought in as much cash as he had expected. After buying textbooks and paying for his spring semester tuition, he had less than a hundred dollars to his name. He smiled ruefully at an errant thought, *'Of course, my fraternity bills are paid through March. By then I'll have a real problem. Oh well, I'll try that Fuller Brush job the placement bureau found for me. It doesn't pay much, but it's spending money.'*

The following week his science laboratory sessions were moved to Tuesday and Thursday afternoons, disrupting his Fuller Brush schedule. Bill waxed philosophical as he quit the door-to-door sales job, thus ending the misery of rejection by housewives in the area - rude women upset him. His easy-come, easy-go attitude covered a real anxiety about his financial condition.

Accepting odd jobs whenever his revised schedule permitted, Bill earned a few dollars' spending money, but as spring vacation approached, his cash reserve was down to twenty dollars. *'Hm, just enough to sit in the MacDonald's poker game,'* he mused, turning whimsy into reality as he picked up the telephone and called the Alaska Tug office.

As soon as he identified himself, the dispatcher became friendly, greeting him with a, "Hi, Slim! You want to talk to Elmer? He's right here."

A moment later the Captain came onto the line with a comradely, "Hello, Slim, are you ready to sail? Ray wants to take a vacation. How's school anyway?"

"Ha! Ha! Skipper, sign me up. I'm broke and spring break starts Easter weekend. When do you sail?" Bill asked hopefully.

"Friday morning. Can you afford to miss a week of classes? Aren't you graduating in June?"

Weighing his alternatives for a split second, Bill sounded spontaneous as he accepted Elmer's offer, "You've got a deckhand, Captain Hairston. Actually I can't afford not to sail. I'll talk to my professors and report aboard Thursday evening. Will you still be at Baker Dock?"

"Ha! Ha! Right, let's skip Dupont this time. We're carrying normal stores, mostly canned food and dry goods. Say, Slim, don't forget your poker stake. I'm looking forward to winning it from you. See you Thursday."

Bill said good-by and hung up, eager to put his academic affairs in order and hopeful that missing a few classes would not lower his grades.

Π   Π   Π

The *MacDonald* sailed from Commencement Bay in a gray pall, overcast skies and a light drizzle eliciting Cookie's trite description of Tacoma weather for the umpteenth time, "Slim, this here's 'Oregon Mist'. You know...it missed Oregon. Hee! Hee!"

She passed a harbor tug off the Browns Point Lighthouse, and Bill stepped onto the wet deck upon recognizing the *Peter Foss*. He exchanged unintelligible shouts with the familiar figure of an old friend on the other boat's deck, finally settling for a casual wave as a proper greeting.

Elmer called down from the wheelhouse, "Do you know Warren Larson, Slim? I haven't seen him since before Christmas when I tried to talk him into working on the *MacDonald*."

Nodding agreeably, Bill replied, "He told me about your offer. His folks are neighbors of my grandmother in Old Tacoma, and even as a kid he told pretty good fish stories. Now he claims that he's building a gillnetter over on Day Island and returning to fishing for a living. The boat's keel could be laid within a year or two."

The skipper shrugged with an air of skepticism on his face, commenting, "Fishing isn't what it used to be. Might be okay for the boat owners though, but I think Warren would make more with Alaska Tug. He could be a mate within the year. How about you, Slim? Want to sail with me this summer?"

"Thanks, Elmer. I'll think about it.   I like the *MacDonald* and you guys on the crew." Bill responded diplomatically as he ducked back into the mess.

The skies darkened, and the rainfall increased as they plowed through the inland waterway between Canada's islands. The night the tugboat entered Grenville Channel, Bill remained in the wheelhouse as an observer, silently paying respects to the *Amanda Jackson* and Pegleg the Cook.

Uncharacteristically, Jack volunteered information on their passage, identifying the scene of last summer's collision with a brief but friendly announcement, "Here's the spot, Slim. The *Amanda Jackson* is six hundred feet below us. We'll see that distinctive headland in a couple of minutes."

"Thanks, Jack. It all looks so different in the winter," Bill replied, not recognizing any landmarks.

$$\pi \quad \pi \quad \pi$$

Bill awoke as his head banged against the bulkhead and one foot bounced over his bunk's sideboard. Reaching instinctively overhead with both hands, he grasped the steel braces firmly and swung his other leg over the edge. Dropping to the deck, he wrestled his clothes onto his swaying torso with one hand while the other held the sideboard.

By the time the deckhand staggered into a mess seat, his stomach was reacting to the boat's motion.

'Nausea and hunger are certainly contradictory feelings,' he thought, and chuckled to himself at his mild discomfiture. Observing Elmer and Dick eating oatmeal and drinking coffee, he signaled the cook's helper to give him the same.

Bill ate slowly, listening to the officers' discussion of the weather and their route for the day. When the engineer asked about sailing alee of Duke Island, Bill perked up.

"Will we be within sight of Cottage Cove, Elmer?" he asked hopefully.

"Yes, but a curtain of rain will make the island a dark shadow. I doubt we'll see much scenery for a day or two. You know Ketchikan is the 'rain capital' of Alaska, don't you? Heh! Heh! Not quite the same in winter, is it, Slim?"

Bill smiled ruefully but nodded as he answered, "It is a mite depressing, isn't it? Still, I'd like to look for that cabin near our anchorage. What time will we pass Cottage Cove?"

The skipper thought but an instant before replying, "After three o'clock, I expect. Right about dusk with all these rain clouds over us. Tell you what, Slim, I'll have Jack interrupt our poker game when we're off Ray Anchorage. You can take your look from the wheelhouse."

π   π   π

Bill leaned into the wheel, bracing his body against the heavy seas in Icy Strait as he thought, *'What will Cross Sound and the Gulf of Alaska hold in store for us if it's rough in here?'*

His reverie deepened as he automatically maintained course, remembering his search for the cabin and musing, *'Heck, I didn't even see Cottage Cove through that downpour. And Ketchikan was just a blur as we sailed up Tongass Narrows. I'm not sure winter in Alaska is so great except that I've already earned enough money to pay my bills.'*

Jack entered the wheelhouse to take his watch, shortly followed by his deckhand - Bill's relief.

Elmer suggested, "Slim, you and I had better get some sleep before we hit the gulf. We're in for some nasty weather when we come around Cape Spencer."

None of the crew members really slept during the ensuing hours since the *MacDonald* bounced and rolled all the way to the Gulf of Alaska, making headway slowly but with determination. Unbidden, Bill went aft to help Harry winch out a full thousand feet of cable, amazed at the action of the whiplashing cable as its steely shrieks blended with the howling wind. He could make out the running lights, but otherwise their barge was but a gray ghost.

Returning to the warmth of the mess, Bill shucked his coat and gloves and grabbed a handful of soda crackers to chew, knowing his stomach could not handle the stew cooking in the galley. Jack sat quietly across from him, pale countenance showing fatigue. Beside him was his young deckhand, ashen face and rolling eyes advertising a case of seasickness barely contained.

The lad turned his head away as Cookie appeared in the galley doorway with a sneaky grin, commenting tongue-in-cheek, "I see you're a real sailor, Slim, eating a snack before dinner. Here, have a chili pepper. It'll settle your stomach."

He produced an open jar and took out a hot pepper, placing it on his tongue with relish and chewing it slowly. Offering the jar to Bill, his face maintained a beatific look of pleasure, only his eyes dancing with deviltry.

"Ha! Ha! Look at the kid, Slim. He doesn't seem to like chili peppers. How about pork chops, kid?" he crooned.

"Shut up, Cookie!" Jack ordered, but he was too late. The seasick deckhand rushed to the door, body racked by stomach tremors. He opened the door and put one foot outside on deck when a towering wave engulfed the *MacDonald*, drenching the lad and splashing inside.

Cookie screamed, "Close that door!" and looked on in horror as he was too late. The cook muttered in desperation, "No, not in here."

Bill and Jack broke into laughter as Cookie got his just desserts for teasing them, his shoes covered with the retching seaman's rancid spew. Both men left Cookie and the kid to tend to the mutual problem, Bill anxious to avoid any sight or smell which would antagonize his own queasy stomach. He owed Harry an hour and decided quartermastering was easier than sitting around. Keeping busy at sea was the best remedy for motion sickness.

π   π   π

"Hard aport!" the skipper ordered abruptly.

Bill complied without hesitation, his gaze fixed on the gyro-compass and its fluctuating needle. The MacDonald's almost westerly heading swung southwesterly.

"Steady as she goes, Slim," Elmer said in consternation, wonder in his voice as he continued, "Look at that wave, it must be twenty feet high. Brace yourself, Slim."

Checking his new heading before looking up, Bill saw water, a wall of the sea just a stone's throw from their bow. As the MacDonald slid into the trough before it, the rising swell encompassed the horizon, its phosphorescent crest well above the wheelhouse.

Suddenly the howling wind became but a low moan, and as the two seamen held on for dear life, the bow lifted into the breaking wall of water. The tugboat shuddered, and her hull groaned as the sea enveloped it entirely, smashing down on the wheelhouse and flowing three feet deep along her open deck. The MacDonald's buoyancy reasserted itself as seawater ran out her scuppers and the howling wind could once again be heard.

"Bring her four points to starboard, Slim," Elmer ordered as he watched the monster wave advance on their barge, its running lights abruptly disappearing behind the wall of seawater. He rang slow ahead before the barge was smothered by the heavy seas, easing tension on their tow cable for thirty seconds before ringing for more power.

"Bring her slowly starboard while I check our position on radar. Sailing into the wind is bringing us too close to that light ahead," the skipper asserted thoughtfully, almost as if he were talking to himself. "Damn! This radar set is acting up. Hold your present course, Slim, while I try for a better picture."

Twenty minutes later the beacon seemed much closer and the seas less challenging. Bill alerted the captain, "Isn't that Montague Island to port? Is this course okay?"

Elmer glanced up and nodded confidently, repeating, "Steady as she goes, Slim. We've plenty of seaway around that light, and the island is sheltering us from the worst of the storm."

Taking the wheel, he ordered, "Wake the next watch. Tell Jack to shorten our towline to six hundred feet before coming on duty."

π   π   π

Bill was shaken awake from his first sound sleep in three days. Harry was talking to him, repeating, "Wake up, Slim. No rest for the wicked, my friend. Come on, wake up."

"Is it my watch?" the drowsy deckhand queried in confusion.

"Not for an hour, Slim, but we're icing up in a blizzard and need help. Come aft when you're awake - and dress warm, shipmate."

Minutes and a cup of coffee later, Bill stepped onto deck, turning aft to avoid the sleet gusting horizontally toward the stern, freezing on his clothing as he took stock of the situation. A short step later his feet flew out from under him, and he slid half the length of the boat, ending up prone at Harry's feet.

"Ha! Ha! Welcome to winter weather in Prince William Sound, Slim. This damned sleet is freezing to everything it touches, including our deck. The boat is getting top-heavy and is in danger of capsizing. You're sitting on eight inches of ice right here. Grab a fire axe and lend a hand," the chuckling Harry concluded as he delivered a lumberjack's blow to the sheet of ice.

"Aren't we likely to damage the deck?" Bill asked rhetorically as he joined his shipmates in hacking the ice. Chunks of ice, great and small, flew in the air, one of the crew wielding a shovel periodically, icial debris cast back into the sea as the *MacDonald* entered Valdez Arm.

Jack shouted in irritation, "Damn! I hit the stanchion, most of the ice is gone. The storm is quieter inside the Arm. Let's take a break, gang."

Bill spent the remainder of his watch cleaning up the afterdeck, his mind a bit confused as he considered his lot. *'I'm no sailor, that's for sure,'* he thought. *'And rain in the southeast islands is certainly preferable to ice in Valdez. Wow! Look at that glacier behind the town. It's bigger than life. Hmm, maybe I'll try fishing this summer down by Ketchikan. I wonder if Elmer or Harry or Warren can help me find a berth.'*

π   π   π

The *MacDonald* plied the calm waters of Puget Sound, sunlight gracing their journey from Point-No-Point south. Bill's watch was ending as they cleared Browns Point and headed across Commencement Bay toward Baker Dock. He descended to the deck and headed for the stern, having promised Harry a hand winching in the tow cable.

During their watch together he had thanked Captain Hairston for the job during his spring break and asked his advice about working on a fishing boat in June. Elmer had reiterated his offer for summer work on the *MacDonald*, and though it made Bill feel good, he politely declined, opting to try his luck at fishing instead.

In a spontaneous if somewhat hesitant bit of fatherly advice, the skipper gave a personal opinion, "Slim, you don't need to be a fisherman anymore than a deckhand. Crimininty, fellow, you'll be a college graduate and can pick a good job. If I had your education, I'd be a lawyer or a teacher or something - well, you know, a professional."

Receiving no response from the thoughtful seaman about to be a college senior again, Elmer concluded, "Of course I'll give you a hand getting on a fishing boat, if that's what you really want."

"Thanks, Elmer. I think that a tugboat captaincy is a first-class pro-
fession. Fancy sounding jobs don't interest me right now, but fishing in
Alaska I need to do," Bill stated tactfully.

ᴛᴛ   ᴛᴛ   ᴛᴛ

Bill threw his seabag over his shoulder and waved a casual
good-by to his shipmates as he descended the gangplank, his mind
reverting to his college studies and making up several classes. He'd
extended a week's vacation to seventeen days and was a mite
anxious about his grades, particularly since he'd missed a philosophy
exam the day he sailed.

"Hey, Slim! Studying already, I bet," Elmer called from the office
doorway where he was standing with Warren Larson.

"Geez, Bill, weren't you even going to say hello to me before
going back to C.P.S. I was ready to buy you a beer, too," Warren
teased him with a bright grin.

"Well, I accept, Warren," he retorted, and looking around saw the
Peter Foss moored behind the *MacDonald's* barge. "Are you free
now? I'll buy both of you a round with my poker winnings."

The skipper laughed as he accepted, "Ha! Ha! You're on, Slim.
That big pot you won last night was mostly my money. Besides,
Warren is meeting his old fishing buddy, Ole Olson, at the Old Town
Tavern. Between the three of us, we'll get you a berth for your Alaskan
fishing trip."

Warren quickly agreed, "Ole owes me a favor or two, which he'll
remember clearly after a couple of beers. Can you leave in early
June, Bill?"

"Sure, let's go tell Ole he's got a crew member," Pardue replied
eagerly, quite ready to use his friends' connections for a job in Alaska.

All three piled into Elmer's old Hudson and drove along the waterfront to Old Tacoma, Elmer and Warren chatting good-naturedly
about mutual acquaintances and maritime events in Tacoma. Warren
turned to Bill in the back seat. commenting, "I'm going to work for

Puget Sound Tug next month. My skipper was unhappy that I was going fishing, so I quit Foss. I had to put off building my fishing boat for awhile."

"Too bad she won't be ready this year. I could fish with you," Bill replied, adding a late thought, "Of course, you favor the San Juans, and I like Alaska."

"Well, my friend, Ole will take you there all right, he loves Ketchikan," Warren informed him as they pulled up before the tavern and stepped onto the sidewalk, both of his friends greeting everyone in sight. Obviously they were very much at home in this neighborhood, and Bill relaxed, sure that his friends would convince Ole to hire him.

π   π   π

The ensuing weeks passed swiftly for Bill, filled with make-up studies, fraternity socials and intramural softball games. His past, present and immediate future were paid out of his spring paycheck, and he pocketed a small reserve to tide him over. Laughingly he called it his poker stake for the fishing boat.

Charles and Babs sat near him in his philosophy class and after one particularly difficult test asked him to join them for coffee and talk. Their mutual confusion on the great philosophers was discovered in that discussion, and sharing ideas seemed a likely method for raising their grades. They fell into a natural routine of meeting after philosophy class.

One windy May day Charles was reportedly in bed with a case of the prevailing intestinal flu, and Babs led Bill to coffee, arm in arm, her charm turned up a notch. She flattered his intelligence, smiled warmly and even batted her eyelashes a few times. He smiled inwardly at all her attention and his reaction to it, having experienced similar feelings during their dates together last year, but he simply attributed Babs' provocative glances to her flirtatious nature.

At coffee the next week, Charles casually mentioned that he was flying to Ketchikan before finals for a couple of days, adding, "My uncle insists I learn a little about his hardware store before I go to work next month. He's going fishing with a gang of his old cronies as soon as I start work. I hate to miss the Senior Prom, but since I'm only a junior, it's no big deal. When are you going to be in Ketchikan, Bill?"

"Captain Olson plans to fish along the way, but I expect we'll dock for fuel and supplies about the end of June. I'll look you up when we're in port. You can buy me a beer," Bill replied with a teasing smile as he rose to leave. He had an intramural sports council meeting, his last of frequent gatherings he'd attended during his tenure as the Theta Chi representative.

His long-legged stride had carried him halfway across campus, just beyond Todd Hall when Babs' clear voice sang out, "Bill, wait for me, I'll walk as far as the girls' gym with you."

She was all smiles as she joined him, her complexion lovely as a light blush tinged her cheeks, and her sweater clung to her chest, rising and falling provocatively with her quickened breath.

"Isn't it just terrible that Charles will miss the prom? Who are you taking, Bill?" Babs asked coyly.

"Nobody, Babs. I'm not much of a dancer, and that shindig is expensive, I just. . ." Bill was saying as she interrupted, pressing his arm impetuously against her soft body.

"It wouldn't be too expensive if we cut a few corners. Wouldn't you like to take me to your Senior Prom?"

"Why, sure, Babs, I'd be glad to," he said eagerly, convinced by her closeness and charming behavior that it was a wonderful idea, his minor discordant thought about money quickly stymied. In fact, all other thoughts deserted him when she leaned against him to kiss his cheek.

As they parted at the gym door, Bill's happy, contented smile turned slowly to one of self-derision, knowing full well she had wrapped him around her little finger without much effort.

He thought, *'I'm being used, her interest will disappear as soon as Charles returns. Hmm, maybe I should inveigle a little smooching before the dance, she's awfully eager to have an escort to the prom. Turnabout is fair play.'*

Leaving the council meeting early to time his passing the gym exit as the physical education class was dismissed, he was unable to find her. He asked a friend if Babs had been in class and got a puzzled look in response, and a no, she wasn't assigned to that class. Obviously her trip to the gym had been a ploy to get the prom invitation.

Walking across the quadrangle he espied Charles and Babs entering Jones Hall, hand in hand. He chuckled ruefully at himself as he continued up Fifteenth Street, muttering a silent sentiment, *'So much for being devious, you Lothario. You're no match for that scheming vamp.'*

ᴨ　ᴨ　ᴨ

Bill stood quietly at Babs' elbow as she conversed volubly with her sorority sisters, the smile on his lips becoming more forced as the evening wore on endlessly. His date was being a social gadfly, and he was relegated to the role of her consort, following her around the ballroom and dancing with her friends. When he had suggested they spend more time with each other, her haughty response was an angry, "Hmph! You're no fun."

Babs led him to the basketball players' table for the third time that evening, and soon after she was dancing with the team captain, whose date glared daggers at the dancing couple on her way to the powder room.

Bill thought, *'At least I don't have to dance with Mary a third time. Jerry's a nice enough guy normally, but tonight he's no friend to either Mary or me.'* Chuckling aloud at his own ability to be manipulated by Babs, he picked up a glass of fruit punch at the refreshment table.

"I don't know what you think is funny, Bill Pardue. That hussy you brought is a cheap flirt," Mary pronounced loudly enough for people nearby to hear.

Bill's humorous reaction produced tears in the girl's eyes as he retorted, "You're only half right Mary. My date with Babs isn't cheap."

Recanting quickly, he apologized, "I'm sorry, Mary. I shouldn't be flippant when your feelings are hurt. What can I do?"

"Butt out, Pardue," a visibly irate Jerry threatened, "Or I'll. . ."

Mary's sobs stopped his "or else" tirade, and she asked plaintively, "Will you walk me home, Bill? I only live a couple of blocks away."

In sugar-sweet tones, Babs spited Mary and Bill, "Yes, Bill. Take Miss Goody Two-Shoes home, and Jerry will take care of me." She pressed her body against the now confused athlete, her eyes issuing an invitation that tied his tongue.

"Of course I will, Mary. Shall we dance our way over to the coatroom?" Bill offered, offering her his arm.

She nodded and they moved across the ballroom, Mary with head high and Bill with a tight smile.

Strolling along the tree-shrouded sidewalk toward her home, Mary relaxed and began talking, "Thanks, Bill, for taking me out of there before I made a bigger fool of myself. Ugh! I could scratch her eyes out...and Jerry's, too. He's so immature."

Bill remained silent and attentive, listening to Mary's therapeutic monologue dutifully while thinking that he was as immature as Jerry when it came to women. In his opinion Mary was a nice girl and too good for Jerry. *'Heck, he deserves Babs and vice versa. Now why couldn't I have thought of that before I spent all my savings on this Senior Prom?'*

꠲ ꠲ ꠲

Bill flipped his tassel over the mortarboard perched on his head and stood contemplating his life as the ceremony was completed. *'An alumnus of the Class of Nineteen Fifty'*, he thought, *'And I have three days to celebrate before I leave Tacoma on the Flying Mermaid. I wonder if I can talk Ole into stopping at Metlakatla for Helen's wedding.'* Her invitation included a real Tsimshian tribal feast, and her personal note said friends were welcome.

"Congratulations, Bill, you've set a good example for me. If you can make it, so can I. Say, I'm a senior now that you guys are alumni," Charley joshed as he shook hands, somehow a better friend now that Babs had deserted them both, becoming Jerry's pinned sweetheart.

"Thanks, my friend. When do you leave for Alaska?"

Grinning widely, Charley responded happily, "Tomorrow, my uncle is rarin' to go fishing with his cronies, and he's paying for my airplane ticket again. Are we still meeting in Ketchikan for a beer?"

"Ha! Ha! You bet, Charley - in a couple of weeks. You can show me the town. Have a good flight," Bill concluded, waving casually as he moved toward the doorway. He exchanged congratulations with classmates as he shook a series of hands before reaching his family where hugs abounded. His sister was hosting a dinner in his honor, Bill being the first Pardue to attend college, let alone graduate.

π　π　π

Sipping a bottle of cool Heidelberg, a lone figure sat perched atop a piling stub at the end of the Old Town Dock, waiting in the dim light for sleepiness to develop. Bill wondered why he had left the tavern early, particularly when he had to wait for two trains to roll past before he could cross the tracks to the fishing boat. "Well," he muttered to his companionable neighbor, a large gray sea gull who was sharing his vigil, "I'm short of money despite the folks' graduation present, and Warren bought me this beer. I'll pay him back if he ever gets up to Ketchikan."

The old gull screeched at the sound of his voice, fluttering wings in a seeming challenge to Bill's presence and lowering himself to the timbered dock, he retorted, "Okay! Okay! You can have this spot back, fella. I'm off to my bunk on the *Flying Mermaid.*"

Bill slept the night fitfully, anticipation keeping him on edge. In the morning he arose as soon as Ole's footsteps sounded on deck. It was still dark although Tacoma's skyline stood out in the pre-dawn light.

Ole grunted in surprise when Bill appeared beside him on deck, suggesting quickly, "Why don't you fix breakfast while I check the boat. Our engine has been giving me fits this week, and I want it operating perfectly when we're at sea."

Taking a bag of groceries which Ole proffered, Bill nodded agreeably and checked its contents, finding homemade bread and cinnamon rolls plus two dozen eggs. He went below and lit the kerosene stove, pulled a package of bacon from the cooler and fried a batch of bacon and eggs. Carrying two plates of food to the cramped engine compartment, he announced, "Breakfast is served, Ole. Coffee'll be ready in a few minutes."

Wiping excess oil from his hands, the skipper ate everything on his plate, commending Bill, "You're a good cook, Slim. That's one of your duties on this boat."

"I know, new member is the cook. Warren told me what to expect, and he said I'd love your wife's cinnamon rolls. He's right, they are delicious."

"You bet they are, and they'll be gone before we clear Browns Point. The rest of the crew will arrive after sunrise, and we'll sail north. I hope to be fishing in the San Juans before the day is over," Ole paused as someone boarded the boat, ordering, "Go topside and see who that is, Slim. If it's Larson visiting, offer him breakfast in exchange for a hand with this engine. I'm the only man in this crew who knows anything about machinery, but I'm still a fisherman rather than a mechanic."

Bill no more stepped on deck than he heard, "How about breakfast, old buddy? My tug doesn't even have coffee yet," Warren gestured in mock disgust at the Tacoma tug moored at the lumber mill next door.

"Sure, Warren, you go fix Ole's engine, and I'll make breakfast for you. Fair enough?" Bill replied, heading back to his stove. One of his shipmates shouted a greeting and waved, signaling his arrival, and Bill figured he might as well start cooking in earnest. Sunshine was striking the hills around them, and the rest of the crew would be along shortly.

The engine ran smoothly all day, the *Flying Mermaid* passing several other commercial fishing boats off the Ballard locks as they sped north. Mike the Greek cackled, and in his old raspy voice called up to Ole, "By golly, Skipper, we are the fastest fishing boat on the Sound today."

In an aside to Bill, he added, "And we'll have to take on fuel in Friday Harbor at this rate."

They fished the eastern reaches of the Strait of Juan de Fuca for three days, striking a school of chinook salmon off Lopez Island at dusk on the first day. The next morning dawned bright and sunny, every boat they encountered coming up dry - no fish. By the time they reached Friday Harbor to sell their fish and buy fuel and groceries, Ole was fed up with the San Juans and announced they'd head for Alaska at first light.

ᛟ   ᛟ   ᛟ

The *Flying Mermaid* ran before a blustery southwest wind up Dixon Entrance into Revillagigedo Channel, its sputtering engine giving everyone aboard a thrill. Bill directed Ole up the shore of Duke Island, while watching a two-man fishing boat to port, believing it to be the same outfit he'd seen last summer. As they passed Duchess Island and entered Ray Anchorage, the young man got his first real look at Cottage Cove in almost a year.

Lying at anchor in the snug harbor, Ole puttered with his engine while the crew fished for halibut from the stern, and Bill and Red trolled for salmon in the sawed-off dinghy. They stayed close to shore alee of the wind, trolling a single line through Morse Cove. Bill caught several rock cod for dinner - but no salmon.

Coming back to Cottage Cove, Red got lucky and caught a thirty pound king, which pulled the tiny craft across the water toward the rill beside the cabin.

Bill laughed at Red's look of frustration as he sank a gaff into the salmon, teasingly saying, "Ha! Ha! He's too big for this dinghy, Red.

You'll have to land him on shore or let him go. Or maybe I can explore Cottage Cove while you row out to the boat."

The latter solution was fine with Red, and Bill tramped over the clearing, discovering that only the cabin showed signs of recent use. He was standing on the gravelly shore when the strangers' boat came into sight, two men paddling the double-ender awkwardly into Cottage Cove. Red immediately set out from the *Flying Mermaid* to pick him up, and Ole fired up the engine, its steady beat reassuring to Bill.

The figures in the double-ender soon became distinguishable as a weathered old Indian and a gray-bearded white man, seemingly strange partners to the waiting young man.

"Throw me a rope and I'll pull you into the beach. Did your motor break down?" Bill called out.

Gray-beard rose and scampered to the bow, his twisted body gnomelike in appearance as he expertly threw a weighted rope to Bill's feet, neither he nor his partner wasting breath with a reply until their boat was secure.

"Thank you, mister. Yes, our engine broke down today, and we are tired from rowing. My name is Gregori Zohkov, and my partner is Tsimchuck."

Bill offered his hand to Gregori, finding a hesitant response but a firm grip as he spoke, "I'm Bill Pardue from Tacoma. I was here last summer with the *MacDonald*. Are you the same fishermen I saw? Do you live around here?"

With a momentary reluctance, the old Indian accepted Bill's handshake, deigning to reply, "Live at Metlakatla and fish here. Tsimshian land all over."

Nodding agreeably, Bill offered, "My captain is a fair mechanic. Would you like him to look at your motor?"

Tsimchuck frowned, but Gregori answered quickly and simply, "Yes, thanks. We can use the help."

ᴨ   ᴨ   ᴨ

Dusk blurred the shoreline of Annette Island as the *Flying Mermaid* and her tow plied the rough waters, approaching the now visible lights of Metlakatla. Gregori had given Ole three cans of gasoline and guaranteed the cannery would buy his fish if he would tow them to town. Tsimchuck had to be home on Sunday for church services. The weather had cooperated as the tandem pair cruised through Danger Passage and Felice Strait, passing Tamgas Harbor after lunch and then rounding Point Davidson into Nichols Passage.

Bill carried two cups of hot coffee up to Ole and Tsimchuck, the latter serving as navigator in the night seas. The Indian had been almost truculent in manner, appearing not to like his rescuers. His directions to the captain were terse, and he ignored Bill entirely, Gregori softening any rebuff by chatting with the young man and satisfying his ever-present curiosity about Alaska.

When Bill returned to his "galley", Gregori had just washed dishes and was cleaning the sink. He offered to help cook dinner, and a friendly conversation ensued.

Bill finally asked a more personal question about the old Indian, pointing out, "Tsimchuck doesn't like me, but my friend Helen told me that Tsimshians were universally hospitable, ready to help one another - including other Alaskans. Why is Tsimchuck so. . .?"

"Helen!. . .You're from Tacoma?. . .Are you Helen Duncan's mystery friend from college? The white man she invited to her wedding Sunday?" Gregori asked in wonder, smiling broadly as Bill nodded.

His gray-bearded friend explained hastily, "Helen is Tsimchuck's granddaughter. He's been very concerned about missing her wedding. Even I can't get a smile out of him."

"Damn! I'd forgotten the date. Ole said he might take me to Metlakatla for the wedding, but. . .how thoughtless of me to forget," Bill muttered, adding, "Helen said I could bring friends. Would that be okay with her family?"

"Yes, you'll be welcome. Tsimchuck's honor demands it, and besides, Helen is one of his favorites. You know, he has ten children, twenty-eight grandchildren and two great grandchildren. Tsimchuck is a venerated member of his tribe and my best friend, but sometimes he can be difficult. He saw you admiring the cabin where we sometimes spend a night and considers you an intruder," Gregori paused as another thought came to mind, continuing, "I wonder if he knows you're Helen's friend? She must have told him your name when she talked about you. She loves and honors him greatly."

π   π   π

Bill pulled his tie off and stuffed it in his side pocket. He was glad he'd worn it to the wedding ceremony, but the clambake gathering along the seashore was much more casual. The sun had been out long enough to warm the light breeze coming up Nichols Passage, and friends and relatives waited around picnic tables for the arrival of the bride and groom.

"Well, Slim, I'm glad we sold our fish last night. We made enough to buy fuel before we leave for Ketchikan today. When will the new-lyweds show up?" Ole asked, already impatient to be on his way.

"Soon, I hope. Say Ole, aren't the fuel pumps locked? Isn't the father of the groom the local distributor? Let me ask Gregori."

Bill walked over to his new friend, who was engaged in a spirited but good-natured argument with one of the wedding party's ushers. He thought once again that the young man looked familiar, but recognition would not come as he studied his features.

The Indian's dark brown eyes caught sight of Bill, words cut off as a broad grin spread over his countenance, and he called out enthusiastically, "Bill Pardue, welcome to Metlakatla. Remember me, Malcolm Angias, from. . ."

". . .Camp Witek on Guam. Malcolm, it is good to see you. Don't tell me you're one of Helen's cousins?" Bill finished his friend's statement as he shook his hand vigorously.

"Of course, and Tsimchuck's grandson. I told Grandpa we served together in the Marines."

Gregori laughed, adding with a teasing tone, "Ha! Ha! I'm not sure that makes you any more popular with the old man. He doesn't care much for white men."

Bill watched the humor in Malcolm's eyes, in his thoughts recalling their months together on Guam. His friend had been a sergeant and a hero, having received a Silver Star and a Purple Heart on Okinawa. Malcolm was reticent about his personal life as well as his medals, no one knowing the details of either, although Bill remembered now that his mail was postmarked from Alaska.

His friend's stocky wrestler's build hadn't changed, his shoulders and hands looking as powerful as ever. However, four years had etched lines in his now weathered face, giving him a more Indian look than during the war. And his crewcut had grown out considerably, shorter than most of his tribesmen but still a bit shaggy. His teeth were unblemished white enamel, a feature Bill had always envied, and his smile was as warm as ever.

Gregori suddenly pointed to a Cadillac coming down the road, announcing loudly enough for everyone to hear, "Here come, John and Helen. Now we can tap the keg."

Bill followed Gregori into the reception line, meeting the members of the wedding party one by one, getting a warm hug and kiss from Helen. She grasped his arm tightly as she chattered excitedly, "I'm so glad to see you here, Bill, and thank you for fetching Grandpa and Gregori along. Grandpa begrudgingly admitted you and your friends were a big help. We received your gift last week, so I didn't expect to see you here. Oh, I have so many questions, we'll have to talk later."

Turning to her watching husband, she introduced her guest, "Dear, this is Bill Pardue from Tacoma."

John smiled sparingly but extended a welcome hand courteously, "We're happy you could attend our wedding, Bill. Helen has told me so much about her best friend at the College of Puget Sound that I feel I know you. I understand you graduated earlier this month."

"Yes, and Alaska drew me back on a fishing boat. Thanks for having all of us to the celebration. You know, John, you're a fortunate man. Helen is a fine woman. I wish both of you a happy marriage."

A quiet thank you and a few casual handshakes later, Bill left the reception line, not trying to catch up with Gregori who was talking to Tsimchuck across the way.

A familiar grip on his shoulder claimed his attention, and a friendly, "Hey, Bill!" brought his gaze around, his eyes meeting the sloe-eyed stare of Malcolm's companion, time momentarily at a standstill as a spark passed between them. Before him stood a young woman, a girl actually, fresh and vibrant in her natural beauty. His heart tripped as a radiant smile played across her lips fleetingly, mutual recognition of their attraction dimmed abruptly by Malcolm's propriety grasp of her elbow, and his introduction casually offered, "Bill, meet Mae Wilson, my girl and one of Helen's bridesmaids."

Mae held out a small hand to the young man, and he held it lightly as Malcolm completed the introduction, "Mae, this guy is my old buddy from the Marines, Helen's classmate at college and Grandpa's good Samaritan yesterday."

Standing next to Malcolm, the girl was of equal height, but seemed almost fragile beside the Indian's brawny form. 'Hardly fragile,' he thought to himself, 'She's got a nice figure and looks mighty healthy. She has brown hair and eyes, I wonder if she's Tsimshian - she doesn't look it.'

Malcolm led his girl away to greet his family - much to Bill's chagrin. The Tacoma visitor was kept busy for the next hour, Helen's brother introducing him to family members. When he stood before Tsimchuck, Bill realized he'd met everyone and grinned in relief.

The reticent old Indian chuckled irascibly, "Ha! Ha! You did very well, young man. All my relatives like you, except maybe John. Helen's talked about you too much, but he'll come around," Tsimchuck paused and held out his hand in friendship, concluding, "And so will I, Bill Pardue, friend of my grandchildren."

Gregori chimed in, "Finally, you old grouch, you remember your manners. Let me borrow our friend and share a beer before he leaves. Ole's about ready to leave."

In the next few minutes Bill was all but rude to Gregori, failing to catch Mae's eye several times and replying, "Huh?" to his friend's questions.

"Ha! Ha! Mae Wilson is a lovely girl, isn't she? She's not really Malcolm's girl, you know, although he'd like to believe so. She lives in Ketchikan with her father since her mother died, but visits her friends here regularly," Gregori hesitated, observing Bill's interest in the girl.

The young man asked dutifully, "What's her father do for a living?"

"Gene is a timber cruiser for the Furrer Mill in Ketchikan. He used to work on Annette Island, but he moved so his daughter could go to high school in Ketchikan. She graduated with honors a couple of weeks ago."

Gregori hesitated again, finally blurting out, "You know, her grandmother was Tsimshian. She's one–eighth Indian," and then adding more calmly, "That makes a difference to some people up here."

Bill smiled and answered simply, "She's a nice girl. Is she related to Tsimchuck?"

"No, her great-grandfather was a friend of Father Duncan's and married into the tribe before they moved to Annette Island. He and his bride spent their honeymoon on the trip out of Canada." Hesitating yet another time, Gregori offered one other piece of advice, "Gene Wilson is a protective father, and Mae is young and naive. If you look her up in Ketchikan, be on your best behavior."

"Thanks, Gregori, I understand. Now I'm going over to say good-by to Mae and Malcolm before Ole has a conniption fit. He's been signaling me for ten minutes."

ᴨ   ᴨ   ᴨ

The fishing boat maneuvered between the barely visible marker buoys into the Ketchikan fishing dock. Everyone in the crew had enjoyed the clambake, eating and drinking their fill, feeling very friendly toward their hosts. In unanimous yet silent consent, the exhausted crew members retired immediately, only the skipper conducting business that evening. He looked up a fisherman friend to get directions for their halibut trip in the morning.

Two faces appeared in Bill's drowsy half-sleep, a pretty girl in Metlakatla and Charley - beer in hand. He dismissed Charley preemptively and drifted into sleep with romance on his mind.

Chapter Three

A none-too-gentle shake awakened Bill, Ole's low voice calling his name and commanding, "Wake up, Slim. You and I have to take the boat out of the harbor, and then you can cook breakfast. I brought some groceries back with me last night, as well as the location of a good halibut hole in Behm Canal."

Dressing quickly, Bill climbed topside into the still morning air, Ketchikan's lights and their reflection off the water being the only illumination at this hour. He asked in curiosity, "Where away, boss? North or south?"

"North, Slim. We have easy sailing for thirty or forty miles. Cast off the lines," the skipper said as the engine caught and idled smoothly.

Bill performed his familiar deckhand's duties without a hitch, coiling and stowing the lines before moving up to stand beside Ole. As the *Flying Mermaid* turned up Tongass Narrows and the city lights fell behind, Bill could see the changing sky to the east, a comforting sign that dawn was approaching.

Ole answered Bill's unasked question, "I won't need any help at the wheel for awhile, Slim. Why don't you cook us breakfast before you wake the other guys?"

꠸   ꠸   ꠸

Two hours later the boat's chief cook and bottle washer completed his chores and went on deck to stretch his cramped muscles. *'That galley is awfully compact,'* was accompanying thought, followed by admiration for the majestic scenery basking in brilliant sunshine. *'There isn't a prettier place anywhere.'*

Chuckling aloud, an image of this very same scenery came to mind - a gray and blustery March day, but his opinion didn't change as he muttered, "Two sides of a coin."

From nearby Red concurred, "I know what you mean. Night and day is another term I've used. It's downright funny how this country can be so different from summer to winter."

Glancing over the schooner's gear-filled bow, Bill asked, "Where is Behm Canal anyway?"

"See that rocky point to starboard? Well, we'll follow the shoreline around it to the northeast. I'd guess our fishing grounds are better than an hour away. Care for a game of cribbage?"

"No thanks, Red. I think I'll relieve Ole at the wheel for awhile. I've been cooped up long enough."

The skipper stuck his head out the door and accepted Bill's offer hastily, "Slim, I heard you. Come here and steer this boat while I get rid of my morning coffee. If you stay a hundred feet off shore, there'll be no problems."

Bill enjoyed his quartermastering, not at all a chore like cooking. After several minutes of touristy viewing, he settled into a more watchful routine, soon observing his shipmates preparing their fishing gear on the bow. He smiled at his good luck, handling the wheel being a simpler task than laying out fishing lines. He was actually disappointed when Ole took over the wheel and told him to relax for a few minutes.

He joined the men standing before the small wheelhouse and listened as Red pointed easterly and explained, "Ole says there's a halibut bank about halfway to that gray cliff over there. When he stops, we'll start laying out lines."

Bill asked, "How long do you figure that we'll fish here?"

"Ha! Ha! Until the hold is full of halibut or we run out of groceries. How many cans of Spam did the skipper buy?" Red joked.

"Ha! Ha! A full case, my friend, so let's hope the halibut and the weather cooperate. Spam and fish will be our entire diet inside of a week," Bill quipped in return, the other men turning up their noses in a gesture of disgust.

The engine's steady beat changed tempo, signaling its disengagement from the propeller shaft, and the fishermen went to work letting out a line as the boat's momentum served a helpful purpose. Abruptly the contrary motor coughed and sputtered, once, twice, and on the third such sound, stopped altogether.

ᛍ   ᛍ   ᛍ

"Damnation!" Ole roared as he stomped below with an irritated scowl on his face. Even newcomer Bill was aware how helpless they were without power; they could neither fish nor control their movement. The gravelly beach astern suddenly seemed very close to their drifting vessel, a single fishing line in the water now serving as a fragile anchor.

Curses resounded from below, Olson the engineer proving to have an interesting vocabulary in both English and Swedish, Red freely translating the latter words and phrases. The starter turned the motor over with a distinctive cough and sputter on the first try - then nothing.

Ole's head popped out of the door, and he moaned balefully, "Who fueled this boat last night? Damn it, do I have to do everything?"

Each of the men looked at his shipmates, shrugging their shoulders and saving their breath as the forlorn skipper added, "That tank's as dry as a bone. I reckon I'd better radio the Coast Guard before we end up on the beach. I hope our battery has plenty of juice."

𝕋   𝕋   𝕋

Bill hurriedly put the galley in order, eager to be on deck to greet the Coast Guard cutter out of Ketchikan. The crew had retrieved their line by hand with difficulty and had then dropped anchor when they were near shore. Decent weather allowed the boat to remain stationary, and the men's tensions eased, prompting their request for food.

Frustration had finally overtaken Ole, and his attitude induced carelessness. When the anchor was in place, he had rushed back to the engine compartment and promptly slipped on a middle rung of the steel ladder. He fell only a short distance, but ill fortune found him as his right leg slid between two steel engine braces, his torso twisting grotesquely as the leg was pinned in the bilge.

Red and Bill lifted him clear of his entrapment and hoisted him to waiting hands. His intermittent gasps gave way to a shriek of pain when he tried to stand on deck. While the men carried him to his bunk in the cabin adjoining the wheelhouse, Bill prepared a bowl of soup for the invalid. He muttered to himself, '*I hope that leg isn't broken.*'

He'd hand-fed the dispirited fisherman, wrapping him in blankets before he returned to the galley to feed the crew soup and sandwiches.

Stepping onto deck, he admired the cutter's approach, her bow knifing through the choppy surface, leaving an impressive wake behind her. As she slowed to a crawl and coasted to within a hundred feet of the *Flying Mermaid*, an officer called out, "Stand by to receive a line!"

Red waved acknowledgment and moved aft, Bill expecting a weighted rope to be thrown to the boat as the two crafts closed. To his surprise, a Coast Guardsman brought out a whale gun, or at least a contraption that resembled one, and fired a projectile at the *Flying Mermaid*. A length of light line fluttered behind the missile as it arched over the interval, lazily falling toward Red. With a more practiced eye than Bill's, the fisherman stood his ground, watching it strike the cabin wall four feet away.

"My God!" he yelled, "It went right through the wall into the Captain's bunk."

Bill rushed to the cabin, bumping into Ole who was slumped against the door frame, white-faced from pain in his injured leg and frightened into stuttering, "Loo. . .oo. . .ook, Slim. That damned spear harpooned my bunk, right where I'd been napping. If I'd stayed in bed, I'd be skewered. This trip is jinxed. I'm going home!"

Π Π Π

In the smothering rain squall enveloping Tongass Narrows to the south, the *Flying Mermaid* disappeared from sight. Bill stood on the Ketchikan dock for a few minutes, lonely now that Ole and the rest of the crew were gone. His thoughts were reflective of that bizarre incident in Behm Canal that ended his fishing career, the disturbing outbreak of war in faraway Korea, his financial situation nearing the poverty level, and his decision to stay in Ketchikan to seek his fortune.

While he occupied a warm bunk in Ole's boat, life in Alaska had seemed secure, a hundred dollars to his name, the clothes in his dufflebag and good health ample assets for survival. Standing alone as he was, tested his self-confidence and eventually brought a rueful smile to his lips. '*Well, I've burned my bridges behind me, and it's time to stop thinking and start doing. Should I seek a job first or look for a room?'*

Dufflebag over his shoulder, Bill headed for the Carlson grocery store where a community bulletin board might provide a lead. Charley had offered his uncle's couch for the night, but his aunt hadn't endorsed the idea, instead suggesting he check at Carlson's for lodging. His friend had also said his uncle needed help in his store, but Mrs. Blakely's enigmatic stare nixed that idea. Nevertheless, he had appreciated Charley's attempts to help a fraternity brother, and he'd enjoyed their night at a local tavern. Next time he'd have to buy the beer.

Bill halted before the Carlson's store entrance, waiting while a short man with solid shoulders and thinning blond hair fidgeted with a magazine display rack next to the open door. Seeing a customer in the offing, the man's lips smiled a greeting which spread to his clear blue eyes. Stepping aside and motioning the younger man to enter with a three-fingered left hand, he asked courteously, "What can I help you with today?"

"I just want to look over your bulletin board, if I may," Bill rejoined with equal politeness.

Studying him as he walked to the board and fingered the room and board cards pinned there, the storekeeper queried, "Aren't you a friend of Charley Blakely's?" At a nod from the visitor, he added, "From college, I hear. I'm Roy Carlson, sometimes known as 'Little Swede'. 'Big Swede' is my brother Olaf, a ferryboat captain. He's on a fishing vacation with Blackjack Blakely. We're all old friends. Welcome to Ketchikan."

They shook hands firmly, Roy's right hand normal and strong. Bill replied, "Thanks. I'm Bill Pardue, up from Tacoma on a fishing boat. I like this part of Alaska and stayed behind when Ole went south this morning. Now I need to find a place to room and board while I look for a job."

With a knowing nod, Roy said, "I guessed that was what you were doing. I have an extra bedroom upstairs in my house. You'd have to share a bath with my brother, but Olaf lives on the ferry more than with us. My wife is a good cook, to boot. Are you interested?"

"Certainly, but I'm short on cash and out of work," Bill stated frankly, afraid his honesty might negate the offer.

"Would one hundred dollars a month seem reasonable to you? Can you afford half a month's rent in advance?"

"Why sure, Roy. That's more than fair. You've got a deal. Can I move in today?" Bill accepted eagerly, aware the rent was low by Alaskan standards.

The storekeeper wrote on a roll of butcher paper and tore off the piece, handing it to the newcomer with further advice, "Take this note to my wife Julia and introduce yourself. Oh yes, pay her fifty dollars, and she'll probably feed you lunch before you walk down to the Furrer Mill. John's hiring men to pull the green chain. You know, the dirty work in the mill."

"Thanks, Roy. Hard work won't hurt me. How do I find your house?"

Bill 's destination was perched on a steep hillside, accessible by a terraced stairway built in three tiers of eighty-four risers. He knew the exact number because he counted them as he puffed his way to a railed veranda encompassing the south and west walls of the two–story house. With a rueful smile on his lips, he saw the access road come up the north side of the property at a precipitous but manageable grade to the Carlson garage.

He was admiring the view of Tongass Narrows and Gravina Island and recovering his breath when he heard a door latch click behind him. A maternal voice sounded from the far innards of the dwelling, carrying through the opening door, "Don't forget your jacket, Aaron. It's going to rain today."

Bill turned to face a hesitating tow-headed lad, startled blue eyes watching him from cleancut and youthful features. The visitor noticed the pre-teen boy was bare-armed, and he thought, *'This must be Roy's son. Not big at this age, but he's all gangling arms and legs, and look at those size twelve feet. He's going to be a lot taller than his dad.'*

"Aaron! Did you put your jacket on? Why is there a draft?" the voice modulating as a motherly figure appeared in the hallway.

The boy addressed the stranger courteously, "Hello, Mister, are you looking for my dad?"

"Hi! No, I'm looking for Missus Carlson," and offering his hand to the lad, he concluded, "You must be Aaron Carlson. I'm Bill Pardue."

As they shook hands, the woman of the house stepped forward with a slight smile, introducing herself, "I'm Julia Carlson. What can I do for you, Mister Pardue?"

Roy's wife was fairly tall and solidly built, and replicas of her son's blue eyes peered at him from behind horn-rimmed spectacles, her blonde hair tied in a bun behind her head. Bill thought, *'Missus Carlson is kind of attractive for an older woman. She must be in her late thirties.'*

"Hello, Missus Carlson, your husband sent this note with me," he stated soberly as he handed over the torn butcher paper.

She laughed gaily, her humor lighting her countenance in contrast to her image of a moment ago, and she sallied, "Oh Roy and his darn butcher paper notes."

Bill reacted with a relieved laugh of his own, "Ha! Ha! Your husband took pity on a stranded sailor and offered me board and room in your home. I'm to pay you half a month's rent if you agree to take me in."

"Of course, you're welcome, Mister Pardue. Come in and look at your room. It's not very large, but it does have a nice view of town and the narrows. How long will you be staying with us?"

As he followed her and the boy upstairs, he replied, "For the summer, I expect. Roy said the Furrer Mill is hiring, and I need a job." Pausing on the upper landing, he complimented his landlady, "You keep a lovely home, Missus Carlson."

As she beamed her appreciation for his observation, Aaron impulsively offered, "Gee, Bill, I can show you the way to Furrer's."

"Aaron, mind your manners. Mister Pardue is our guest's name," corrected his mother.

"No, folks. I'm just plain Bill. And thanks Aaron, I can use a guide to the mill. Is it far?"

"See, Mom, we men don't stand on formality. Do you play chess, Bill?"

Smiling at her son's eager friendliness, she spoke to her new boarder, "Call me Julia, Bill, and come down to the kitchen for a sandwich after Aaron has shown you the room and the bathroom you'll share with my brother-in-law."

♫   ♫   ♫

Against the constant background of whining saws, Bill stood alongside the moving belt carrying freshly cut Sitka spruce from the blades. He had started work five minutes after his arrival at Furrer's, filling in for an absent millworker. Three dollars an hour and time-and-a-half for overtime, of which there was plenty during the summer, seemed a good wage to him.

Of course he was working on the "green chain," pulling four-by-eights at his station while his senior co-workers handled two-by-fours, but he reminded himself that hard work would be good for his soul as well as strengthen his body.

Picking up one end of a heavy twenty-four foot piece of lumber and dragging it to his stack, he put down the butt and shuffled the timber forward. He thought, *'Nothing scientific about this work, but then I have time to dream about Cottage Cove and my new life in Alaska.'*

Suddenly the piece was jerked to a stop, and as Bill turned around, he heard a sneering cackle and then a snide remark in a familiar tarheel accent, "Heh! Heh! Got you, Greenhorn," A big bruiser from North Carolina named Rick Honeycutt was anchoring his timber, releasing it with another sneer as he moved back to his own pile before the foreman saw him.

Bill continued working as he watched Honeycutt out of the corner of his eye, considering how to deal with the fellow. Rick was six-four and two hundred and fifty pounds of mean and irascible bully, thinking himself as the cock of the walk. He even thought himself a ladies' man although Bill considered his brutish face anything but handsome.

Wondering to himself, Bill thought Rick might look more presentable if he kept his perpetual five o'clock shadow in hand. *'Oh well, I'm not likely to top that moose in a rough-and-tumble fight, and I don't*

see any girls around. Maybe I should keep a two-by-four handy, if he
gets to be a pain in the butt,' a chuckle rattling out of his throat aloud.

"What's so funny, Greenhorn?" Rick called across the stack of
four-by-eights in growling tones, seeming to read Bill's mind.

The shop foreman walked past Bill, murmuring approval to the
newcomer, "You're doing just fine, Pardue."

Oblivious to the animosity between the two men, the boss
signaled the glaring bully with a beckoning index finger, announcing
for all to hear, "Rick, you've been clamoring for a chance at sawyer.
Come with me and let's see if you can do the job."

A broad smile creased Honeycutt's face and with an "I told you
so" look to his fellow workers on the green chain, he followed his boss
out the door. Bill breathed a visible sigh of relief, both for avoiding a
confrontation on his first day of work and for having peace and quiet
on this crew. Confirmation of the latter point was quickly evident in the
relaxed smiles around the shed. He thought he'd be happy in his
summer job, and he looked forward to living with the Carlson family.

As Bill crossed the open yard, a woman's voice called his name,
"Yoohoo! Mister Pardue, you need to fill in your employment card, and
Mister Furrer would like to meet you." The gray-haired office manger
waved cheerfully as he answered her summons and headed for the
open door.

After completing the simple form against the backdrop of mill
noises outside and a muted conversation in the adjacent office, Bill
asked, "Missus Johnson, when will Mister Furrer be free to see me?"

"Oh, right away, Mister Pardue. His daughter Alexis just returned
home from a visit to a college friend, and they're catching up on family
news. He said to bring you right in."

Knocking lightly, the office manager opened the door and walked
forward to hand Bill's employment form to John Furrer at a small desk
of unfinished spruce. As Bill was to learn in his association with the
mill owner, Furrer was unpretentious and straight as an arrow in personality as well as business. He was of the old school that said a
handshake was as binding as a written contract, and his smile was a
sure offer of friendship.

Bill took a good look at the man as he followed Missus Johnson into the office and was impressed with his solid appearance. Clad in plaid shirt, denim trousers and hobnail boots, his sinewy, gnarled hands somehow matched his craggy outdoorsman's face, piercing gray eyes overshadowed by a shaggy gray mop of hair. *'An Alaskan he is for sure,'* thought the newcomer.

As John Furrer rose and shook the extended hand, he greeted the young man, "Welcome to Ketchikan, Bill." At that moment Bill's gaze fell on a beautiful girl seated across from her father, her smile as exciting to him as Babs' had been before that dance. His grip tightened briefly as he looked into violet eyes, alive with interest even though Bill was scruffy with sweat and sawdust.

"Ha! Ha!" Furrer laughed delightedly at Bill's reaction, "This is my daughter Alexis - my pride and joy. Lexy, meet Bill Pardue, newly arrived from. . .", and scanning the card hastily he added, "Tacoma. Bill, when did you graduate from college?"

"Last month, Mister Furrer. I came up on a halibut schooner last week."

Furrer interrupted, "Were you on the boat that ran out of fuel?"

Grinning sheepishly, Bill nodded in silent affirmation.

Alexis covered the young man's discomfiture with a diverting question, "Which university did you attend, Mister Pardue?"

"The College of Puget Sound is my alma mater, Miss Furrer. Tacoma has been home, but I like Alaska, and I'm going to try my luck in this area. It's beautiful in the summer," he responded.

"Ugh! Give me California any time. Palo Alto is simply wonderful."

Bill agreed readily, "The entire Bay Area is great, and the Stanford campus is tops, but there are an awful lot of people crowding into the San Francisco area. Even San Jose is becoming a real city, and it used to be farming land."

John interrupted in curiosity, "Why are you working on the green chain? With your military record and college degree you could have found work in management or sales."

Bill smiled ingenuously and explained, "I had a couple of opportunities - insurance and oil, but I want to find something of my own in Alaska. It's the land of opportunity."

"See, Lexy, here's a young man that likes Alaska better than the forty-eight states. Why can't you appreciate our finer qualities?"

Casting a loving glance at her father, she teased, "You're the most wonderful thing in Ketchikan, Daddy. I love this wilderness because you do, but don't expect me to love the rain or Ketchikan's isolation from the real world."

The father smiled indulgently at his only child, observing playfully, "I believe that fancy education you're getting is ruining a good native Alaskan."

Glancing up at Bill, he apologized, "Sorry we've kept you listening to a family difference of opinion, Bill. I like to say hello to new employees and let them know my office door is always open. I enjoy visiting with you men, so feel free to drop in anytime."

"Thanks, Mister Furrer. I'll remember your offer."

"And call me John, all the guys do. See you tomorrow," the mill owner concluded.

᛬ ᛬ ᛬

Bill came out of his reverie abruptly, Aaron appearing before him on the gravelly road, asking eagerly, "Did you get the job, Bill? I mean the regular job. I told Mom you went right to work."

"Ha! Ha! Yes sirree, I'm pulling the green chain. Not a big deal, but a regular check will pay my bills. What did you do this afternoon?"

Aaron smiled with pride as he replied, "I caught six salmon over on the creek and sold them along Creek Street for four bits each. Oh, I kept one for Mom. We're having it for dinner tonight.

"What will you do with all that money, my friend?" Bill asked in teasing but curious tones.

Aaron hesitated, turning a little bashful as he shared his secret, "I'm saving it for an airplane ride. Dad says I can go flying on my twelfth birthday. I want to be a pilot and fly all over the world."

Bill nodded in sober reflection, aware of the boy's eyes seeking approval, finally advising, "I think you can do anything you set your mind to, Aaron Carlson. Flying is certainly a responsible career in these modern times. Good luck!"

"Has my son been talking about flying again?" Roy remarked as he topped the hillside stairway. His arm encircled his son's shoulders as he joined them and spoke in fatherly tones, "I guess I'm not raising a storekeeper, am I, Son? You have a dream of your own."

To his boarder he offered, "Come on in and meet my brother Olaf-'Big Swede.' He returned from that fishing trip today and is sailing to-morrow on his ferry run."

Bill met Roy's brother a few moments later on the landing outside their adjoining rooms and wondered how the two men could be brothers. Olaf was appropriately named Big Swede, standing six-three in his bare feet, muscular shoulders stretching his bathrobe's fabric to its limit. He had a full head of blond hair neatly trimmed about his ears, with bright cheerful blue eyes smiling a welcome toward the new boarder. He was as casual and irreverent as Roy was methodical and conforming, although both possessed a redeeming sense of humor.

"The bathroom's yours, and there's a little hot water left," the smiling man said as they shook hands. "Glad to meet you, Bill. I'm Roy's brother, Olaf. I hear you've spent the afternoon on the green chain - hard but honest labor. Julia says dinner is in ten minutes, and I'm never late for one of her meals," he stated appreciatively and dis-appeared into his room.

"Okay, Olaf, I'm hungry, too," Bill stated as he went to his dresser for clean underwear and then hurried into the bathroom.

When the dinner bell sounded, both men rushed downstairs to the dining room, Olaf's familiarity with the house landing him in his seat first. Bill neatly avoided any faux-pas at the table by sitting next to the big man and aping his manners. Roy said grace before the newcomer could reach for the food, the dinner ritual taking but a moment.

"Amen!. . .Pass the potatoes, Dad," Aaron spoke quickly, beating his uncle's reach for the bowl. To Bill he explained, "It's Carlson self-defense, Bill. Uncle Olaf loves mashed potatoes, and I want my share."

"Shame on you, Aaron," Julia reprimanded her son with good-humored banter. Glancing at Olaf she added, " There's more potatoes on the range when your uncle finishes this batch."

The men at the table dug right in, conversation for a time limited to Julia's monologue of the day's events.

When she switched to a question for her new boarder, Bill swallowed a mouthful of food painfully, and politely replied, "Yes, Ma'am. I'm working at Furrer's Mill."

Olaf grinned as he filled his plate again, beating the distracted boarder to the salmon as well as the mashed potatoes. Bill smiled ruefully as he cleaned his plate while answering all of Julia's questions in detail, being rewarded with an extra big piece of apple pie with a slice of cheddar cheese beside it, her brother-in-law receiving only a sliver of the dessert.

She laughed gaily at Olaf's look of consternation, finally ad-mitting, "I'm joking, brother-in-law of mine. I made a lemon meringue pie just for you, but you should share it will Bill."

It seemed that the rest of the Carlson family seldom ate lemon pie, either deferring to Olaf's voracious appetite or not liking it, Bill couldn't discern which with all the familial raillery across the table this evening.

He excused himself after agreeing to accompany Aaron on a fishing expedition on Sunday, full of good food and pleasant company, content now to test his new bed. It had been a long and eventful day for the newcomer to Alaska, and he was hopeful that he would soon cease being a chechako.

॥   ॥   ॥

Summer flew by, or so it seemed to Bill, his first two paychecks cashed and a few dollars put aside in a savings account downtown. He had gone fishing with Aaron every Sunday, helping him expand his hoard of coins intended for his birthday flight, and he had gone to Charley's for a beer a couple of times. He had even talked to Alexis Furrer in the mill office a time or two, but he was satisfied with his quiet life as a millworker and boarder. His friendship with the Carlson family grew stronger, Julia smiling approval at his staid, hard-working and savings personality. He viewed his new life with amusement, feeling a little like Mister Hyde with Doctor Jekyl on vacation, knowing himself well enough to dispel any claim to being saintly.

He had taken to stopping by the store after finishing his shift at the mill, helping Roy close up shop, accepting a bottle of Coca Cola for his efforts. His interest in the grocery business flattered his friend's ego, but Bill learned a lot about Ketchikan and the territory in their casual conversations.

It was easy to share his dream of Cottage Cove with his new friend, and soon they began a daily game of estimating the supplies necessary to live a winter on Duke Island. The methodical store-keeper eventually tore off a humongous piece of butcher paper from the roll on the counter and wrote down each and every item they se-lected. Roy stored it under the cash register, the list known only to the two conspiring friends.

One evening Alexis entered the store, greeting Roy like an old friend as she ordered three steaks from the meat cooler. Surprised at finding Bill sweeping the aisle, she smiled prettily and kidded him, "Doesn't Father pay you enough, Bill?"

"Ha! Ha! Naturally not, Alexis. No worker ever believes he gets paid enough for his labor," Bill retorted.

From across the store Roy quipped in mock sarcasm, "Don't think you're getting more than one Coke for helping me, Bill."

The youngsters laughed dutifully, and as Alexis continued to smile at him, Bill asked tentatively, "Would you like to take in a movie with me some evening?"

"Sure, I'm free Friday night. We could go to the soda fountain after the film. That's where most of the gang gather."

Bill nodded agreeably, suggesting, "I'll pick you up at seven o'clock. Is that okay?"

Alexis nodded, still smiling as she said, "See you then, Bill. Bye!" Accepting a package from Roy, she left the store. Bill ignored his friend's eyebrow-raised curiosity, thinking platonically that it was time for him to make a few friends. Besides she was awfully pretty.

π   π   π

Bill was striding hurriedly across the mill yard Friday afternoon on his way home to bathe and change clothes, when the owner called out his name, "Bill! Bill Pardue! Have you got a minute?"

Reluctantly the young man changed course to the office, thinking it likely that the boss knew about his date with Alexis and wondering if he was going to be lectured on gentlemanly behavior. Roy had told him that Alexis' mother was dead, and John was a doting father, having raised the girl as a single parent.

Missus Johnson handed Bill a steaming cup of coffee as he entered the office, smiling pleasantly, and he thought, conspiratorially at him.

"Thanks, Missus Johnson. The air is cool when the sun goes behind those clouds. Something warm in my stomach is just what I need."

Directing a probing gaze at Furrer standing beside the lady, he nodded and answered the original question, "Yes, I have a few minutes, John, but not much more. What can I do for you?"

"Well, young man, I hope I can do something for you. I have a sales position open and thought you might consider accepting the job. Much of the work would be representing my company in the Seattle, Portland and San Francisco markets. You're a college grad and should find the work easy, and in a year or two you might move into the office with me. It's a good opportunity," Furrer concluded.

"Thank you, John, but I just left Tacoma to live in Alaska. Any long term commitment to work in the States is not for me. Actually my goal is to find a place where I can grow with Alaska. I believe statehood is coming and will open up this country."

"I thought you might feel that way, Bill," the businessman said, not unpleased with the straight-forward reply, adding with a smile, "But you're the best man I have in the mill for this job. Give it some thought anyway. I'm in no hurry."

Bill left the office wondering about Furrer's job, a nagging suspicion that the offer was tied to his date with Alexis dominating his thinking. *The position sounds tailor-made for a prospective son-in-law in the business. 'Ha! Ha! I'm only taking his daughter to the movie theater. My imagination is no doubt overactive, but John Furrer hasn't said ten words to me since that visit in his office. And now I'm a good man for management?'*

᛫᛫᛫   ᛫᛫᛫   ᛫᛫᛫

Always appreciative of a good western, Bill had enjoyed the latest Jimmy Stewart film, "Winchester 73." He had found the Furrer home without any problem, and had visited with Alexis and her father before they walked to the theater.

The girl confirmed his suspicions as they walked arm in arm along the sidewalk, "Excuse Daddy, Bill, he likes to talk to my dates. Every young man I go out with is given Father's once-over. He told me you turned down his sales job. Too bad, we could have seen each other if you traveled to San Francisco for the mill."

Bill was pleased with her interest in him and suggested, "We've got the rest of the summer before you go back to Stanford. How about going fishing with Aaron and me on Sunday?"

"Oh, with the Carlson boy? No thanks, Bill, I'm not a fisherman. You could ask me to the King Salmon Derby dance next Saturday," she countered.

Bill agreed eagerly, "That's a great idea, Alexis. Will you go with me? Maybe you can meet me at the store after work next week and tell me about the dance. Roy will treat us to a Coke."

They cut short their discussion when they reached the soda fountain, Bill meeting a dozen of Alexis' friends during the ensuing hour. Recognizing several family names, he thought, *'These kids are typical teenagers - not a care in the world. Ha! Ha! Of course my date is their age, and I'm not much older.'*

Leaving the soda fountain after an hour of socializing, the two strolled up the street, a boisterous trio of millworkers standing on the street corner. One of the men stepped forward to greet the couple, Bill quickly recognizing the bully, Rick Honeycutt.

His nemesis was surprisingly cordial as he spoke, actually removing his cap to say hello to Alexis, "Good evening, Bill, Miss Furrer. It's a nice night, isn't it?"

Bill answered in kind, "Yes, we're enjoying our stroll. I take it you're acquainted with the boss's daughter Alexis."

"We haven't met formally, but I've seen you at the mill, Miss Furrer. I'm Rick Honeycutt, one of your daddy's sawyers." He paused for a moment as she silently nodded in response to his self-introduction and finally blurted out an invitation, "Would you consider going to the King Salmon Derby dance with me, Miss Furrer?"

Bill observed Alexis' decline like the lady she was, her lips smiling courteously, but her eyes cool and disapproving as she replied, "Thank you, Mister Honeycutt, but I'm attending with Mister Pardue. Perhaps we'll see you there. Good night."

Rick flushed as the couple walked on, Bill catching a flash of malevolent temper in the bully's expression, realizing the man's anger was directed at him. *'Oh well, we didn't get along anyway,'* he thought, and promptly lost interest in all, save the pretty girl on his arm.

π   π   π

Friday afternoon the foreman pulled Bill aside with a message to report to the boss immediately. Wondering at such a summons to the office, Bill entered with a question in his eyes for Missus Johnson. With her usual motherly smile, she called over her shoulder, "Mister Furrer, Bill Pardue is here."

"Come on in, Bill," John's voice rumbled through the partly opened door, and upon seeing the young man step forward, he introduced his companion, "Bill Pardue, meet Gene Wilson, the mill's timber cruiser. He needs help scouting a stand of federal forest timber which is up for bid next month. Are you interested in climbing a mountain or two over in Carroll Inlet? It should be educational."

A weather-beaten yet gentle face with gray eyes and dark hair looked up at the young man, lips creasing into a pixie-like grin as he explained his need, "It shouldn't take but three or four days, Bill. We have to hurry if John wants to submit a bid on time. You would be my packer and have a chance to learn a little about cruising timber at the same time."

Bill accepted the gnarled and calloused hand in a firm grip, feeling a muscular response from the lean but sturdy man standing before him and quickly agreed, "The job sounds interesting. When do we leave?"

"Monday morning first light. I have chartered a plane to fly us in and then to return for us on Friday morning," Gene expounded.

Furrer broke in with a chuckle, "Ha! Ha! You can still escort Alexis to the dance, Bill. Is your daughter going, Gene?"

"I don't know, John. Mae just returned from Metlakatla yesterday, and all we've talked about is the wedding," Gene replied.

Bill's face brightened in recognition of Mae Wilson's name, and he exclaimed, "Gene Wilson! Of course your name sounds familiar, I met Mae at Helen's wedding. Malcolm Angias told me she lived with her father in Ketchikan. Pleased to meet you, Gene." He shook the older man's hand a second time with friendly enthusiasm.

"Well, I expect you must be Helen's friend from college. Mae told me how pleased the Duncans were to have you at the wedding. My daughter was impressed when old Tsimchuck shook your hand - and smiled." Gene responded.

With a chuckle and nodding affirmation, Bill admitted, "Being a friend of Helen and Malcolm, two of the old man's favorite grandchildren finally broke the ice. Gregori told me Tsimchuck seldom talks to white men - let alone chechakos."

John Furrer quickly inserted his opinion, "You're no longer a chechako, young man. You've made a lot of friends in Alaska. Say, about that dance tomorrow night, maybe you and Alexis can take Mae with you."

Bill looked directly at Gene as he queried in doubtful tones, "Would she like to attend? Isn't she dating Malcolm Angias?"

"They're good friends is all. Mae is enrolled at the University of Washington this fall and will be leaving for Seattle next month. But to answer your question, why don't you walk home with me and we'll ask her."

With a nod of release from Furrer, Bill followed his new friend out of the office, chatting with him as they walked up the street.

ᛏᛏ   ᛏᛏ   ᛏᛏ

The float plane circled lazily over Ketchikan, gaining altitude before swinging easterly over the Gateway City. Clear and windless weather had opened a flight path over the mountaintops of Revillagigedo Island toward Carroll Inlet, Bill appreciating the aerial view as the pilot pointed out topographical landmarks with enthusiastic pride in his island homeland. Only Gene Wilson seemed unaffected by the scenic panorama passing below, intent on his notepad and the map spread over his lap.

Bill reminisced as they soared over the pristine landscape, recalling his pleasure as Alexis drove her father's Chrysler up the street to the Wilson apartment. Charley had agreed to escort Mae to the King Salmon Derby dance on a double date, walking over to her place to meet Alexis and Bill. The waiting couple appeared beside the car as Alexis braked to the curb, everyone exchanging greetings as Mae scrambled across the back seat.

During the short trip to the dance hall, Charley and Alexis were as talkative as Mae was silent, Bill happy to join in the conversation as the opportunity presented itself.

Studying the waterways below as the pilot continued to identify landmarks, Bill recalled his mixed feelings of Saturday evening, inevitably comparing this affair with his prom experience. Alexis was not the manipulative hussy that Babs had been at that other dance, but she did spend an awful lot of time with Charley.

Dancing with Mae proved to be a distinct pleasure, the girl putting Bill at ease with graceful movement and small talk. He remembered shrugging mentally at the time. She seldom spoke when all four of them were together and yet carried on a newsy dialogue with him when Charley was dancing with Alexis. He learned Malcolm's younger brother Arthur had joined the Marines and was in San Diego at boot camp, the newlyweds had returned from their Juneau honeymoon before Mae had left Metlakatla, and her father was moving to Seattle in the fall to be near her. Gene had taken the job of Furrer Mill's salesman that John had offered to Bill.

'Ah well,' Bill thought, 'So much for thinking it over. John didn't waste any time in hiring someone else.' With a mental twinge of guilt at the envy on his mind, he mumbled aloud, "I want to homestead Cottage Cove anyway."

Gene responded with a grin, "And where is Cottage Cove, Bill?"

Returning a grin in kind, Bill said, "Off Ray Anchorage on Duke Island. Have you ever seen that small cabin on the south shore?"

"Yes, I recall it vaguely. Used by fishermen, isn't it? It's a pretty setting, Bill. You ought to see a lawyer about your veteran's rights to homesteading," Gene commented and then pointed ahead with an extended finger, "There's Carroll Islet now."

Bill nodded, his mind wandering back to the dance, an unpleasant memory taking over the image. Returning from the rest room, the young man had overheard voices coming from an adjacent alcove, recognizing first Charley's laughter, and as Bill stopped in his tracks, Alexis said in hushed tones, "I think we should return to our table. Our dates will be patiently waiting. Tee hee!"

Bill was turning away when Charley laughed derisively, "Ha! Ha! Let them sit. Bill had his nerve, asking me to bring an Indian to the dance. She's as wooden as the cigar store variety - no fun at all. Why did you agree to double date with her along?"

"Well, she's not really my friend, and my father and Bill made the arrangements," Alexis replied in plaintive tones.

Charley muttered in criticism, "Well, Bill is okay, but his judgment of people can be lousy. I think he actually likes Indians. I don't understand him."

Bill's shame at eavesdropping turned quickly to cold anger as he strode away, body rigid and eyes staring straight ahead. He almost passed Mae, who grasped his arm and queried, "What's the matter, Bill?"

Unwilling to repeat what he'd overheard and thinking irrelevantly, Mae doesn't even look Indian, he forced a thin smile to his lips and admitted, "I'm upset with Alexis and Charley." After a few moments of silence, he added, "I think it's time to go home."

As Mae nodded, Charley's voice came from behind him, sounding relieved in agreement, "Let's call it a night, folks. I'm going fishing with my uncle tomorrow."

Bill's attention returned to the plane as it banked sharply to the left and settled into an approach over glass-smooth water. Its floats soon touched down, cutting a swath with a sizable wake astern. As the pilot nosed his plane toward shore, Bill reckoned his education as a timber cruiser was about to begin.

ᴛᴛ   ᴛᴛ   ᴛᴛ

Gene proved to be a good companion over the ensuing four days, silent when working in the forest but a decent conversationalist beside their campfire. His familiarity with local birds and animals matched his knowledge of the trees around them. The timber cruiser was civil in answering questions about what he was doing as he worked, but volunteered little vocational instruction during their sojourn. Yet Bill watched and learned from an expert by example, appreciative of a new experience as well as a bigger paycheck. His savings account was approaching the total cost of Little Swede's "list of possibles" kept under his store counter.

As he lay drowsing in his sleeping bag beside the glowing embers of the camp fire on their first night, the forest stillness erupted in a beastly roar and thundering crash. Bill reared up in shock, struggling to escape his bedding as chuckles emanated from his partner.

Gene's voice rippled in playful humor as he gibed his young companion, "Ha! Ha! Some chechako you are, Bill. That bear was just as scared of your snoring as you were of his roaring. He took off up the mountain like a shot. A black bear probably, only testy when cornered. How's your ankle?"

"It's okay, but I'd be running in the other direction if I could have escaped my bedding, sprained ankle or not," Bill replied sheepishly.

"Ha! Ha! You mean swimming, don't you? What's a city boy like you doing in Alaska? John told me he'd offered you the sales job, but you turned it down."

Bill laughed at himself and explained his goals, no longer sleepy and glad to hear his partner chatting freely. He concluded a virtual monologue on Bill Pardue with an explanation of his sprain, "I should have watched where I was going this afternoon, but my right ankle turns over now and again - an old basketball injury."

Gene's nod was almost visible in the deep purple twilight as he warned, "Safety is critical when you're alone in these woods. That's why I asked for a partner on this job. Furrer wants a speedy survey of this timber stand. Now go back to sleep. It's your job to fix breakfast in the morning."

Bill's ankle held up on the job, careful use of the joint and Gene's empathetic assignment of chores making it almost normal by their last evening at Carroll Inlet.

"Thanks, Gene, for having me along, and for putting up with a cripple to boot."

The older man's weathered face creased in a wrinkled smile, and in humor he responded, "You're welcome, my friend. That sprained ankle actually was helpful since you kept out of my way in the forest - being careful, I mean. Ha! Ha!"

Bill chuckled without any retort, and Gene's countenance sobered as a companionable tranquillity enveloped the camp site. Gene hesitated, finding the right words to express his feelings as he broke the silence, "Thank you for taking care of my girl at the dance. Mae told me that your friend didn't like her. She was grateful for your understanding and for escorting her to the door."

"Charley isn't much of a friend sometimes, and Alexis' behavior only made the situation worse. I was relieved to escape that date without a fuss. Those two deserve each other. Your daughter was a lady throughout the evening."

Gene agreed proudly, "She's always been a wonderful daughter. Her mother died of tuberculosis when Mae was a child, and we've taken care of each other ever since. That's why I decided to work in Seattle. Mae's going to the University of Washington to study nursing. Am I being too protective? I want to support her decision, but people can be cruel because of her Indian heritage."

"I think it's great that you two can be a family in a new city. Your support will give her more time to study. Will you come back to Ketchikan when Mae is a full-fledged nurse?"

"Yes, or Metlakatla. Whatever Mae decides is fine with me. Her great-grandmother was a Tsimshian princess who married a friend of Father Duncan 's. The newlyweds moved to the island with her tribe in 1887. Mae is one-eighth Tsimshian and proud of it," Gene concluded in an almost combative tone.

Grinning broadly, Bill quickly agreed, "You won't get any argument from me about your daughter. She should be proud of her ancestry, not many of us are descended from royalty. Besides, Mae is as intelligent as she is beautiful. You're a lucky father."

"Ha! Ha! You're right, of course. It's just that Mae has always thought Alexis was perfect - and her special friend. She belittles herself in comparison, and I can't criticize Alexis - her friend and John's daughter. We've all been friends for a long time."

Bill concurred readily, "Alexis is nice enough. She's very sophisticated, but she lacks the character your daughter has. And you're right, Mae has to learn the difference between the two traits."

π π π

Bill felt the white caps slap their plane's pontoons as the pilot glided gently onto the wind-blown surface of Tongass Narrows. When the plane shuddered with real contact, he thought it was a propitious time to return. The weather had changed overnight, with a dark gray cloud blanketing the Alaskan islands. Another day in the wilderness would have resulted in a very wet camp.

As they debarked the aircraft, Gene spoke for the first time since breakfast, "Bill, let's drop our gear off at the freight office. I want to introduce you to a lawyer friend of mine. We'll probably find him having lunch on Creek Street. He drinks too much, but he knows territorial law."

Bill nodded and followed his partner up the street, asking as they crossed the bridge, "What's your friend's name?"

"Don Wilson, and he's neither the radio announcer, nor a relative. But ask him if he knows Jack Benny, and he'll do a perfect impersonation of the Benny's sidekick. Now remember, Bill, he may appear a clown, but he's a very capable attorney."

Moments later a man called out from the porch of a seamstress' shop, "Hello, Gene. How are you doing?"

Gene smiled as he turned toward the balding, thin man sporting a thick mustache, and replied, "Hi, Curly. When are we going to play stud again?"

Guffawing loudly, the dandified denizen of Creek Street offered, "Come on down to our place tonight. Bring your friend along. Some of the guys are having a poker party - draw or stud. You might. . ."

A blowzy woman interrupted in a loud but pleasant voice, " Gene Wilson, where have you been keeping yourself?" Before he could see her clearly, let alone answer, a heavily made-up half-dressed woman of many years stepped into the doorway and continued, "How is that lovely daughter of yours? Give her my love."

Gene laughed as the apparition vanished within the shop, calling out, "Ha! Ha! We're just fine, Dolly. Thank you," and turned to the man, declining his invitation, "Sorry, Curly, but I'm having dinner with my daughter this evening. It's been good seeing you and Dolly."

Waving a casual good-by as they walked on, Gene explained in *sotto voce,* "Yes, that's our most famous resident on Creek Street, Dolly Arthur, or Big Dolly as she's known. Past her prime, but she still knows everyone in town. Curly is her companion but not as well liked as Dolly. They both think the world of Mae, so they're all right in my book."

Gene led the way up the boardwalk and turned into a midstreet tavern, its precarious appearance enhanced by the rickety pilings holding it aloft. Creek Street reminded him of Salmon Beach in Tacoma, a fishing village he had often visited with a fraternity brother. Picturesque was an understatement for either locale, the quaint wooden houses perched above a gravelly beach seemingly from another era.

Sitting center stage with a gathering of cronies was a figure quickly recognizable, albeit a reasonable facsimile of the radio personality. Don Wilson rose to greet his old friend Gene and then offered his hand to Bill. Tongue in cheek, Bill delivered his punch line on cue, "Gee, Don, do you know Jack Benny?"

The tavern audience was immediately rewarded with the humorous impersonation Gene had predicted, patrons quieting their chatter to appreciate Don's performance. Noting the smug looks on both men's faces, Don concluded, "Say, I bet Gene put you up to that question, didn't he?"

"Guilty as charged, Counselor," Bill admitted as the tavern hum returned, "But he also told me you were the best lawyer in town."

Sputtering with suppressed mirth, Gene spat out, "Don, Bill misunderstood my praise. I said you were the best lawyer I knew - and the only one."

"Ha! Ha! You no doubt told him I was a comedian as well. What can I do for you, young man? How about a beer?"

Bill forthwith explained his interest in homesteading a site on Duke Island as they sat eating smoked salmon and drinking beer, ending up their meeting by hiring Don Wilson to prepare claim forms for him.

As the two friends returned to the plane company's freight office for their gear, Bill's persistently frowning expression drew a bit of cheerful humor from Gene, "So his fee of a hundred dollars is your week's pay at the mill. Think of Don's fee as part of your investment, and Don's bar bill on Creek Street. Ha! Ha!"

Grinning sheepishly at the grain of truth in his friend's gibe, Bill shrugged his shoulders expressively, figuring out loud, "I need to work another month to afford my homestead. How's the weather around here in September?"

ᛏ ᛏ ᛏ

Bill leaned against the ship's wheel, playing the quartermaster with a bit of nostalgia as Big Swede looked on. The ferry handled differently than either the *MacDonald* or the *Flying Mermaid*. He thought, *'I guess they are boats and Olaf's vessel is a ship. I believe my host is a little nervous with me steering and misty fog all about us. I'd better give him the wheel.'*

Motioning for relief, Bill said, "Thanks for letting me get the feel of your ship, Captain. She's a good craft for these inland waters."

Smiling at the compliment, Olaf replied in kind, "You handled her well, Bill. You can sail with me anytime."

A spontaneous grin brightened the young man's face as he nodded and left the bridge. Bill soon found a peaceful niche in the su-

perstructure which lay alee of the cool sea breeze and stood contemplating his mission.

Don Wilson had made inquiries about land on Duke Island, and
using Bill's veteran's status as a lever, had filed claim on Cottage
Cove. Because the tribes were contesting land rights in the territory,
Don was sending Bill to Juneau with copies of the papers which he
would re-file personally. The lawyer shrewdly guessed that the
Alaskan government's generosity might be curtailed before long, and
he told his client to contact all the bigwigs in the capital during his
visit. Tying names and faces together might be useful in proving up on
his homestead.

Gene and Mae had followed his application with a sponsor's interest, having him to dinner the Sunday before they moved to Seattle
and listening to his enthusiasm during the entire evening. Mae and he
had become friends during the brief period, occasionally walking and
talking on their strolls about town. The subjects of Cottage Cove and
college life soon broadened into personal likes and feelings. Bill had
missed her company during these past two weeks.

He disdained any interest in Alexis, even when she stopped by
the store looking for company after Charley went back to Tacoma to
turn out for football. Soon she was gone also, and with Aaron in
school, Bill itched to get on with his life. Roy and Julia claimed it was a
severe case of homestead-itis, and he couldn't disagree with them.

Quitting the mill had been easier than he had expected, the
boring work gladly ended, and John Furrer supported his goal with a
bonus - a Winchester 30.06 from his gun collection. He had lost his
"boss's pet" status after the dance fiasco but earned part of it back
when Rick Honeycutt had offended Alexis in the mill yard. He had felt
sorry for the would-be Lothario when the haughty beauty had rebuffed
him before his friends, but when he had grown truculent and spiteful,
Bill had jumped between the two angry people just as John had
stormed out of the office door. The hapless sawyer had been fired on
the spot.

Bill thought, 'I was sure lucky. Rick was too confused to notice
me until it was all over. If looks could kill, wow! I suppose that's why

Alexis tried to make up with me, but her behavior was at fault. She could have shown a little compassion for a courter.'

Shivering in the autumn air in spite of wearing a sweater and a coat, Bill moved aft to the heated passenger lounge, thoughts still on his ambitious plans. He bumped into a figure standing before the door, lips forming an apology as he was pushed aside.

Rick Honeycutt swung a fist at him without speaking, his gleeful grin giving him away, and Bill ducked as the heel of Rick's hand struck the back of his head. Surging forward in self-defense, Bill shouldered the bruiser aside, stopping behind a steel support, not quite sure what to do next.

Fortunately, a deckhand appeared and ordered, "No fighting, gents! Save your differences for shore."

Bill nodded agreement and moved through the open door past spectators without appearing to hurry. His only thought was, *'Saved by fate again. Someday I'll have to fight that guy.'*

Bill left the ferry at Juneau with Olaf, suspecting an arranged escort when he saw Honeycutt standing beside the gangway, but glad to avoid trouble. He obtained a room near the capitol buildings and immediately implemented his lawyer's instructions. Remembering Don's advice, he followed a sign toward the Governor's office, stopping in the hallway to ask a distinguished-looking gentleman for directions.

With a glint in his eye, the man stated positively, "Hmph! That old office is stuffy. Why don't we talk right here. I'm Ernest Gruening. What can I do for you?"

A slight flush in his cheeks didn't deter Bill as he accepted the proffered hand and said, "Glad to meet you, Governor. Greetings from Don Wilson and John Furrer. Both men insisted I drop by your office for a visit. I'm Bill Pardue, up from Ketchikan to file a homestead."

"Welcome to Juneau, Bill. Anything I can do to help with your filing?" Governor Gruening asked in helpful tones.

"Just remember that I'm a veteran and have a claim being processed on Duke Island. I hope it goes through without delay," Bill replied, adding a request, "Is there anyone else around that I should visit?!'

"Mister Bartlett, our territorial representative, is in Washington. Hmm, have you met any Tsimshian tribal elders? They consider Duke Island their land," Gruening queried.

"Yes, I've met Tsimchuck, and I served with Malcolm Angias on Guam. I was introduced to about everyone in Metlakatla at Helen Duncan's wedding. But they don't know I'm a homesteader."

"Hopefully, they'll be good neighbors. Say hello to my friends in Ketchikan when you return, including Jack Benny's sidekick. You saw his impersonation, I expect?"

"Yes, he's a good comedian, himself. Thanks for your time, Governor. Good-by," Bill said as he shook hands, and the two men went in opposite directions. He had one more chore today, delivering a letter to a lawyer friend of Don's, before calling it a day. The ferry left at eight o'clock in the morning, and he was ready to go home to Carlsons' place.

ᛏ   ᛏ   ᛏ

Sitting in the dining room after one of Julia's special dinners, Roy spread their butcher paper list over the table, both men half rising to study it. Using his right index finger, he pointed to each item with a red asterisk, explaining, "These hardware articles are packed in my storeroom. The blue asterisks denote groceries which we can pack when you're ready, and the circled items are on order. We have to wait for their arrival or find them in town. Have you thought of anything else?"

"No, Don says I can't make any improvements until he hears from the land office in Juneau, but I'm going to insulate the cabin anyway. I will need that circled item for sure. Have you heard of a boat which I can afford?" Bill asked.

Roy nodded and replied in the manner of an accountant, "Itemizing your needs like we did made good sense. We'll manage.

Your credit at the store is good. Now about a boat, there's an old Tlingit coming by the store tomorrow to see you. Dicker for an hour or so and then make a deal with him. He's offering a ten–foot open boat with two outboards, a fifteen horse Johnson for speed and a two and a half horse Evinrude for trolling. You know our biggest problem will be fuel for those engines. Metlakatla probably is the best source, or maybe Gregori will agree to supply you with a few cans. Anyway, you should have a hundred dollars left in your savings account, and you can earn a few dollars selling fish and meat."

Grinning at his friend's meticulous business methodology, Bill quipped, "Thanks, Roy, I can tell I'm going to have fun."

In a serious tone, Roy proclaimed, "You know, I envy you, my friend. Most men don't see as much adventure in a lifetime as you'll experience this winter. What a wonderful opportunity!"

Chapter Four

Bill munched on the sandwich which Julia had packed for him, glancing intermittently at his watch as his ten-footer nosed through fog and a light drizzle off Mary Island. He had followed in the wake of a coastal steamer past Hog Rocks, but his fifteen horsepower motor couldn't match the speed of the ship. Heavily laden with supplies, the open boat was soon alone in Revillagigedo Channel, and the homesteader became his own navigator.

As his eyes sought out the nearby shoreline through continuous precipitation, he thought, *'My watch says three o'clock, but who can be sure in this light. I haven't seen anything but gray haze all day. Well, at least the sea is relatively calm. My boat is still afloat, and I'm making good time. Hmm, should be in Cottage Cove by dark.'*

Continuing to hug the shoreline, Bill carefully avoided shallow waters and rocks near Mary Island. He swung southwest as he cleared Edge Point, crossing Danger Strait and the open waters between Cat Island and a string of rock islands to the east. Light slowly diminished under the gray pall, daylight all but gone before the sailor could breathe a sigh of relief. There was the dim outline of his cabin in the distance, suddenly visible as the fog thinned in the twilight.

Startled as his Johnson sputtered and coughed to silence, Bill moved with alacrity to his small Evinrude, dropping propeller and shaft into the water and pulling sharply on its starting rope, happy to hear its immediate response. He tilted the Johnson to minimize drag while the boat resumed its course. He figured to refuel the outboard after reaching his destination, speed not as important as the few minutes of daylight left.

As it turned out, darkness was complete when Bill beached his boat in front of the cabin. Using both of his kerosene lanterns, he carried all of his supplies to the cabin before pulling the boat above the high water mark and tying it to a stump.

By the time he had a blazing fire burning in the decrepit iron cooking range, his teeth were chattering, and his hands were numb. He didn't feel comfortable until his flushed fingers were firmly wrapped around a porcelain mug filled with hot coffee. As he relaxed, he finally realized he was home for the winter.

π   π   π

Weeks passed industriously as Bill insulated the cabin, explored the forest around the cabin and fished to supplement his larder of foodstuffs. He returned from Morse Cove one noontime to discover a stranger ensconced on his stoop, waving a casual greeting to him. There was no boat in sight, and the homesteader wondered at the mystery of such a visit.

"Hi, Neighbor!" the gnarled and bearded old-timer shouted hoarsely in a voice seemingly unused to conversation.

As Bill left his boat tied to the mooring stump, he responded in welcoming tones, "Hello yourself. Welcome to Cottage Cove. I thought I was the only settler around here. Where did you come from?"

A hint of a smile creased the visitor's lips as they shook hands, enough clearance to display a set of fine white teeth. Reassessing the man's age, Bill concluded his salt and pepper beard and what hair he could see under the woolen stocking cap masked a younger face than he'd originally guessed. The stranger's grip was firm, and while his stature was diminutive, his physique exuded sinewy strength.

"I'm Ed Hill. Have a snug cabin over on Judd Harbor - about seven or eight miles by foot - over there," he spoke deliberately as he pointed southwest. Bill thought again that his voice rasped from disuse and wondered anew at his visitor.

"Pleased to meet you, Ed. My name's Bill Pardue. I'm homesteading this property. How long have you been living at Judd Harbor?"

"Oh, I came up from Tacoma in '39. Knew the fella who built this place. He was okay, but I don't get along with Tsimchuck and his partner - just avoid them. He called me a squatter once. Course he's right, but I didn't like it. He'll be upset to see someone living in the cabin. How are you going to handle him?"

Bill chuckled in agreement, "Ha! Ha! I expect you're right, Ed, and I don't know how to answer you. Tsimchuck and Gregori are welcome here as friends - so are you. I know he considers this place as his fishing cabin, but if my papers come through, I'll hold title. By the way, we have something in common, I grew up in Tacoma. Do you have family still there?"

"Nope! Nary a soul. Don't talk about my youth much - it's long gone. Say, I hung a quarter of venison from your ridgepole inside. You'll need a smokehouse if you're here for the winter, weather being so contrary and all."

"Thanks, will you spend the night? We could get better acquainted," Bill offered graciously.

"Nope, I've got chores at home, and I'm pretty much a loner. Talked enough for a month of Sundays already. Seldom say more than hello."

Bill responded with an understanding smile, "I've experienced the same thing since I arrived, but I like to talk. You will stay for fish and chips, won't you? I'll share my last potato with you."

"Sounds delicious. I ran out of potatoes weeks ago, and since you want to talk, you can tell me how you came to be here," Ed said with the same sparse smile characteristic of the recluse.

An hour later, Ed Hill took his departure with as little fanfare as his arrival. Bill had talked throughout the meal, his reticent neighbor using single words economically, and when the young man paused for breath, Ed had spoken a quiet thanks and ended his visit without any ceremony.

Bill thought as he watched his new friend disappear into the forest, *'He didn't tell me anything about himself, and he didn't invite me to his place. He's downright secretive about his past, but maybe he's just a real hermit. Well, I'm going to call on him anyway. He's my only neighbor.'*

π   π   π

Bill was enjoying one of those rare wintry days when sunlight touched upon the Alaskan rain forest as the purring beat of an airplane caught his attention. Sinking his axe into a block of firewood, the shirtsleeved young man stepped away from the cabin, shivering as he left the shelter of its leeward wall. Scanning the skyline with interest at a sound novel to Cottage Cove, he espied a brief flicker of light, assuredly sunlight reflecting from a metal surface, discerning movement before form as the plane approached the cabin.

Wings rocking in a wigwag greeting, the familiar float plane with Ketchikan markings buzzed its position, banking slowly over Ray Anchorage as a hand waved energetically in greeting from the passenger window. Bill jumped in joy as he waved back, recognizing

Aaron Carlson and remembering the lad's promise to fly over Cottage Cove on his birthday flight. Was it November 24th already?

Circling over the bay and dropping lower, seemingly just above the whitecaps, the plane approached the cabin a second time, banking sharply as a fluttering homemade parachute was thrown clear. Climbing on a northerly heading, the plane wigwagged good-by as the package thudded into the ground thirty feet from Bill. He ran to the burlap-wrapped bundle, laughing and curious, his boyhood feelings of Christmas morning revived. What was Aaron's gift?

Dropping to his knees beside the disheveled and rent bundle, he ripped the fabric asunder to find a frozen turkey, misshapen by its hapless collision with the rocky soil, but still in one piece. A thick waterproof packet came loose as Bill tore the rest of the burlap away. The thought of mail sobered him as he carried the gift to his cabin.

Breaking the envelope's seal, Bill extracted six letters, three without postmarks. He chose to open the letter from Aaron first, reading his young friend's school news and planned flight to Cottage Cove on his birthday. The boy thanked him for the aviation book which Bill had left with his folks as a birthday gift. A postscript invited him to Christmas dinner in Ketchikan. Julia's note confirmed the invitation and then spent a page worrying about his health and well-being on "that God-forsaken island." Roy scribbled a one-line greeting on the back side of his wife's notepaper, including a hello from Olaf as well.

Nostalgia bordering on homesickness pervaded Bill's thoughts as he read the Carlsons' words a second time. "It's sure nice to hear from my friends," he muttered aloud, startled by the sound of his own voice. His mind laughed at his whimsical mood as he recalled his habit of talking aloud to himself and wondering why those few spoken words should have surprised him. 'Ah well,' he thought, 'I don't get mail every day.'

Bill opened a newsy letter from his mother, discovering that Charles Blakely had come to dinner one Sunday. . .he was such a nice man. Her many questions about Ketchikan and this mysterious Cottage Cove brought a ghost of a simile to his lips, and reinforced the idea growing in his mind. He would draw a map of Southwest Alaska and his new home, to send to his folks. He wished he could go home for Christmas, but visting the Carlsons would be fun and he could telephone Tacoma as well.

Charley being on his mind, he opened the only real surprise of the drop - an early Christmas card. His fraternity brother and erstwhile pal wrote that football was not for him, his grades were more important. Smiling devilishly, Bill translated the fraternity-style glibness to mean he hadn't made the team. When Charley mentioned his visit to the Pardue home and said nice things about his parents, Bill shook his head in wonder. Charley always knew exactly what to say to preserve their friendship.

'How can anyone stay mad at that guy?' Bill thought as he picked up a letter postmarked Seattle. No return address couldn't disguise the source as Mae's neat handwriting was easily recognized. She wrote of her father's success and her university classes briefly, devoting most of the single page to her volunteer work at the campus clinic. She said that she was eager to take a real nursing class next quarter.

Bill reluctantly laid aside the personal messages and picked up the remaining two letters, opening first the Juneau-postmarked envelope containing a form stating that his homestead claim was being processed and then reading Don Wilson's note assuring him that his title to Cottage Cove was forthcoming. The lawyer mentioned a trip to the capital in December when he could expedite the paperwork.

Shrugging aside his irksome feeling at the double-talk and the nefarious thought that both messages were nothing but hot air, he began writing responses to all his correspondents. He would give them to Elmer Hairston when the *MacDonald* traversed Revillagigedo Channel in a day or two. His old towboat had passed through on its northerly trek one morning last week, but Bill hadn't seen it until too late. Besides a friendly visit and posting his mail, he needed some gas and a couple of batteries for his radio.

With this thought in mind, Bill packed a day's supplies and set out for Duchess Island, planning to fish as close to the shipping lane as weather would permit. Calm seas and good fishing blessed the

**Bill's homemade maps, of Southeastern Alaska
sent to his family in Tacoma (1951).**

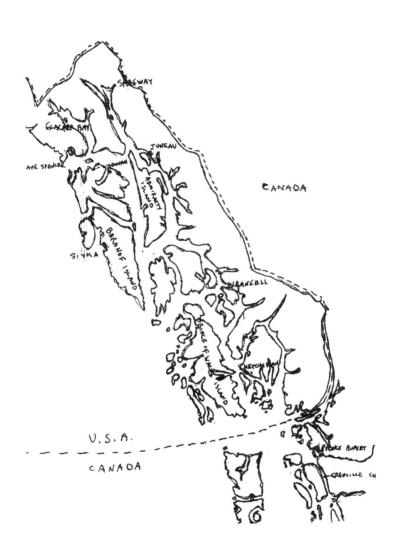

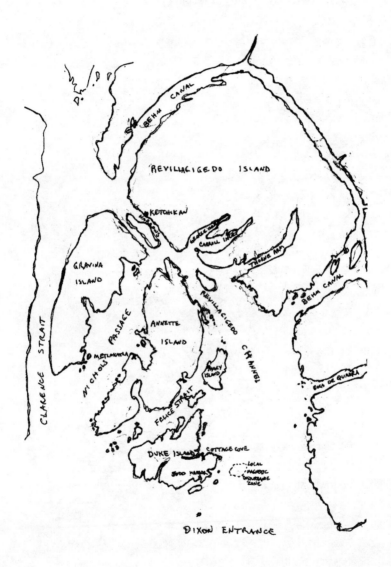

BEHM CANAL

REVILLAGIGEDO ISLAND

KETCHIKAN

CARROLL INLET

THORNE ARM

BEHM CANAL

GRAVINA
ISLAND

PASSAGE

ANNETTE
ISLAND

REVILLAGIGEDO CHANNEL

METLAKATLA

NICHOLS

MARY
ISLAND

BOCA DE QUADRA

CLARENCE STRAIT

FELICE STRAIT

DUKE ISLAND

COTTAGE COVE

JUDD HARBOR

LOCAL
MAGNETIC
DISTURBANCE
ZONE

DIXON ENTRANCE

sailor all day, but he saw no ships in the channel, electing to continue his vigil overnight on Duchess Island.

Bill sat on the eastern shore with a fire to his back and scanned the horizon for ship's lights. He nodded off, awakening when he became chilled, and stoked his campfire, living with this routine until dawn.

After a cold breakfast of biscuits and fried cod, he resumed fishing, trolling eastwardly for a stray salmon. Two miles out he cut his motor and mooched for bottom fish, more interested in proving his theory of the *MacDonald's* schedule than catching a halibut. Hungry and discouraged as a threatening front darkened the sky prematurely, Bill pulled in his line and started his Johnson, heading for home. He found the wind had stiffened as the boat plowed through the choppy waters toward the dark outline of Duke Island.

A casual glance over his right shoulder caused him to blink his eyes, concentrating on a distant light. *'Is it a ship, a beacon or just a campfire?'* he asked himself. Uncertain but hopeful, Bill set his motor to idle and watched the growing lights, soon identifiable as a ship. When he distinguished a second set of lights behind the ship, he turned up the power and set a course to intercept the oncoming vessel. *MacDonald* or not, he was going to hail her, gambling that he had enough gasoline to reach home if the ship refused to rendezvous with him.

An hour later he was within a mile or two of the oncoming tug and barge and signaled with his flashlight, simply waving the beam in a tight circle in the direction of the approaching vessel. After his third signal, the towboat sounded a deep-throated blast which Bill fancifully presumed to recognize as the *MacDonald 's*. He concluded it was comforting to be an optimist on this dark night.

A powerful searchlight illuminated the whitecaps between the two boats, and the tug's diesel engines quieted to gentle rumble, a voice calling faintly, "Hello, the fishing boat! What's your problem?"

Hearing Elmer Hairston's voice relieved Bill's worries to no end, and he shouted a reply, "Bill Pardue here, Captain. Looking for a free meal. May I come aboard for a visit?"

"Hell yes, Slim! Throw Ray a rope when you come alongside," the skipper yelled, ordering in more normal tones, "Bring her starboard slowly, Harry."

Bill adjusted to the *MacDonald's* new course and moments later threw a rope to the waiting deckhand, declaring to figures outlined by the cabin lights, "It's sure good to see you guys. Come here and grab a couple of halibut."

Ray replied, "You're crazy to be out on a night like this and with a storm coming in, but it's good to see you too, Slim."

Dick, the chief engineer, grasped his hand and pulled him aboard, grinning in welcome as he joshed, "Ready to sail on another trip with us, Slim?"

Jack Anderson slapped his shoulder in a friendly fashion for the surly mate, muttering a greeting, "Welcome aboard, Slim. Cookie's frying some pork chops for you, and the skipper will come down to the mess after he finishes plotting a new course."

"Thanks, folks, it's good to feel the *MacDonald* under me again. Let's go eat," Bill replied, adding as an afterthought, "Say, Jack, I need gasoline. Can you help?"

Captain Hairston's voice replied, "Ray, get a five gallon can of gas out of the engine room. What else do you need, Slim?"

Shaking Elmer's hand as he stepped over the mess doorsill, he replied, "I could use a couple of batteries for my radio, and I'd appreciate it if you'd mail some letters for me. Are a couple of halibut fair trade?"

"Sure, Slim. Cookie has us eating fish and chips all the way to Tacoma. Are you staying at Cottage Cove?" the skipper responded.

Cookie called out from the galley, "Don't tell me you actually live out here in the middle of nowhere."

To all the crew gathered for dinner he explained, "I've homesteaded Cottage Cove with my veteran's rights claim, and unless someone stops me, I'll be a titled landowner by spring. Right now I'm fishing while the weather's good, and tomorrow I'll be hunting in whatever weather passes over Cottage Cove."

Harry stuck a grinning face around the corridor entrance, shaking his head as he addressed the captain, "Mate says the sea is getting rough. He wants to resume course south in five minutes," adding a quip to Bill, "Good weather for ducks out there, Slim."

The young man stood up quickly, calling out to Cookie, "Pack a brown bag for me, old buddy. I've got to be going."

Elmer laughed and frowned simultaneously, "Ha! Ha! Sorry we couldn't visit longer. You take it easy returning ashore. I'll point my spotlight toward Duke Point until you're well underway. So long!"

Everyone scurried around to help Bill board his bouncing ten-footer, and with gas, batteries and dinner at his feet, he started his Johnson and left the *MacDonald* with a wave of his hand, already soaked beneath his oilskins as he bounced through turbulent seas.

Holding his seat with one hand, he steered with the other; trying to follow along the beam of light cast by the *MacDonald*. Minutes later he felt suddenly isolated as the spotlight blinked out. The tug was three miles astern, and Bill estimated that he was at least five miles from Duke Point when his outboard sputtered. He cranked up the Evinrude and cut off the Johnson, accomplishing a minor miracle as he poured gas into the near–empty tank while steering the Evinrude with his knees.

Another ten minutes found him running with full power again, manipulating the flashlight and reading the compass when wind and sea sent his boat askew. He managed to eat both pork chops in his lunch, but seawater had tainted Cookie's fresh bread, and he threw it to the fishes. At one point he slowed down to bail water out of his boat with an old coffee can, another onerous routine necessitated as foul weather blanketed the open craft.

When the wind quieted and the surf crashing on rocks became a factor, Bill realized he was off course. Swinging to starboard and holding the surf noises to his port side, he guessed, *'Maybe I goofed, or maybe the magnetic disturbances in the channel affected my compass, but either way I'm off course. I wish I could see more than phosphorescent foam atop waves breaking around me.'*

Suddenly hearing more wind than surf, he swung aport and said a little prayer. Sneaking a glance at his compass confirmed he was heading for home, and he wasn't going to second-guess himself now. Bill was confident but tense as he used noises from the wind and the sea to skirt the shoreline of Ray Anchorage.

Remaining patient was a tedious chore, but Bill figured to himself, '*I dasn't turn into shore too soon, or I'll end up on the rocks. Better to overshoot Cottage Cove than come up short.*' No sooner did that thought cross his mind than a dervish of white water appeared a few feet ahead of the boat.

Bill dodged the hazard expertly, the submerged rock obstacle fixing his location. Low tide and an exposed rock meant he was only a few hundred yards from his place. Another minute, and he'd turn into shore.

He switched to the Evinrude and slowly crept closer to the dark mass of the island. Moments later his bow brushed a submerged rock, and he cut the motor, tilting it out of harm's way. Paddling furiously to shore, lady luck stayed with him to the end, his mooring stump but a few feet from his landing.

᛫   ᛫   ᛫

A day of rest and relaxation seemed a terrible waste to the fatigued sailor, but a small price to pay for his nerve-wracking adventure. He finished reading Ayn Rand's, *The Fountainhead*, remembering woefully that his small library of books and magazines was dog-eared with usage. All the newspapers he'd brought with him had been devoured in flames long ago, used when he was impatient to start a fire in his stove. Cookie had enclosed an outdated *Seattle P.I.,* which he was determined to keep around the cabin until he'd perused every item several times. Living alone allowed a lot of time for reading and playing solitaire.

He rose to stoke the fire, adding a piece of firewood to the small firebox and picked up the empty water pail. Dashing in shirtsleeves to the creek and back, Bill laughed aloud as he reckoned that he had failed to avoid a single raindrop in his quest for fresh water. Gee, I could have filled this pail by holding it out the door.

Shaking himself like a wet puppy as he stood inside the cabin, he set the pail down and returned to the stoop with a musing expression on his face. Sure enough, his eyes were keen even when his mind didn't pay attention. The halibut which he'd strung from a nearby spruce branch was gone.

'Some varmint must have stolen my fish while I read,' he thought as he crossed the grassy field to search for signs. Amongst the roots and up the bole of the evergreen were claw marks, and a few feet away, Bill found the clear track of a bear. Initially assuming it was a large animal which had prowled his land today, his estimate became more realistic as he followed the beast's trail into the woods. Both the size of the paw print and the length of the critter's stride suggested a small bear - hardly more than a cub. Bill had heard there were black bears on the island, and he wondered if they hibernated. He knew he needed a meathouse, or he'd be feeding an unwelcome companion all the time.

ⴲ   ⴲ   ⴲ

Early the next morning, Bill bundled up in warm clothing and carrying his loaded rifle, set off on the bear's trail. His quarry's spoor had been washed away in many places and was soon lost by the amateur trailsman. The bear had been heading toward the hill above Duke Point, so Bill continued in that general direction.

Practicing a hunter's quiet movement, the young man skirted a thicket of evergreens. He climbed a small knoll, going around a mighty spruce, and stepped onto a deadfall to survey the hillside.

Movement at his feet alarmed Bill, and a horrendous noise combining elements of a grunt, squeal and roar erupting from the cavernous jaws of a brown bear startled him breathless. He leaped backward in an automatic reflex, his left leg falling between the twisted roots of the long fallen spruce giant. Without pausing, he pulled loose and rolled down the slope, coming to rest beside the thicket minus much of his trouser leg.

Lining his rifle on the deadfall, he realized the racket of breaking branches and the flailing motion flowing downhill through the thicket was the bear running for dear life. Come to think of it, he'd glimpsed the animal's flight as it roared. Bill laughed at the recalled sight of the two solitary figures scaring each other half to death.

He called forth in stentorian tones, "Keep running, little bear. . . and leave my fish alone!"

Bill saw no reason to fear the animal and decided it was time to head home. Live and let live was his magnanimous thought - a boost to his injured pride.

Stepping forward on his left leg, he felt a twinge of pain in his thigh, and glancing down at the exposed limb, he saw a wood splinter embedded in the muscle tissue. Blood was oozing slowly from the wound, and Bill decided to leave the oversized sliver intact and walk home. He reasoned that he'd lose more blood if he removed the splinter out here in the wilderness. Gritting his teeth in pain, he stumbled into his cabin an hour later, wondering if he had made the right decision. His boot seemed to be full of blood, and his head was swimming.

Stirring embers to life in the stove, Bill placed a crumpled-up page of his precious newspaper in the embers and shoved a dozen pieces of dry kindling atop the tinder, covering the pile with two small pieces of pitchy wood. As the fire came to life, he restored the stove lid and set a teakettle of water on the range to heat.

With shaking fingers Bill undressed, removing his trousers and ripping off the remnants of his longjohns leg. Each brush against the splinter was like touching a raw nerve, and he worried about his wound anew. Laying out a blanket on the floor, he gathered a medical olio of useful items, beginning with his first aid kit, a bottle of alcohol, a metal cookie sheet and a couple of clean rags.

The teakettle stopped whistling when he set it on the floor and opened the front of the firebox. Stoking the flames with more wood, he sterilized a razor blade held by a pair of pliers in the red-hot embers. He closed the stove door and dropped both items on the cookie sheet, before collapsing unceremoniously on the blanket.

Bill doused the wound with alcohol, gasping despite his determination to grin and bear it. Picking up the razor blade, he once again gritted his teeth as he cut a half inch gash in his taut skin at the splinter's entrance. Now he grasped the sliver and pulled gently upward, but his fingers slipped on the bloodied wood fragment.

Shrugging his shoulders at his pain and the lack of success, he moaned aloud, "Ohhhh. . .ouch, that hurts. I'd better get this hunk out before I lose any more blood."

He hefted the pliers in his right palm, studying his predicament one last time before acting. With dogged intent he set the jaws to grip the sliver, and tightening his hold with both hands, he heaved upward. The splinter resisted but a second and then burst from the wound, Bill sprawling backward in painful shock.

His eyelids fluttered on the edge of consciousness, but he forced himself erect to pour more alcohol an the open wound. His mind raced with thoughts, first aid memories recalled in rapid order, let it bleed for awhile to cleanse the wound, keep it disinfected, make sure no little sliver remains in the leg. . .don't pass out.

Finally the doctor-patient washed his hands in alcohol and used his fingers to feel the swollen area, finally pressuring the wound closed. He noted the bleeding had stopped, and then he strapped a pressure gauze pad over it. He hoped his ministrations were good enough to avoid infection. Bill slowly wrapped the blanket over his body and collapsed into a dreamless sleep.

ᵮ   ᵮ   ᵮ

Awakening to a chilled room, Bill reluctantly used another piece of his newspaper to rekindle a flame in the stove. Without leaving his makeshift bed, he drank two cups of water and ate his last three baking powder biscuits before settling back on the floor for a nap.

Ten minutes later his mental alarm clock brought him back to the real life of a homesteader and daylight. He rose on one leg to sit in a chair and sighed with relief that his bandage was still clean. He touched his wrapping and the skin around it with only minor pain. Puttering for an hour, he managed to stow his doctoring tools and brew a pot of coffee.

Weariness came sooner than he liked, and he moved to his bunk with the pot beside him, a full cup of the strong brew and his last page of the newspaper devoured before he drifted off.

The room was still warm when Bill awoke and swung both legs over the side of his bunk. A twinge in his wound reminded him to balance on his right leg as he stoked the fire and warmed a can of Campbell's Chicken Soup. He sipped a half cup of cold coffee while the pot was reheating, smiling for the first time since his accident. Maybe life was okay after all.

TT   TT   TT

The sound of voices outside the cabin roused the napping patient, his injured leg holding up as he limped to the door and opened it.

"Ho! Ho! What a scruffy character we have found, Tsimchuck. Is living the life of a hermit so bad, my friend?" Gregori jibed as he greeted the disheveled young man.

A broad grin split Bill's countenance as he replied, "Gregori, Tsimchuck, you are a sight for sore eyes. Come in, come in."

As he stepped backward on the wrong leg, he staggered momentarily, Gregori rushing to his side and grasping his left arm in support. With Tsimchuck's grip on his right arm, Bill was all but carried to his seat beside the table, and the Indian began removing his bandage.

"Hmph! Good work for a chechako," Tsimchuck grunted as he inspected the crusted scab now covering the wound, adding with a commanding nod, "Now I'll fix a proper bandage."

Bill was too happy to argue with his visitors and began talking a mile a minute, all three men smiling at the lonely man's monologue. As he droned on sonorously, Gregori prepared a fish stew and a fresh pot of coffee while Tsimchuck cleaned the cabin and spread the partners' blankets in the corner.

Pausing for breath, the grinning invalid joshed, "Gee, if you're staying for awhile, you can chop some firewood for me."

His friends both laughed, Gregori responding, 'We're here for a week anyway. Tsimchuck suggested you need a way for your boat. We'll split a Sitka spruce if you'll catch our supper tomorrow. That leg of yours looks fit enough for fishing."

π   π   π

Bill hunched down into his parka and rewound Helen's gift about his ears and nose. The Tsimshian scarf fended off a gust of wet and icy air which curled around his face as Gregori quartered the light west of Metlakatla. The three friends were on the last leg of their journey.

Grateful for his friends' personal care at Cottage Cove, he reckoned he owed them a more physical debt for the solidly built spruce way beside his creek. His boat now rested high and dry out of the water, safe from storms while he was working to ensure his homestead title in Metlakatla and Ketchikan.

He wanted to talk to the other Tsimshian elders about his claim, like the good neighbor he wanted to become. With his friends' support, he hoped to get a letter of endorsement or at least a character reference from the tribe. Gregori had agreed to give him the latter, and Tsimchuck had agreed to cosign it, but both men urged him to visit Metlakatla and have an audience with tribal leaders.

Besides, Bill looked forward to seeing Malcolm and Helen as well as visiting the doctor about his healing leg. Strength was returning to his muscles, but pain was still present when he pushed himself. He'd have to remember to walk without a limp, or he'd earn an unsavory nickname from his Indian friends. He'd noticed Alaskans were quick to assign names and characteristics to chechakos.

Malcolm Angias waved from his own boat which was moored at the cannery dock. Obviously he had recognized his grandfather and his partner and soon yelled across the windy sea, "Is that you, Bill Pardue?"

Bill stood and waved back, shouting in response, "Hello, Malcolm, are you coming or going?"

As the two boats touched fenders, Malcolm grinned a welcome and answered normally, "Neither, my friend! I want to hear all about your adventure on Duke Island and expect a full report at dinner. Can you stay with me?"

"Thanks, but Gregori has a bunk ready for me. However, we've all been eating each other's cooking, and we look forward to your offer for dinner," Bill quipped in reply, an earnest inflection in his voice.

"Ha! Ha! Touche! My cooking hasn't improved. Say, maybe Helen will offer to cook for us bachelors. She asked about you the other day."

Silence fell as the four men unloaded the catch of halibut from the boat, Tsimchuck and Malcolm delivering the fish while Gregori secured the craft.

"Come along, Bill," he ordered sternly, "It's time to visit the doctor. We can see how well your leg is. Tsimchuck will arrange a meeting with the elders for this evening. Don't expect any miracles, and you'll enjoy the experience. Not just anybody is granted an audience, but Tsimchuck and Malcolm are powerful men in the tribe - respected and honored."

π π π

Helen's husband John roared with laughter as Bill poked fun at himself with his bear story. Everyone had enjoyed the after-dinner tale, even Gregori and Tsimchuck who had heard it so many times. The story-teller was particularly pleased with John's amusement, because it symbolized Bill's acceptance as a family friend rather than "that fellow Helen knew in Tacoma."

"There is an old saying among my people," John intoned soberly but with a sly smile, continuing as everyone looked toward him, "A chechako who befriends a bear owes his friends a beer."

Amid the pseudo-boisterous approval of the gathering, Bill acquiesced with but a minor demurral, "John, you tell a taller tale than me, but I accept the obligation. I'll buy you guys a root beer right after our meeting."

The men rose, gathering their jackets and filing outside. Bill thanked Helen for the hospitality, and she spoke words of encouragement, "Good luck with the elders, Bill. You have many friends in Metlakatla - John included."

Nodding in appreciation at the last comment, Bill complimented the newlyweds, "You have a fine marriage, Helen. I couldn't be happier for you and John."

Hurrying down the street to match strides with his friends, he asked Malcolm about his cousin, "What do you hear from Arthur? Isn't he in Korea with the First Marine Division?"

Shaking his head in a mixed expression of sorrow and pride, Malcolm responded, "He was, but he was wounded in action - a real hero. He's at the Presidio in San Francisco now, recovering from shrapnel and burns. The doctors saved his right arm, but he won't have full use of it again. He should be home in the spring."

Tsimchuck spoke clearly, reflecting his own feelings of family pride, "Arthur earned a Silver Star and Purple Heart in Korea, just like Malcolm did on Okinawa. He is a true Tsimshian warrior."

Malcolm quickly contradicted his grandfather, "Oh, Grandpa! Tsimshians are peaceful people, not warriors. Arthur and I were just being good Americans, like Bill here - doing our duty."

Tsimchuck smiled serenely, and ignoring his grandson's denial, repeated, "Warriors and heroes! One and the same, don't you agree, Bill?"

"Of course, Tsimchuck. Your family and friends have every reason to be proud of their stalwart Marines. All Alaskans know they represented our nation with honor and courage."

Bill felt a bit nervous as they mounted the steps to the council room door, not sure what was expected of him this evening. Several elders waited just inside the door, greeting him with smiling respect as they reintroduced themselves - uncles and cousins of Helen and John Williams, Malcolm Angias, and in one case, Mae Wilson. Tsimchuck placed a mug of coffee in his hand as everyone socialized in the small lobby.

Finally Bill glanced meaningfully at Malcolm, eyes asking what to do, but his friend only shrugged and sipped his coffee. The elders were still in good humor as they drifted away, but not into the meeting room. One by one they left the building. Soon Tsimchuck, John's father and Mae's cousin were the only elders beside the young homesteader.

Jack Williams chuckled at Bill's confused expression, handing him an envelope as he explained, "The Tribal Council can't endorse your claim in any official capacity since they're on record as opposing the territorial act, but as you observed during the last half hour, you have a lot of friends in Metlakatla. This letter of reference praises your character and states our friendship. Since Duke Island and homesteading aren't mentioned, most elders signed it. We'd rather have you for a neighbor than any other chechako."

"Thanks, Mister Williams, and the rest of you, too. Tell the. . ." Bill began to reply, hesitating for a long moment as ship's horn sounded in the harbor.

Malcolm quickly spoke up, "That's the ferry, Bill. Don't worry, it won't leave until eight o'clock in the morning. Gregori will get you on board before it leaves. Let's go to my place and have a real beer."

With a relieved sigh, Bill expressed his gratitude anew, "Good! Please tell the elders thanks for me. Lead the way, Malcolm."

⊓ ⊓ ⊓

A blast of icy air off the Gulf of Alaska swept over the ferry deck where Bill stood waving to Olaf and Aaron Carlson. A snowflake landed on the young man's nose. His hand brushed it away casually, his thought being that Ketchikan could be in for a white Christmas.

First in line on the ferry's ramp, Bill stepped onto the landing, shaking hands with the Big Swede and then giving the excited and grinning boy a bear hug.

Aaron was fairly bursting with news, his voice partially muffled in Bill's coat, "I talked to Mister Furrer, and he said you could work tomorrow, and Mom invited him to dinner because Alexis is staying in Palo Alto for the holidays, and I bought you a present for Christmas. It's a. . .".

"Whoa! Ha! Ha! You better wait to tell me what it is until Christmas Eve when we open gifts. It's sure good to see you again, Aaron. When can we go fishing?" Bill asked, casting a conspiritual wink at the boy's uncle. His schedule in Ketchikan was certain to be a busy one.

Two days before Christmas, Bill was pulling lumber from the green chain when the foreman appeared to relay an order to report to the boss. He hurried across the yard in shirtsleeves. Slipping through the door quickly and shivering from the cold, he uttered, "Brr! It's a bitter day outside."

Missus Johnson handed him a mug of coffee, and with a silent smile pointed to the inner office, whereupon Bill wrapped two hands about the warm earthenware cup and walked forward.

"You wanted to see me, John?" he asked as soon as the mill owner looked up.

"Yes, Bill. I have an errand for you to run. Gene and his daughter arrived at the airport a few minutes ago and are taking a taxi to my house. I'm expecting an important telephone call any minute and can't leave the office. Will you take my car and meet them at the house?" John waited for Bill's affirmative nod before concluding, "Help them get settled and take the rest of the day off. Gene can pick me up later. Oh yes, tell the Wilson's that Julia's invited them to Christmas dinner.

Since I've given everyone a paid holiday tomorrow, I'll see you at dinner."

Bill had lit the logs in the fireplace and opened the drapes before the Wilson's taxi drove up to the front entrance. He swung the door wide and stepped off the porch, calling out, "Welcome home, folks!"

Father and daughter responded simultaneously with a "Hello Bill!" Gene's jovial voice accompanied a warm handshake and a slap on the back while Mae's surprised and subdued tones were barely audible.

Cocking his head to one side in a quizzical pose, Bill astonished himself when he quipped, "Is that the only greeting I get, Mae Wilson?" and opened his arms wide.

Without hesitation, the girl placed her hands on his shoulders and stood on tiptoes to kiss his cheek, declaring cheerfully, "It is good to see you, Bill, but why aren't you living at Cottage Cove?"

"I am, but I got lonely out there in my cabin and decided to take the Carlsons' up on their Christmas invitation. I didn't expect to see you until next summer," Bill replied as he hefted two suitcases and followed Mae into the house while Gene paid the cab driver.

"Oh, the fire is lovely, and cozy, too. I guess I'm a bit homesick for Ketchikan. Seattle is nice enough, and university classes are interesting, but it's not home for me. Oh, I saw your friend Charley playing basketball at Seattle University. I mean to say the College of Puget Sound team was there. Charley scored several baskets, but your alma mater lost anyway. Seattle U. has a really good team, you know."

As Mae took a breath, her father suggested, "Why don't you and Bill visit while you unpack, Mae? I'll take John's car and check into the office. Say Bill, did the boss say anything to you about us going back to Carroll Inlet and cruising another stand of federal timber next week?"

"No, but I'm available until Don Wilson returns from Juneau. Put in a good word for me, will you, Gene?"

"Of course, Bill. You two go ahead and visit now. I'll call after I talk to John."

Mae kissed her father's cheek, sending him on his way with a "Bye now, Dad! Be sure and look up your cronies in the mill."

Bill accompanied Mae around the house, helping her unpack their luggage in two of the upstairs bedrooms and then watching her brew a pot of coffee in the kitchen. Perched on a high stool near the pantry, he commented, "You know your way around the Furrer home, Mae. Are you still good friends with Alexis?"

"Yes, we were childhood playmates, often pretending to be the mothers we didn't have. I hope we'll always be friends. You know, Alexis is a warm and caring person, but she still pretends. Society life and lots of the 'right' people for friends are very important to her. She wrote me that she was going skiing with her Stanford friends after Christmas - it was the 'in' thing to do. She doesn't think of herself as thoughtless because her father always indulges her."

Bill nodded in agreement, returning to an earlier subject, "How come you were at a Seattle U. game? Aren't the Washington Huskies your team?"

Laughing humorously, she made a miaouing face, wrinkling her nose and mouth as she replied, "Ha! Ha! Yes, and they are very good. But you know how I feel about basketball. I only went because my date had tickets. By the way, Charley came into the stands after the game to say hello. He said he'd be working for his uncle again this summer, and then he asked about Alexis. He went down to Palo Alto at Thanksgiving to see her. I do believe he's smitten, Bill."

"Good, they can have each other. Charley's a fraternity brother and all, but he can be as thoughtless as Alexis. Let's drop this subject. Tell me about your classes."

After they had both exhausted their favorite topics of nursing and Cottage Cove, Bill remembered to tell Mae about his accident and his trip to Metlakatla and his visit with their mutual friends. He was interrupted as the telephone rang, the girl talking to her father for a moment and then handing the phone to him.

"Hello, Gene. Are we going up to Carroll Inlet?" Bill asked eagerly.

The receiver made his friend's voice sound twangy as he answered, "Yes, John just finished that important call from the forest ranger, and we're slated to leave the day after Christmas. The boss is going along for the ride. We have to stay here tonight and plan the job. Ha! Ha! John says you're to enjoy your vacation while you can. So long!"

Bill hung up the phone and asked, "Would you like to walk around town now and have dinner with me afterward? Your dad seems pretty busy."

"Oh yes, thank you," Mae accepted with alacrity, a frown quickly expressing concern as she added, "Maybe I could fix dinner here, restaurants are so expensive."

"Ha! Ha! No you don't, Mae. I've got a few dollars to splurge on a pre-Christmas celebration. Where would you like to eat?"

Mae smiled her pleasure, answering without delay, "Creek Street. Father has never taken me there to eat. He thinks I'm too young. . .", and seeing a doubt in Bill's eyes, she leaned forward, expression animated as she challenged him boldly, going on a typical female offensive, "Do you think you're dating a child, William Pardue? Maybe I should stay home. You men!"

Rattled by this unusual aggression in Mae, Bill acceded to her choice but still expressed concern, "Okay, Mae, but I'll probably get in dutch with your father."

Studying the mischievous glint in her glance and the coquettish blink of her lashes, he added, "I know you're a woman. That's why you'll have to behave yourself on Creek Street."

He caught a self-satisfied look of triumph light her face as she quickly turned away and realized his normally demure young friend could be a vixen when she chose. He thought to himself that he was no match for her when she played the woman's role. *'When she wants to be, she's a mighty persuasive gal.'*

Having made her point, Mae was a fine companion on a tour of the town. She even suggested a Coke in the soda fountain and exchanged newsy greetings with all the young people gathered there.

As they strolled along Creek Street, curiosity and second thoughts combined to quiet her manner.

He led her into the restaurant where he had met Don Wilson, figuring it was as respectable as any along the boardwalk. They had been seated for a few minutes, conversation sparse but comfortable as Mae took in everything she'd never been allowed to see before.

Suddenly she grinned and gave a tiny finger wave to someone at the door behind Bill. The familiar blowzy voice of Dolly Arthur boomed out, "Mae, you're becoming a beautiful woman and a sight for sore eyes," and recognizing the girl's escort, she continued, "And your daddy is letting you date this handsome young fellow? Bill, isn't it?"

In her naive good manners, Mae exchanged kisses with Dolly, said hello to Curly and invited them to sit down. Bill was amused at his own attitude. He was a little appalled at the turn of events but proud of Mae's open friendship with Big Dolly.

Seeing Dolly's hesitation, Bill supported his date with gallantry, repeating Mae's words, "Join us, folks. I surely look forward to dinner with two beautiful women. And you're welcome too, Curly."

Curly held Dolly's chair as she sat down, and then glancing at the two young people, he winked at Bill and teased, "Gosh, Bill. You and I could play stud after dinner."

Dolly silenced her man with a normal tone of voice, "Quit joshing these younguns, Curly. I doubt if they need our company at all," and turning to Mae with genuine affection she added, "But I'm glad you asked, dear. The last time I saw Gene, I told him he'd raised a real lady."

The owner came to the table and deferentially asked for Dolly's order and actually bowed when she introduced him to Mae Wilson. A moment later their regular waiter placed an ice bucket replete with a bottle of champagne between the women, compliments of the house.

Pouring a sip in one glass, he held it out to Mae, and before Bill could figure out how to object, the girl tasted it.

"Hmm, that's very nice. Thank you, Abner," she said to the owner standing anxiously nearby. Bill knew Dolly was respected along Creek Street but was surprised when Mae was treated so well.

Dolly sensed his wonderment and explained, "Gene saved his life in the woods years ago, and I nursed him for a few days. Even loaned him money to start this restaurant. Nothing's too good for us or ours. Alaskans can be loyal people, Bill."

As Mae drank the last of her champagne, the waiter appeared beside the bucket and bottle, and Dolly waved him away, taking Mae's glass from her hand and turning it upside down on the table. A few moments of silence were broken when the girl acknowledged the censure with a "Yes, Ma'am."

When Dolly nodded and smiled, Mae turned to the still frowning Bill and commanded, "Not a word out of you!"

Pleasant conversation, fine food and good service mellowed Mae a bit as she halfway apologized, "I'm sorry for barking at you, Bill, but I don't like being frowned at."

Dolly patted Mae's hand affectionately and leaned forward to say, "I'm sorry, dear, if I offended you. I just had a mothering urge. You are. . ."

A loud and insulting voice called from the bar, "Hey, Dolly, is that your new girl sitting with that jerk Pardue?"

Bill jumped to his feet to face the obviously drunken Rick Honeycutt, Curly restraining him as Abner and his bouncer escorted Rick to the door. Three of his buddies left with him, laughing as Rick jeered, "Oh, pardon me, it's just the Wilson half-breed."

Shaking in anger, Bill stood frozen for several moments as his temper gave way to reason.

"Come along, Mae. I'll take you home now. Dolly, Curly, I've enjoyed your company this evening. Thank Abner for his hospitality," Bill concluded as he took Mae's trembling hand in his own and led her to the cloakroom.

Their brisk walk home was an uncomfortable silence, Mae unhappy and confused and Bill busy with a plan of retribution. First he had to see the girl home safely and then seek out Olaf Carlson. His reverie was interrupted as they mounted the steps to the Furrer front door, and a quiet sob escaped Mae's lips. Bill took her into his arms and held her gently as she murmured, "I'm sorry, Bill, I'm sorry."

Raising her chin with his index finger, he disclaimed her imagined fault, "You did nothing wrong to be sorry for, Mae Wilson. Dolly's absolutely right - you are a lady."

He kissed her lips briefly and told her, "A good night's sleep will make you feel better. Don't pay any heed to that drunk's insults. Good night, Mae."

A half hour later Bill strode down Creek Street with the Carlson brothers flanking him, Roy insisting on accompanying them in their quest. He looked forward to acting as Bill's "second" as he put it, agreeing that the fight was between him and Honeycutt. The brothers would keep the bruiser's cronies out of the fracas.

Several people recognized the trio and seemed to know their intent, but everyone stayed clear, offering neither help nor hindrance until Curly stepped out of the shadows with a terse announcement, "Honeycutt's inside this bar with a half dozen friends. How do you want to handle this, Bill? I'm dealing myself in."

"Rick's mine. Keep everyone else out of it," he ordered as he entered the dimly lit room and walked over to the noisy table where his antagonist was seated. Men scrambled out of his way as he advanced to the table's edge, placed his left palm on its hard surface and with his open right hand, slapped the jeering Honeycutt with all his strength, bringing the back of his hand across the bully's mouth on the return swing.

Rick's drunken manner evaporated as he reared out of his chair and charged around the table, Bill dragging a chair from behind him and hurling it into the oncoming fighter's knees. Memory of Rick's insults kept the young man's temper white with controlled rage and excluded any scruples about fairness or pity.

As the big brute stumbled over the chair, Bill aimed a hard kick at Rick's head, a broad boot flattening the man's nose as he rolled under an adjacent table. Bill seized a chair and raised it over his head with both hands, bringing it crashing down over Rick's head and shoulders. Surprisingly, the big man was still on his feet when the aggressive challenger drove his right fist into his already bloodied nose. Honeycutt's reflex backhand drove the younger man back with a split lip and hazy vision, a stranger's hands pushing him into a ham-like fist. A dozen blows fell upon each fighter, Bill finally dodging aside and tripping the clumsy behemoth as he charged by, his throbbing left leg reminding him that he had to end the fight soon.

With surprising agility considering his leg's weakening and his head's wooziness, Bill attacked, landing on Rick's back and driving his face into the floor. He pummeled the fallen man's head and shoulders unmercifully until Rick reared back, sending his tormentor into the crowd. Hands barely touched his back this time, the sound of a thud, followed by one of Rick's friends collapsing in a heap, telling the whole story.

Honeycutt grasped him in a bear hug, sure his superior strength would win out, but Bill was having none of it, clapping both palms alongside the bully's head, effectively boxing his ears. Wriggling loose, Bill stomped his opponent's toes, and slipped under his right arm. Grasping a huge wrist with tenacious strength, he threw his body over Rick's back, his weight coupled with momentum breaking the hapless bruiser's arm as he was flipped head over heels into the bar, all the fight gone out of him.

Olaf's powerful fingers gripped his arm, holding him back as he kicked at the downed man, "Enough, Bill, he's had enough. Calm down, my friend, you've won."

Bill staggered to the bar and looked in the mirror, wondering where all the cuts and bruises had come from. '*I don't remember being hit in so many places,*' he thought as he felt twinges all over his body.

The bartender was screaming that someone had to pay for the damage, so Curly took a small wad of bills out of Honeycutt's pocket and threw it on the bar. Roy added a couple of twenties to the pile, and the bartender bought a round on the house, the combatants completely forgotten.

Olaf and Roy braced Bill, marching him home with firm grips on both elbows. Julia muttered, "Tsk! Tsk!" as she repaired the damage to Bill's face and ordered Roy to prepare a hot bath. Deciding no stitches were needed, she sent him to soak in the tub with a mild reprimand but a look of approval. He heard her tell her husband, "That boy reminds me of you as a young man, Roy. He's no chechako any longer."

𝗧𝗧 𝗧𝗧 𝗧𝗧

Bill woke to the sound of angry voices downstairs and immediately knew that Gene Wilson was calling him to account. He dressed as rapidly as his stiff and sore muscles would allow and combed his hair into a semblance of order although his mirror confirmed nothing could help his bruised face.

Gene's angry voice carried through the house as Bill limped slowly down the stairwell, "Why did he take her to Creek Street in the first place? How could he stand by while Honeycutt called my girl names? Where is that coward, Olaf? I want to tell him a thing or two."

In a moment of respite, Mae's tearful voice could be heard, "I told you, Daddy. Bill's not at fault. I made him take me to Creek Street. Dolly will tell you he was a perfect gentleman."

"Hah! Where is that perfect gentleman now? Hiding upstairs or in. . .?"

Gene's mouth gaped as he saw the battered young man standing at the foot of the stairs behind Julia and Mae, at a sudden loss for words at the spectacle.

Mae looked over her shoulder and gasped, an expression of pain, pity and pride blossomed into a radiant smile. She rushed to him and threw her arms around his neck, unabashedly kissing him on his lips. Blushing a pretty pink as she felt everyone's stares, she stood her ground, and though Bill was taken aback, he held her tightly in place, liking the warm feeling touching his heart as well as his body.

Gene sputtered, "What the hell's going on, Bill? Mae, what are you doing?"

Silencing the girl with a gesture, Bill replied, "I apologize for upsetting you, Gene, but I had to see your daughter home safely before I could deal with Honeycutt."

"Why were you and my daughter on Creek Street? I trusted you to show good sense."

Bill winced, but answered calmly, "I'm sorry, my judgment could have been better, but Mae did nothing wrong. Your daughter's a lady."

Gene shrugged his shoulders, calmer as he agreed, "I believe Mae's account. She never lies to me. I reckon I was wrong to call you a coward. You look like a truck ran over you."

Olaf finally spoke, "Gene, you should see the other fellow. Honeycutt was still out cold when we brought Bill home. Roy and Curly will tell you a more fanciful tale, but Bill won his fight."

"You whupped Honeycutt?" Gene asked in disbelief, "That rough-and-tumble fighter?" Shaking his head in awe, he mumbled, "Well, what about that?"

As everyone relaxed, Aaron sidled into the room and asked, "Gee, Bill, how did Mae make you take her to Creek Street?"

A ripple of laughter answered the boy's question, even Gene smiling at the youth as he said, "It seems my daughter is a woman, Aaron. I'm sorry for carrying on so, folks. Bill, I should have listened to Mae and shared her faith in you."

"Does that mean I'm still working for you after Christmas?" Bill asked teasingly, and as Gene nodded, he continued in the same vein, "Is it okay if Mae goes fishing with me today? Aaron can be our chaperone."

π   π   π

Julia proved herself a master cook on Christmas Day, voracious appetites sated as chairs were eased back from the sumptuous banquet. Good cheer was abundant, except maybe when John Furrer mentioned his daughter's absence. Even when Olaf teased Bill about his black-and-blue coloring, everyone laughed with natural humor.

Mae and Bill conspired to clear the table and wash the dishes, everyone agreeing that Julia had done enough. When the last pot was in the cupboard, the young couple donned coats and slipped away.

Mae held a simple gift for Dolly, and Bill carried a bottle of champagne for Curly as they set out to wish them a merry Christmas.

Walking through town, Mae and Bill shared a moment of companionability so rare in the busy holidays. A brief visit to their friends' noisy house accomplished, they walked back up Creek Street to the park overlooking the creek's gushing waters.

Both were subdued in their first time alone since that fateful evening, Bill finally pointing to a wet stone bench by the creekside. Neither deigned to sit, preferring to stand behind the bench and admire the view. Bill placed an arm around Mae's shoulders and spoke, "I meant everything I said to your father yesterday. We're friends, I know, but I feel something much stronger. I think you did vamp me the other night. Will you be my girl and wear my fraternity pin?"

She answered with a breathless sigh, grabbing his coat lapels in her fingers and raised her lips for a sensual kiss. Tasting blood she hastily withdrew, looking over Bill's split lip with concern, then playfully daubing it with her dainty lace handkerchief. "No more kissing, my hero. I think I did more damage than Rick Honeycutt. I want to hear all about that fight. You haven't really said much."

Taking the hanky from Mae and putting it in his pocket as a keepsake, he fastened his fraternity pin on her sweater, and closing her jacket, he deposited a peck on her forehead. Hand in hand they strolled to the Carlsons on a circuitous route, Bill relating the full story, egged on by Mae's look of adoration. She knew instinctively how to get what she wanted out of him - and Bill knew exactly what she was doing.

Chapter Five

Bill leaned over Aaron's shoulder and surveyed the coastline of Duke Island from a thousand feet, enjoying his young friend's gift to him of a flight home. Nostalgia touched lightly on his emotions as he recalled his holidays with the Carlsons, particularly his romantic moments with Mae. He fingered the hand-knitted scarf she had given him at Christmas, not as charismatic as Helen's Tsimshian talisman, but somehow much dearer to him.

The more mundane gifts of money which he had received from his family in Tacoma and his generous paycheck from the mill had combined to make him feel rich just two days ago. His lips twisted in a wry grin as silent laughter filled his thoughts, recalling Don Wilson's "lawyering" bill the homesteader paid as he accepted the initial ownership document for Cottage Cove. Proving up on the homesite claim would eventually produce a deed to the land.

'*Well,*' he waxed philosophically to himself, '*I can't spend money out here anyway. I hope these supplies are sufficient until Gregori and Tsimchuck visit in the spring.*'

Aaron tapped his shoulder and then pointed to his home on the shore ahead as the pilot maneuvered the plane into a landing approach, the boy asking hopefully, "Can I come and stay with you after school is out? Dad said he'd talked to you."

"Sure, Aaron! In fact your father hopes to come along for the fishing – maybe late May. Even Olaf may join us for a couple of days," Bill responded, pausing as the twin floats bounced off whitecaps in Ray Anchorage.

The lad bemoaned present weather conditions, "Heck! I wanted to see your place today, but the pilot says we have to hurry before the water gets too choppy for a takeoff."

The aforementioned gentleman silently pointed to the newly-built way, a signal for Bill to climb onto the plane's port pontoon and unload his supplies. Aaron followed to hold the tail snug against the slip, the pilot loath to stop the idling propeller. Minutes later the boy crawled back into the aircraft cabin, soaked to his hips in seawater but smiling at his adventure.

Bill pushed the plane away from the way, watching in place as the pilot gunned the engine and plowed through choppy seas. A final exchange of waves marked the aircraft's abrupt rise into the air as whitecaps released it, and the plane headed straight toward Ketchikan.

All alone for the winter months was the homesteader's dis-agreeable thought, somewhat dispelled as he was startled by his bear friend standing in the meadow behind the cabin. The brute offered no challenge to the young man as he toted his supplies into the cabin, seeming to be content with being a watchful greeter.

Talking to the bear he now called "Brownie," Bill kept his voice calm and friendly, never taking his eyes off his erstwhile companion. Deciding that Brownie's expression was doleful, lip-smacking and hungry, Bill unwrapped a chunk of halibut and cut it in two pieces, taking the bigger half outside. As he walked slowly toward the bear, he continued talking and watching, finally depositing the piece of fish on a stump near the tree where he hung meat.

As Bill backed away, Brownie advanced to the stump, nose actively twitching as he smelled the tasty morsel. Satisfied that his benefactor's odor on his dinner was no threat, Brownie seized the halibut chunk in his jaws and slowly sauntered into the forest.

"Well, Brownie, I guess my first task is to build a meat shed, or you'll help yourself to my daily catch," Bill announced to the departing brute, his companion in solitude.

π   π   π

Snowflakes stung his bare face as the wind blew hardily, a blizzard still raging around his cabin. He took a smoked cod from his newly built smokehouse, noticing the marks of his whipsaw on the raw spruce boards. Inside the wood was covered with a coating of soot, but when he closed the door, the outside looked much fresher, only rain and snow weathering its surface. He had alternated cutting lumber and fishing for several days, finishing the stout structure just before the snowstorm hit with full force.

Brownie had been conspicuously absent ever since his return, and Bill wondered anew if black bears hibernated.

After packing cod and biscuits in his jacket pocket and bundling himself in three layers of clothes, Bill went hunting for a deer he had spotted at dusk. Finding the animal's sign by the stream, he followed a fairly clear trail into the forest, and eventually to a deadfall where it had spent the night – not far from Bill's accident site.

Remembering with a smile the motto of safety first, Bill continued on the fresh track, staying downwind as he crept stealthily forward. Freezing instantly at a movement ahead, his eyes scanned the forest as he sought to identify his prey. Soon another movement caught his attention as the deer walked unalerted in his direction.

Muffling the release of the rifle's safety with both hands, he removed his right glove ever so slowly, watching the animal's twitching ears for any sign of alarm. When the buck turned its head away, Bill noted a pair of two-pronged horns. He lifted his rifle to his shoulder, arresting the motion as the buck seemed to sense danger, displaying a skittish behavior.

Lining his sights on the buck's left shoulder, he squeezed the trigger as the bead fell on target, a shot resounding in the tranquil woodland. The rifle barrel jumped as the bullet knocked the buck down. Bill worked the bolt and switched the safety in one smooth motion. He ran forward, keeping his eyes on the spot while watching his footing and stumbled on the still form of his quarry moments later.

His bullet had entered behind the left shoulder of the buck, and evidently struck the heart and lungs since the animal was bleeding profusely.

Leaning his rifle against a tree, Bill removed his other glove and set about butchering the buck first slicing the throat and jugular vein and then gutting the carcass. Like all frontiersmen, Indians and white men alike, Bill planned to use every bit of his kill – meat, hide and horns.

π   π   π

Switching the quarter of venison to his right shoulder and his rifle to his left hand, Bill plodded down the rugged slope, sure Ed Hill's cabin lay beneath the waft of smoke rising from the trees ahead. His roving eyes found the reclusive fisherman before spotting his cabin, his neighbor perched on a rock at the edge of what was obviously Judd Harbor. In the process of reeling in a small rock cod, Ed became aware of Bill's approach and waved nonchalantly and dexterously flipped the squirming fish into a tub of seawater.

"Hi, Bill. Thought maybe you'd pulled out. I was over to your place last month, and nobody was home," Ed greeted him with a smile. His expression became a grimace as he rose on one leg, picking up a homemade cane to hobble forward. Stumbling on loose gravel, he braced himself with his bandaged and gimpy leg, a painful cry escaping tightly sealed lips.

"Whoa, Ed, let me help you. What's wrong with your leg'?" Bill asked as he dropped the venison haunch and slipped under Ed's right shoulder.

"Oh, I slipped against some barnacles last week, sprained an ankle and scratched my shin. Ankle's coming along, but the cut is infected. Glad to see you, Neighbor. My meathouse is empty, and I'm tired of pancakes."

Wordlessly, Bill grunted his understanding and supported the hobbling old man to his cabin. The conversation remained sparse as Bill hung the venison in the meathouse and cleaned three small cod for dinner.

Washing his hands thoroughly in soap and water, the young man knelt before Ed and directed, "Doctor Pardue is on the scene. Let's look at that leg. Maybe practicing on my own leg last fall will be useful."

With a reluctant nod, Ed agreed, "Go ahead, Bill. I reckon my own medicine is lousy. I hate to admit to needing help, but I am glad you're here."

Unwrapping the soiled remnant of what appeared to be an undershirt, Bill found an inflamed wound which looked and smelled putrid. Three gashes and a dozen scratches marred the shin above the swollen ankle, the deepest cut oozing puss. Bill lifted Ed's foot and rotated it slowly, feeling for broken bones before stating, "I believe you're right, Ed. Nothing seems broken, but you have an infection. Where's your first aid kit?"

The older man pointed to his bedside stand, admitting, "I don't have a lot of medicine. Rubbing alcohol and iodine are over there."

Bill poured hot water from the teakettle into a dishpan, and with soap and his own clean handkerchief, began cleaning the hermit's wounds, finally placing the steaming hot rag over the infection and pressing it against the leg.

"Urgh!" screamed Ed at the heat and pressure, tears glistening in his squinting eyes as his fingers gripped the chair's legs, knuckles turning white as he fought the pain.

After a few minutes the hankie was washed and resoaked in heated water before being returned to the open wound, this time accompanied by Bill's gruff order, "Hold this rag in place while I doctor the other scratches."

A liberal washing with rubbing alcohol was followed by a light application of the tincture of iodine. Finally Bill observed, "There, your scratches and cuts seem okay except for this nasty one. Let's disinfect it."

An hour later the exhausted patient was helped into bed, immediately falling asleep. Bill straightened the cabin and prepared fish and chips, the potato his contribution to the meal. Remembering his neighbor's fondness for the vegetable, he had carried it over in his jacket pocket as a treat.

As light faded and the food was ready, Bill shook his patient awake and handed him a hot cup of coffee. Ed ate his dinner with gusto, falling asleep as soon as he set his coffee cup down. This scene was to be repeated over the next couple of days as Bill fished, cooked and then fed his patient. He hunted for deer one time but failed to find any game close to the cabin.

After a noon meal of fish and pancakes, Ed hoisted his leg across Bill's chair and asked, "Will you check it again? I believe it's healing."

Bill's examination was cursory as he agreed, "Yep! And you're getting your strength back, too. Keep that wound clean, and you'll be fishing within the week."

Ed nodded and gulped out his appreciation, "Thanks! I owe you one, Bill," and with a rueful grin he added, "Guess I'm not as self-sufficient as I thought. You're welcome at my place anytime, Neighbor."

π   π   π

A blast of wet, frigid air staggered the lone figure standing by his boat slip at Cottage Cove this first day of March, 1951. A gray blowing mist blanketed land and sea, and wind-whipped seas of the usually placid bay were roiled into a white froth. Bill's simple tasks of checking his tied-down boat and filling his water barrel had taken only ten minutes, but he was chilled despite his three-layered outfit of winter wear.

As he turned to face his cabin and the blustery wind, its ululating howl was pierced by a ship's horn. *'Why, that's the MacDonald,'* he thought in a flash, *'And it's in the harbor. I wonder what's wrong – maybe heavy swells in Dixon Entrance?'*

Bill peered long and hard into the foggy atmosphere shrouding the bay, finally making out the dark shadow of a familiar barge. An occasional metallic clink penetrated the howling of the erratic southwesterly storm front, but neither voices nor engine sounds could be heard.

On a spur of the moment, Bill decided to challenge the elements and visit his friends on the tugboat. Damping the fire in his stove and securing his cabin with extra care, he took a gunny sack of smoked halibut from the meathouse and carried it to his boat. Releasing the craft into the choppy waters was simple, but managing to start the outboard and maneuver it into offshore waters was a harrowing experience, a real test of his seamanship.

"Hello, *MacDonald!* Anybody home?" Bill shouted, and a faint and indiscernible reply came back through the stout wind.

Spotting a waving figure leaning out the wheelhouse window, Bill called, "Hi, Skipper, may I come aboard?"

"You bet, Slim! Harry's waiting for you on the stern. Did you bring your poker money with you?" Elmer joked, his voice clear as the smaller boat moved alee of the tug. Coming into the quiet nook between the anchored pair of vessels, he nosed up to the *MacDonald's* stern. Harry used a pike pole to snag his mooring line, promptly securing it to a cleat. Bill cut his engine and clambered over the rail with his sack of smoked fish and a second rope. He wanted to be sure his boat was here when he decided to go ashore.

Harry promptly shook his hand and with a conspiritual grin drew the visitor forward to the mess door. An empty seat in the poker game beckoned him as greetings were exchanged. Handing the cook's helper his sack and removing his outer layer of clothes, Bill pulled out a twenty–dollar bill and plunked it down on the table.

"Ha! New blood in the game is just what's needed," Ray chortled in anticipation, Bill's rusty laugh sounded strange to everyone, including himself.

Grinning cheerfully as he folded his hand, he quipped in more normal tones, "I'm glad I didn't win the first pot – it's bad luck. Now deal me some winning cards, Cookie." The lonely young man settled back to enjoy his first real social gathering in two months. Win or lose, he was happy as a lark.

Elmer slid into the empty seat left when Cookie began to prepare a meal and promptly changed the modest run of luck which Bill had followed for an hour. When Cookie broke up the game to serve dinner, Bill lost yet another pot to the skipper and pocketed but a handful of change.

"Well, I finally got my money back, Slim. Sorry we can't give you a chance to recoup your losses, but everyone is hitting his bunk early. We're upping anchor at 4:00 AM and heading south. A tanker reported twenty foot seas in Dixon Entrance at noon today, but the weather report calls for improvement by daylight. We'll cross tomorrow, storm or not. How are you doing with your homestead?"

Bill stretched his visit to the limit, relishing the friendly conversations with crew members but soon found only Cookie and the duty watch left awake. Ray helped him load his gunny sack containing useful odds and ends and a sack of potatoes into his bobbing boat and then cast off his lines when the Johnson sputtered to life. Jack directed him home on the beam of the towboat's spotlight, the return trip seeming less traumatic to the contented young homesteader.

π   π   π

As the series of southwesterly storms abated, cool air and clear skies prevailed. Bill fished close to home, conserving his gasoline supply when he learned the *MacDonald* had none to spare. It was still enough to hear the beat of an airplane engine from a great distance, and he was quick to spot its tiny form off to the north. The pilot wig-wagged the wings and waved through the cabin glass as he passed over the open boat, dropping a parachuted bundle near his cabin.

Reeling in his bottom line took an unreasonable amount of time, and when a fish struck his bait, he tried to jerk the hook free. He found that he'd set the barb solidly into a small dogfish, and with practiced patience cut the embedded steel free of the now dead fish, casting it back into the sea.

The treasure hoard bundle lay almost on his doorstep as he hastened to unwrap several layers of butcher paper to reveal a frozen chicken before finding a newspaper, copies of *Argosy* and *Time*, a Zane Grey novel and a packet of letters.

Ensconced in his homemade rocker, he read all afternoon and much of the next day, work shamelessly neglected despite good weather over the island. He laughed at himself and his loafing attitude, happy for a break in his routine, thinking to himself, first the MacDonald crew and now reading news from the "outside." That his cup runneth over was an amusing thought as he continued to read.

He took *Mac's* letters first, arranging all three in chronological order before perusing them. Next came a single letter written by all four Carlsons, a letter from his mother and a note from Charles Blakely. Simple items from Ketchikan, Seattle and Tacoma were very interesting to the isolated young man, none of the articles being out of the ordinary – boring to most readers.

The sound of an outboard motor brought him out of his reverie, and donning his jacket, he strode to the beach. A boat not dissimilar from his own was cruising the bay, Bill recognizing the figure of Ed Hill as it crossed the cove to his mooring stump.

"Howdy, Neighbor! I'm returning your visit – and some venison," Ed said with a smile as he stepped ashore and stomped around on his healed leg, "And healthy to boot!"

"Hi, Ed. You missed all the excitement. I got some mail a couple of days ago, and I had a visit from the *MacDonald* last week. Cottage Cove seemed like Grand Central Station for awhile," Bill reported happily.

Ed's frowning reply was instantaneous, "Glad I wasn't here. Can't stand so many people. Say, did you get any newspapers? Reading about the 'outside' is okay as long as I don't have to be there."

Bill found it necessary to share his rocker as both men read every article, few words exchanged that day or the next.

Finally saturated with such a douse of reading material, Ed sighed as he laid down the "Help Wanted" section, saying, "Well, I should be fishing. What say we partner for a week and take our catch over to Boca de Quadra? The cannery's not in operation now, but we can trade for gasoline, beer and a home-cooked meal or two. Hee! Hee! Don't mean to insult your cooking, but. . .".

π   π   π

And so it was that Bill and Ed struck off across Revillagigedo Channel, their boats filled with halibut and empty gas cans. Bill looked up at the light clouds and over choppy waters, reflecting, *'I'd call this fair weather today. That is, if you don't mind the rain and a little breeze. We've been running six hours, and the cannery still isn't in sight. We'd better check our gasoline supply.'*

Signaling Ed to pull over alee of a rocky point where the water appeared calm, Bill stopped his Johnson and asked, "How much farther, Ed? Have we got enough gas?"

"Well, it's around that point up ahead – less than ten miles. Water's pretty calm. Why don't I tow you for awhile?" Ed replied, concern sounding in his tone as well.

A half hour later Ed's outboard sputtered to a standstill. He swished his remaining gasoline in a five gallon can and with a careless shrug poured its contents into the outboard's tank – a pint or two. Bill passed his nearly empty can to his partner, saying, "Take this dribble too, and let's make a run for it. It's getting dark."

Side by side the two boats cleared Orca Point at half speed, homing in on the cannery dock across the sound. Bill's Johnson ran dry a mile from their destination, but he waved Ed forward, using his Evinrude to complete the journey.

Ed was met by a fellow named Karl, and Bill's first words popped out before introductions, "Do you have gasoline?"

Karl laughed and kidded the partners, "You fellas don't want to row home, eh? Yes in answer to your question, and I'll buy your catch of halibut also. A tender is due by in the morning. Welcome to what we call the end of the world, gentlemen."

Winking at Ed Hill, he added, "I haven't seen you since last fall, Ed."

The older man merely nodded, so Bill spoke, "I'm Bill Pardue, a neighbor of Ed's. I'm homesteading in that cabin on Cottage Cove."

"Sure, I know the place – Indian built it. You must be one of those veterans who got lucky. I heard only a handful of homesites were approved in Juneau. The tribes' complaints evidently were heeded, and a lot of land was held back. Maybe the territorial government will offer more land this summer. Well, let's get these fish weighed and in my cooler. The first beer's on me."

That evening Ed's reclusive nature went into remission, the dozen or so people spending the winter at the cannery not inhibiting his tongue in the least. Bill heard a variety of stories from his now-talkative partner. Karl finally told him, "Ed comes in here twice a year with fish and a yen to socialize."

He added as an afterthought, "I've visited his place on Judd Harbor, and I've bought salmon at sea, both times when working on a tender. Never heard a dozen words out of him on either occasion, but he's a talker when he has a couple of beers. Well, he's about ninety percent hermit, but that's his right, I reckon."

ᛏᛏ   ᛏᛏ   ᛏᛏ

Sated with all the company he'd kept over his partnering venture with Ed, Bill was content to work in solitude around his cabin for several days. Fair weather and the need for a good workout eventually goaded his conscience, and he set out to explore the two hills southeast of his homestead. There was no trail except an occasional game run, but Bill was familiar with the area where he and his bear had scared each other.

It seemed ironic that the explorer spotted several deer, when as a hunter he seldom saw any. With venison and halibut in his meathouse, he ignored all opportunities for fresh meat, intent on seeing the southeastern slopes and Revillagigedo Channel.

Traipsing through dense underbrush beneath a canopy of huge evergreens was invigorating, and Bill began to feel like a strong and independent frontiersman – not a chechako. As the uphill slope leveled off, the underbrush all but disappeared, and he realized he was on the South Hill summit, the view here just as spectacular as from Duke Hill. Finding a comfortable spot to eat lunch and view the scenery was not difficult, and he seated himself on the mossy ground, settling back against a solid spruce tree.

Bill unwrapped a large chunk of smoked halibut and laid it on butcher paper next to him, alternately nibbling flakes of it and a crumbly baking powder biscuit. His mind drifted into a subconscious reverie as his body relaxed, and he observed nature with a glassy stare. Moments of such daydreaming passed before his conscious mind sensed heavy breathing beside him, a clear snort sounding when he reached for a piece of fish.

Startled into awareness, he turned his head toward the sound, and his eyes met those of a mottled black bear a scant six feet away. Pretty sure that the brute staring back was his missing friend, now thinner and hungry-looking, Bill lifted the halibut with his left hand and gently cast it to the bear's feet. His right hand held a firm grip on the rifle frozen in place across his lap.

"Go ahead, Brownie, it looks like you need a meal more than I do," Bill uttered in gentle tones, trusting the bear to recognize his voice as well as his smell. *'At least we're not scaring each other out of our wits,'* was his accompanying thought.

Brownie threw his head back, shaking his dampened fur, a gesture which could be taken as either a nod or a challenge, Bill wasn't sure what to think. One last twitch of his nose, and the bear seized the fish in his powerful jaws and lumbered away, back along the route toward Duke Hill which Bill had just traversed. *'Wow, I bet Brownie has been following me through the woods,'* a tiny voice said in his head.

"Well, Brownie, next time give me a little more warning," Bill announced to the departing bear, broad rump disappearing into the underbrush. Rising as he admonished his friend, he wisely set out in a different direction, more northwesterly in direction and hopefully a faster route home.

ᵯ   ᵯ   ᵯ

With frontier practicality, Bill whiled away the rainy spring, first swapping fish for gasoline and potatoes from Tsimchuck and Gregori, then potatoes for venison from Ed Hill, and finally venison for fresh vegetables from a tender cruising north from Seattle. It was late May before he was short on supplies, tired of fish and generally bored with his lot.

Bill had not lost his dream for Cottage Cove, but he did wonder how he could make a living on Duke Island after he had proven up his homesite. His mental imagery had been active but unproductive in regards to any workable plan.

One sunny morning during a break in the stormy weather patterns, Bill was motoring across the bay toward Duke Point to see if any salmon were running around Duchess Island when he heard an airplane engine. His Johnson outboard had drowned out the sound of its approach until it was close overhead, and as he looked up, he could see hands waving from the passenger window.

The pilot banked the plane sharply over the bay, circling the open water as it lost altitude. Bill promptly reversed course, thinking that a mail drop would be a wonderful diversion when the plane's engine changed tempo, and he watched it settle into a landing approach. It touched down a half mile away, and taxiing into the wind, headed toward his place.

Bill opened his throttle wide and raced for a rendezvous with his visitors before a mishap occurred. The tide was still very low, and the underwater rocks off his beach were a hazard. He signaled the pilot to hold off shore, closing the distance between them quickly. He advanced that last few yards carefully, his ever present phobia with spinning propeller blades keeping danger in the forefront of his thoughts.

Olaf Carlson stood on a pontoon holding a guy wire on the plane while seizing the boat's rail. Aaron swung down to step into the bow, a hasty "Hi" lost in the unloading of the plane as his father handed him bundle after bundle from the cabin. Bill counted fourteen, or was it fifteen, packages delivered before the boy scrambled aft to give him an unabashed hug. Roy spoke to the pilot and then climbed down to the pontoon, closing the cabin door before he and his brother shoved the boat clear and jumped into it.

The pilot immediately gunned his engine, taxiing around them and roaring eastward in a spray of white mist – a picture book takeoff. It seemed he had a boon of wishes satisfied in company and supplies as he happily chattered – competition for his Johnson.

An hour later the four friends gathered around a pile of bundles on the cabin floor, Bill gesturing to Olaf and Roy to sit in the chairs and Aaron on his bed, offering aloud, "Are you guys ready to eat? I can fry up some steaks – halibut or venison."

Roy opened a small package and spread the butcher paper wrapping on the table, and with a gleeful nod, stated, "I've got a treat for you. Julia sent ham and cheese sandwiches for all of us and asked me to extend her love and best wishes."

"Wow! I haven't tasted ham or cheese in five months. Bless Julia!" Bill retorted.

"And I brought a quart of Olympia beer in my knapsack. Let's celebrate!" Olaf declared as he produced the bottle.

Sandwiches and beer were consumed with ravenous appetite by everyone, Aaron allowed to join the adults with a small glass of Olympia. Happily he prated, "Thanks, Dad, this Oly sure tastes good. I'm sure having fun, Bill, you sure could make a good living here entertaining fishermen."

The lad's innocent remark struck a chord with his homesteader friend, who looked from Aaron to Roy to Olaf and muttered sincerely, "Why didn't I think of that? Aaron, that's a great idea. What do you say, Roy? Olaf?"

Big Swede deferred to his businessman brother, who replied thoughtfully, "Pardue's Lodge, home of King Salmon and Queen Halibut, where adventurous fishermen travel to catch the big ones – the trophies. How does that sound, my friends?"

Besides the comradeship of the next two days, the group fished together and constantly brainstormed Bill's blossoming dream. They set up the canvas tent they had brought in the plane, enlarging "Pardue's Lodge" to accommodate three to six people, and Roy drew a detailed plan on his butcher paper.

"You need capital to expand facilities, perhaps a floor for the tent and a two-hole outhouse would be a good start. And you'll need another boat – maybe a skiff would do. Would you be interested in a partner?" Roy asked contemplatively, the excitement of such a project eliciting his quasi-offer.

"Whoa! Not so fast, my friend, let's wait to explore the possibilities when I'm working this summer in Ketchikan. Say, wouldn't we need a deal with your pilot friend or someone like him?" Bill queried in wishful thought, jumping in alarm when Olaf's roar erupted from the outhouse.

Brownie's plaintive squeal sounded across the yard as Bill ran out of the cabin, a devilish grin creasing his face at the sight of a standoff between man and animal. Both seemed ready to run at the drop of a hat, but neither wanted to be the first to retreat, or both were scared stiff, he didn't know which.

"Ha! Ha! It's just Brownie, Olaf. He probably smelled fresh halibut and wants a bite – of the fish, not you, my friend," Bill explained in his teasing manner.

"Gee, can I feed him, Bill?" Aaron offered eagerly, adding with a more questioning tone in his voice, "He's tame, isn't he?"

"Ha! Ha! Tame isn't the correct term, Aaron. I'd say he was not unfriendly, nor dangerous unless riled. Yes, you can throw him the halibut you caught this morning, but don't get too close."

The lad took the fish from the meathouse and carried it into the field, holding it like an offering to the gods. When Brownie became agitated, shuffling his paws and tossing his head about, Aaron halted. At Bill's command he threw the halibut toward the bear and stood still.

Brownie lumbered forward, sniffing Aaron's scent and cocking his massive head, seemingly studying the boy and the fish simultaneously. Satisfied with his inspection, he jawed the halibut and nonchalantly waddled into the forest with his dinner.

"Gee, he really looked me over. His eyes are so big," Aaron uttered in awe.

"Well, partner, his eyesight isn't too great, but Brownie will know your smell the next time you two meet. Come on inside, folks. We'd better eat our share of the morning's catch for dinner. You've all got same packing to do this evening since your plane is due at daylight."

ᴨ   ᴨ   ᴨ

Intermittent rain fell during the days following the Carlsons' visit, somewhat warmer now that June was here. Bill fished long hours, wet weather or not, smoking salmon in great quantity for sale in Ketchikan. He planned to load his boat and sail north in a week or so.

Trolling off Duke Point one noon, he heard the familiar drone of an airplane engine in the clouds, five minutes passing before he could see it circling overhead. Moments later the pilot banked sharply east and wig-wagged his wings.

'Hmm!' Bill thought as he set off for home, *'He must have seen me. What's up today? That pilot is a daredevil to fly in this weather.'*

When he repeated the scenario of last week, he discovered two men replete in fishing gear, standing on the plane's pontoon. Belatedly he recognized Blackjack Blakely as his voice boomed out, "Hi, Bill. Charley says hello. He's working this weekend so his dad and I can try a hand at fishing. Meet the elder Charley."

He paused as he viewed a boat full of fish and continued cheerfully, "I see the salmon are running."

The Blakely brothers treated Bill with an interesting combination of respect for a businessman and deference to a fishing guide, along with a casual contempt for a hired hand. Whereas the Carlsons shared housekeeping chores while they were guests, Bill found his "paid" lodgers expected to be waited on hand and foot.

Washing dishes while the Blakelys took a twilight walk gave the young man an opportunity to reflect on being an innkeeper. He thought, *'I guess I'll have all kinds of people here if I start taking paying lodgers. Hmm! I don't have to like everyone who spends his fishing vacation with me. That hundred dollar credit at Blakely Hardware will be earned like every other fee I charge – with hard work. Well, maybe we'll get along better now that I've told them their cots are in the tent. Ha! Ha! I guess I can put up with boorish behavior as long as they follow my rules.'*

The door burst open and Blackjack rushed inside, spouting, "There's a bear out in the field," and seizing Bill's rifle from the wall, jacked a shell into the firing chamber, muttering with glee, "What a trophy for my den."

Bill saw red, his temper flaring out of control, his reaction without thought or consequence as he shoved the older man against the wall unceremoniously. Snatching the 30.06 from his hands, Bill growled in threatening anger, "My place is no hunting lodge, Mister Blakely, and Brownie's no trophy for your wall. He's no threat to me or my guests as long as we use common sense. Don't you have enough courtesy to ask permission before handling another man's gun?"

Bill concluded his wrathful exhortation in a calmer voice and removed the live round from the chamber, putting the rifle back on its rack.

He left the flabbergasted and speechless Blackjack in the cabin and strode out to join Charley the Elder who was watching Brownie beg for fish.

"Sorry about that, Bill. I told him not to get excited. Your friendly bear poses no threat. I think he's hungry," Charley opined.

"You're right, of course. Brownie stops by a couple of times a week to beg for halibut. I should have warned you and your brother. However, there will be no hunting by guests at Cottage Cove. I don't care much for trophy hunting. I only shoot game to fill my meat locker. By the way, we'll eat a tasty venison stew for dinner tomorrow – typical fare at Pardue's Lodge."

Blackjack approached the chatting pair and stood diffidently observing Brownie, shifting nervously from foot to foot, not quite sure how to act or what to say. When Bill retrieved one of today's catch from the meathouse, Blackjack quickly offered, "Sorry, Bill. Hrmph! Say, can I feed your pet?"

Bill acceded with a nod of deference and a small grin, handing him the halibut with a word of caution, "Don't get too close to Brownie. As I told the Carlsons, he's not tame even if he is friendly."

ᴛᴛ   ᴛᴛ   ᴛᴛ

Sunny skies brightened the Alaskan landscape, lucent hues of blues and greens dotted with earthen browns and grays, variations of white accenting the choppy seas and tiny puffs of vaporous clouds overhead. Breaking the pristine silence of his wilderness was Bill's call to the Blakelys, "Don't forget your fresh salmon, Blackjack. And remind Charley his dufflebag is in the cabin. I'll pack your gear in the boat."

After Bill had laid down the law to his guests, their behavior and attitude had improved, the three men eschewing hard feelings as they worked together at sea and socialized in the evenings. Forgetting Bill's flare of temper, Blackjack instead gloried in his adventure of feeding a black bear. His story grew as he practiced telling it until he had Brownie eating out of his hand, Charley and Bill laughingly accepting his tall tale.

A friendly arm fell across Bill's shoulders as he stowed two hundred pounds of smoked salmon in the boat. Blackjack threw a gunny sack of fish in the boat, thanking his host profusely, "Thanks a million for a great time, Bill. I'll add thirty five dollars credit to your account for the smoked salmon, and I'll recommend Pardue's Lodge to all my fishing buddies. When will you be looking for paying customers, my friend?"

"That's great, Blackjack. I'll need help when my lodge is ready, and remember that I'll verify your bear-feeding tale if there's a single 'Doubting Thomas' in Ketchikan. I hope you'll be a regular customer, I've enjoyed your company," Bill replied magnanimously, having forgotten their differences as Blackjack had.

Charley joined the camaraderie, inviting himself back for a visit, "Me too, Bill. If my son stays in Ketchikan like he's talking about, I'll have reason to. . .".

All three men turned in unison at the sound of their expected aircraft, spotting the seaplane flying in low over Revillagigedo Channel on a straightaway landing approach.

It wasn't until Bill motored around the tail assembly that he saw Mae climbing out of the cabin to balance precariously on a pontoon as she waved a greeting. Blackjack extended a chivalrous hand to help her into the boat, Bill meeting her halfway in a warm embrace, their prolonged kiss drawing chuckles from their companions.

"Hey, Bill! Aren't you going to let my girl up for a breath of air. Besides, I rate a friendly hello at least," Gene teased the young couple, not at all surprised at their affectionate greeting. He had suspected as much since the Christmas holidays.

Bill grinned sheepishly and replied with a blush echoing in his voice, "Hi, Gene. Welcome to Cottage Cove."

The transfer of salmon and the Blakely brothers to the plane was accomplished in a couple of minutes, and then Gene pushed off as he jumped into the boat. In a now familiar pattern, the plane revved its engine and moved toward open water for its takeoff.

Gene talked all the way to shore as both of the young people appeared shy, perhaps overwhelmed by their spontaneous welcome embrace. Eyeing the tent as he stepped ashore, he said, "Roy told me he had given you a tent for guests. Were the Blakelys paying lodgers?"

"Yes, and Blackjack bought most of my smoked salmon, too. However, I have a lot of improvements to make before setting up a regular business. There are three separate underwater rocks that have to be blasted out of the way before seaplanes can come into shore safely, and my tent needs a decent foundation," Bill informed his friends. Switching subjects abruptly, he continued, "You and I can sleep in the tent, and I expect Mae will be more comfortable in my bed – I mean in the cabin."

Bill blushed as both Wilsons chuckled at his faux pas, the young man thinking his tongue had betrayed a Freudian wish. Mae certainly was beautiful this morning.

π   π   π

Accepting Mae's offer to prepare supper, and deferring to her need for space to demonstrate her superior cooking talents, Bill walked her smiling father over his homestead. He pointed to the location of three submerged rocks which endangered his boat as well as taxiing seaplanes during low tides, commenting, "The water out

there looks innocent enough, but when the tide's out, all three ob-
stacles are just below the surface. In fact, one day this past winter
they were all visible on a stormy morning. Do you have any ideas,
Gene?"

"Well, I know a contractor who builds logging roads in rough
country. He's mighty handy with dynamite, and he swims okay. I
wonder if he's a diver, too," the older man mused before sounding a
warning, "It'll cost you a pretty penny, lad, but don't even think abut
doing any part of the job yourself. I decided long ago to extend my life
expectancy and leave dynamite to the experts – like Einar Gustafson."

"Ha! Ha! Don't worry, I have a healthy respect for explosives –
and for diving," Bill rejoined.

"How about earning that pretty penny next week? I need a partner
this summer cruising timber for John Furrer. I'm through selling
lumber down below. Give me that Alaskan outdoors anytime."

"What about Mae? And the University?" Bill asked with a trace of
concern in his voice.

"My daughter turned eighteen last week, and she's quite
capable of managing her own affairs. In fact, she has reserved a dor-
mitory room with a friend from the nursing school."

Bill threw up his hands and snorted, "Damn! I forgot Mae's
birthday. It is the fourth, right? What can I do?"

"Ha! Ha! And we saved her birthday celebration for this evening so
you could be with us. Relax, Bill, she thought you might have forgotten, and she said it was all right. Mae just wanted to share a
special day with you," the proud father explained with a straight face.

Reaching into his pocket, he grinned with eyes twinkling as he
handed Bill a silver chain and locket, teasing again, "Even in my
advanced age, I remember how a woman thinks. Mae means
she'll forgive you, but she'll be disappointed. Anyway, I bought this
trinket in Seattle just before we flew home, and Mae hasn't seen it.
You take it and give it to her after supper. You owe me one, my
friend."

Mae's clear voice echoed in the open field, calling the men to
"Come and get it!"

As he entered the cabin behind Gene, Bill thought the aroma was delightful, far better than any cooking attempt by himself. And then he looked over the tidied interior and was astounded anew. His place had never looked so good.

"Bill Pardue, you look like you've never seen a clean room before. Stop gawking and sit down," Mae ordered, obviously pleased with his reaction.

As she stepped over to the stove, Bill slipped the chain and locket under the paper napkin at the head of the table. He stated, "Oh no! On birthdays a pretty girl deserves service – and a kiss," whereupon he lifted her chin with one finger and bent over to kiss her lips gently, ending with "Happy birthday – belated greetings included."

Mae blushed happily and allowed herself to be seated by Bill at the head of the table. He placed the stew and biscuits on the table under the girl's watchful eye, finally seating himself at her side.

Their glances met and held as they unfolded napkins, Bill finally dropping his gaze to her gift. Mae followed suit and gave a tiny squeak of pleasure, looking from father to beau before picking it up. Bill was quick to his feet and placed it around her neck, awkwardly juggling the clasp to closure. He disentangled the fine silver chain from his fraternity pin, being very circumspect with his touch on her blouse's open throat, wishing her father wasn't watching him so closely.

TT   TT   TT

The next morning Bill offered Mae a grand tour of his corner of Duke Island, happily loaning Gene his boat for the morning. The youngsters headed into the forest on Bill's faint trail to Duke Hill and the ridge running south.

Mae asked a multitude of questions about his homestead, his winter's solitude and his lodge plans. When they reached his accident scene, she finally brought up the subject of his pet black bear.

Humor was mixed with a little worry in her repartee, and Bill's laughing response left a wrinkle of concern on her brow.

"Will we see Brownie today?" she queried.

Nodding affirmatively, he declared, "I expect so. I packed smoked salmon and biscuits for lunch, and Brownie will probably show up for his share. I brought my rifle along in case we meet some other critter in this forest."

An invigorating breeze blew the fluffy white clouds over a blue firmament, and a verdant canopy of spruce and fir swayed overhead. The sun's rays appeared to come and go like specters of the forest as the young couple climbed Duke Hill. Bill led the way, occasionally pausing to point out scenery or offer a respite to Mae.

After one such rest stop without a semblance of a view, she laughed playfully and said, "Ha! Ha! I'm not tired, are you? Race you to the top!"

Running at her heels, he joined in the banter, "All right, so you're as strong as an ox and can keep up with me. You have a lot of stamina for a half-pint – and a girl to boot."

He stumbled on a downed limb, and catching his balance, he surged forward, only to be brought up short by a standing Mae.

Her soft voice registered late, Bill freezing in place and listening, ". . .lunch with us. Eh, Brownie?   Bill has a piece of smoked salmon for you. Where is it, Bill?"

He dug into his knapsack and withdrew a chunk of fish, handing it around Mae. She took it in hand and advanced three steps, proffering it to the bear while Bill stepped into the small clearing beside her. Brownie pawed the ground only six feet away, Mae's monologue gentling his nervousness. She then leaned forward and dropped the smoked salmon before his twitching nostrils, straightening up to a motionless stance.

One last sniff and Brownie bit into the salmon, lumbering into the underbrush within arm's reach of Bill, whose eyes grew rounder in disconcerted alarm at Brownie's closeness.

Moments passed before he shook his head and spoke, "I thought he was going to rub shoulders with me – literally, that is."

"You should have seen your expression, Bill. Amazement can't quite describe it. But the Carlsons are right, Brownie is your pet bear," Mae teased him gently.

"And your friend, too! I thought you were going to put that salmon in his mouth. Didn't he scare you at all?"

She smiled in relief, admitting, "Yes, but you told me Brownie was friendly, and I just gritted my teeth and talked to him. I was afraid my scent might set him off, but it seems anyone with food is a friend."

Bill casually put his arm around Mae's shoulders and gave her a light hug of approval, which combined with his, "Good work, sweetheart", produced a distinctive reaction. She turned under his arm and gave him a hug, holding her grasp firmly as she stood on tiptoe and kissed him warmly.

In an instant he reacted, and as the two lovers shared a close embrace, he peered into her eyes with a mixed expression of tenderness and ardor. A woman's smile creased her lips, accepting his passionate kiss without coyness, the two young people pledging a silent vow of love.

Bill drew a deep breath for control as he spoke in an emotionally charged voice, "Mae Wilson, you're wonderful. I love..."

"I love you too, Bill. I've loved you ever since the festival dance. Hee! Hee! I was so sure you were infatuated with Alexis and didn't really see me."

"How could I not look at you? You're lovelier than Alexis, or any other woman for that matter." Pausing for a moment, Bill teased her, "Of course, you were awfully prim and proper all evening."

She laughed, "Ha! Ha! That's true while I was with Charley, but I was always nice to you. You just didn't notice until I played the vamp, and then when you came downstairs at the Carlsons all bruised and limping, I decided you were the only man for me. Bill dear, I promise not to vamp any other man if you'll marry me."

"Uh. . .sure. . .but. . .", Bill spluttered plaintively.

Interrupting him with a nervous smile, Mae nodded, "That's a yes, darling. Now don't start spouting platitudes about money, school and 'things,' just tell me you love me, and I'll follow you anywhere. Hee! Hee! Particularly to Cottage Cove. I love it here."

"Honey, it is too rough for you here, and I need a year to improve it into a respectable fishing lodge," Bill worried aloud.

"Oh no you don't, Bill Pardue! Marriage means sharing our lives, and I can hold my own as a cook, nurse and fisherman. I can even chop kindling. I have seven hundred dollars in savings, and Daddy will help us if I. . .we ask him," Mae hesitated with a pleading tone.

Smiling at the "I – We" conversion, Bill kissed Mae on the forehead, musing, "Thinking as a couple takes a little getting used to, doesn't it? Dearest Mae, I'm not too proud to accept a loan from your father or to run up a bill at Carlsons, but asking you to spend an isolated winter with. . ."

"Yes, I will, and enjoy every minute of a six-month honeymoon. Wouldn't you like to be all alone with me for weeks on end?" Mae asked as she drew him back into a close embrace, her kiss demonstrating untold possibilities.

After a few moments of passion, Bill surrendered, "I give up! I'll ask Gene for your hand right after lunch."

"Oh, men! Thinking of your stomach first is not very romantic. Is this the kind of life I can expect from you?" Mae kidded as she stroked his cheek lovingly, giving him a casual peck. She took food from his knapsack, and they shared a snack, interspersed with a kiss or two as they stood atop Duke Hill and purviewed their domain.

π   π   π

Bill hurried across the field to help Gene secure the boat, Mae ducking into the cabin with a wave to her father. Both men realized that Gene was capable of handling the task by himself, and when the young man lingered at the landing asking about fishing, Gene leaned back on the timbered way and waited for the nervous Bill to settle dawn.

"Hmm! Gene. . .er. . .Mae is a wonderful girl, and. . .well, we'd like to get married. I mean, we love each other, and she loves Cottage Cove. Uh. . .I. . .we'd like your blessing," Bill concluded and watched Mae's father apprehensively, his friend's presence somehow missing in the stern figure standing before him.

Moments passed as Gene studied the young man, a father's eye spotting Mae waiting expectantly in the doorway. Letting the youngsters suffer in silence, Gene teased them unmercifully until happy laughter slipped out. He first squeezed his future son-in-law's hand in a crushing grip and then threw one arm over his shoulder while offering the other to his onrushing daughter.

"Of course, you two lovebirds have my blessing. What took you so long to catch him, Daughter? Your mother only needed a couple of months with me."

Mae bubbled with a happy rejoinder, "Between calling Bill names last summer, and us living in Seattle all winter, my style was cramped some. However, I vamped him proper today. Pretty soon he'll believe our marriage is his idea."

"Well, it is!" Bill averred faithfully.

"Ha! Ha! I guess that means I don't lose a daughter, but gain a fishing camp. Come along, Son. We need to discuss my building a couple of bedrooms on the cabin – my wedding gift. I'll be damned if I'll sleep in that tent on my next fishing vacation."

Chapter Six

Bill returned to Ketchikan with Mae and her father, their engagement news awakening Julia's maternal instincts. The two women
closeted themselves in the Carlson kitchen to plan a September first
wedding. Gene went to the mill to see John Furrer, Aaron was
helping their pilot friend, Ed Luden, fly supplies into one of the Stikine
River gold camps, and Roy was working.

Cast adrift, Bill wandered down to the Carlson store and talked to
Roy, their brainstorming soon evolving into another butcher paper list
under the cash register. When business picked up before noon, Bill
left his friend to wait on customers, and strolled over to Creek Street
with his dream on his mind. Sauntering along the boardwalk
behind Abner Hall's place, he stepped around a drunk sprawled on
the doorstep.

An open palm was extended, and a blurred voice begged, "Got a quarter for a cup of coffee, Mister?"

Bill glanced down at the bedraggled figure, speechless as the man's eyes met his briefly in mutual recognition. Rick Honeycutt looked like death warmed over, Bill thought, and his face had aged twenty years from too much booze. And then a twinge of remorse pricked his conscience, not of liking nor of pity, but of self-recrimination that he may have helped change Rick into a drunken bum.

"Rick, get up! I'm going to buy you breakfast, but first you get a bath," Bill ordered curtly.

"Go to hell, Pardue! I don't need your charity, get out of here before I whip your butt!" Honeycutt retorted angrily, for a moment sounding like his ornery old self.

Unceremoniously grasping Rick's jacket in a firm grip, Bill dragged the stumbling beggar over to Bessie's laundry. Despite Rick's litany of dire consequences for his tormentor and the cackling laughter of the old laundress, Bill pulled dirty clothes from Honeycutt's body, distaste and determination marking his face at the chore. Bereft of clothes before the old woman, Rick quickly submerged himself in the gray sudsy water of the laundry tub.

"Clean and patch his clothes and don't give them back to him. I'll be back in ten minutes," Bill ordered Bessie as he exited from the laundry.

He walked directly to the fishing docks where a tender was docked and asked for Karl, sighing with relief when his friend from the Boca de Quadra cannery greeted him.

"Karl, I bet you need men in the cannery. I have a fellow that's down on his luck and needs work. Can you use him?" Bill said earnestly.

"If you recommend him, my friend," Karl halted as Bill frowned, guessing his dilemma. "Say, you don't mean Honeycutt, the bum you whipped last winter, do you?"

After considerable persuasion and a personal plea, Karl assented, agreeing to give him a job on the tender, far removed from the temptation of booze.

Hurrying back to Bessie's, he found his old nemesis ensconced in a cocoon of hot soap and water, seemingly asleep in the tub. However, he opened his eyes as soon as Bill asked the laundress if she'd feed the two men. Reiterating his threats of vengeance and muttering ungrateful obscenities when Bessie was out of earshot, Rick nevertheless ate heartily when hotcakes and bacon were served.

Bessie produced his clean clothes, patched and ironed, and left the room so he could don them in belated modesty. Handing Bessie two dollars and smiling his thanks, Bill growled, "Follow me, Rick," and walked up Creek Street. His truculent companion not only cooperated but kept his mouth closed, more curious than obedient.

The barber watched apprehensively as the two men entered his shop, finishing a haircut hastily to serve the two bristling foes.

Bill spoke tersely to Rick, "Sit and hold still!" and then likewise to the barber, "Shave and a haircut!" Both parties complied quickly, making the young man feel like a drill sergeant in the Marines. Rick looked almost like his former self in moments as Bill observed scraggly hair disappear from his face and head. Paying the relieved barber, he once again led Rick away, eventually waving him up the tender's gangplank where a waiting Karl nodded, asking, "Honeycutt, you want to work?"

"Yes, sir! I'm a hard worker," Rick replied hopefully.

"Okay, you're hired. Go aft and report to the mate, Honeycutt."

Without a thank you, a by your leave or a backward glance, the new hand hurried away.

"Well, Bill, don't look so surprised. You asked me to find a job for him, and you should know that the Honeycutt type never appreciates kindness. I believe your first inclination to whomp him was probably sound," Karl commented with a smile.

"Thanks anyway, my friend. See you later," Bill said good-by with some self-satisfaction, thinking as he walked back to Carlsons that he felt good about himself – appreciation or not.

π   π   π

Mae relayed a message from her father to Bill, telling him to report for work as soon as possible. It seemed Charley had oversold lumber production to a Japanese firm, and the ship was loading it right now.

A quick kiss received and a sack lunch in hand, Bill found himself hurrying down the hill as the shift whistle sounded. Popping his head into the office, he saw Missus Johnson busy on the telephone, but she smiled and waved him onward, never pausing in her conversation.

He walked into the lumber shed and found John assigning men to a makeshift crew, Gene taking over the sawyer's position. John welcomed the added manpower with a relieved smile, "Good to see you, Bill. Take over the green chain from Willy and send him up here. We're working non-stop until that ship is fully loaded."

Bill soon found himself running a four-man crew, including himself, Charley Blakely, Honeycutt's tarheel buddy, Max Gilloy, and a quiet Negro who looked out of place in Alaska. His husky frame and large calloused hands belied his placid demeanor, suggesting strength and a hard worker beneath the man's stoic expression.

The steady buzz of the saw blade cutting a spruce log was interrupted by a crack and a zing, the shrill sound coming to an abrupt halt. Bill answered Charley's quizzical expression, "Gene's blade lost a couple of teeth. Must have hit a nail or some other hard obstacle. Those teeth are like bullets when they come loose. Hope no one was hurt. Let's eat lunch while the line's shut down."

Charley moved next to Bill, smiling his good-natured smile, and commenced speaking, "Good to see you, Bill. Your family says hello, and so do the guys in the fraternity. Say, would you like to trade sandwiches – my tuna for your ham and cheese? How's life on that Godforsaken island of yours?"

Through a mouthful of food, Bill mumbled with a chuckle, "Half a sandwich – I like tuna. Thanks for the message. Cottage Cove is fine. Let's have a beer when we get off work."

Bill had watched as he talked, noting animosity in Max's eyes as he glared at the Negro, the southerner finally settling down on the stairs as far from the man as possible. *'Or as far from me as he can,'* Bill thought. *'He was probably the fellow who pushed me from behind during the fight with Honeycutt. Oh well, let's leave bygones alone.'*

Walking over to the Negro standing alone, he introduced himself, "Hi, I'm Bill Pardue. Would you like some coffee?"

A deep bass voice responded, "Thank you, Mister Pardue, but I don't have a cup. I'm Amos Jones."

Handing the man his half-filled thermos top, Bill responded, "Here, finish this off, Amos. And call me Bill. When did you start working for John Furrer?"

His broad grin flashed fine white teeth as he took a full swallow of the tepid coffee saying, "Thanks, this tastes good. I started just tonight, Bill. That fellow on the saw hired me. Do you think I can work here regularly?"

"Well, you're a good worker, Amos, and I'll tell the boss, but I'm only temporary help myself. I have a veteran's homestead on Duke Island."

Face animated with interest, Amos asked, "I came north to look into homesteading. I'm a Korean veteran – got wounded at Inchon. Does that make me eligible for land?"

Bill nodded affirmatively, answering thoughtfully, "Yes, but I don't know what land is being offered by the territorial government. If you have time tomorrow, I'll introduce you to Don Wilson, the attorney who helped me."

Amos nodded eagerly, both men responding to the buzz of the saw blade and subsequent movement of cut lumber through the mill.

π   π   π

Bill leaned back on his gnarled old log, his booted feet warmed by the fire as his back adjusted to a couple of weather-worn knots. Gene had turned in shortly after supper, having announced a moratorium of timber cruising for a spell, "Back to civilization tomorrow, Bill. I have to introduce Blakely to our Seattle customers next week. I guess you get a chance to work for a living – on the green chain."

Chuckling with his future father-in-law, who rolled up in his sleeping bag for the night, Bill stared fixedly at the moonlight on Thorn Arm. Drifting into a pre-sleep reverie, he thought, *'Two weeks in the wilderness weren't bad. I enjoyed both jobs we've completed for the mill since that night we cut lumber for the Japanese ship.'*

Reflecting back to that day, Bill remembered walking home with Charley, listening to his repeated attestations of love for Alexis. After a romantic weekend in Monterrey during Easter break, she had agreed to wear his fraternity pin.

Smiling in thought, *'Charley is obviously crazy about Alexis, but I wonder how she feels about being a "couple". Hmm, her father must approve of the match since he's hired Charley as his salesman.'*

A spark popped out of the fire onto his boot, Bill brushing it aside casually as he began to turn in. Soon he was dreaming of Mae and his own preoccupation with love and marriage.

ᴨ ᴨ ᴨ

As their seaplane circled Tongass Narrows in a landing approach, Bill spotted a tugboat and barge tied to the municipal pier, soon confirming the familiar vessels as the *MacDonald* and its tow.

Gene volunteered to take his bags to the Carlsons while Bill visited his friends, an offer readily accepted, the young man hurriedly crossed to the neighboring dock. A friendly wave identified the deckhand Ray, standing on the barge's deck.

His voice carried easily in the morning air, "Hi, Slim. I thought I recognized you in that airplane. Coming in from Duke Island?"

"No, Ray. I just got back from a job on Thorn Arm. Got to work for a living this summer. What are you doing tied up in Ketchikan?" Bill asked.

"Harry took sick up near Glacier Bay day before yesterday, and then his coughing got real bad yesterday. Skipper pulled in here during the night and had an ambulance take Harry to the hospital. Everyone's ashore now except Dick and yours truly. Ah well, I'm too bushed to go over to Creek Street. Standing double watches is a younger man's job," Ray complained.

Then grinning contritely, he added, "Of course, that's a sight better than being in Harry's shoes. How about a cup of coffee? Elmer should be back any time now."

Ray and Bill were munching on stale roast beef sandwiches and drinking day-old coffee when footsteps on deck preceded a murmur of voices, soon distinguishable as those of Elmer and Jack. Mate Anderson entered the mess and greeted Bill laconically, in his usual style, as contrasted by a backslapping greeting by Captain Hairston.

Elmer asked, "Has Ray told you about Harry? He's laid up in the hospital with pneumonia, but the doctor says he'll be okay in a few days. Damn! We're behind schedule and short...say, Slim, how would you like to work a round trip to Tacoma?"

Bill nodded gleefully, agreeing readily, "Sure, Elmer, I'm free right now." His expression sobered as he added, "My fiancee may have plans, but I can use the money. She'll understand that I want to visit my folks since they can't come to our wedding."

His friends immediately grilled him on his love life, Bill including news on Cottage Cove and Pardue's Lodge. As a half dozen crew members joined them over coffee, the skipper glanced at his watch and announced, "Let's sail at noon. Jack, go find Cookie and drag him aboard. Ray, you make the rounds of Creek Street. I want to leave with a full crew."

Bill rose, offering, "I'll go see Harry and then pick up my gear. I can check the downtown businesses for crew members."

"Good idea, Slim," and Elmer produced a small wad of bills, concluding, "I doubt that Harry has any cash with him. Give him this loan when you tell him our schedule."

ᴛᴛ   ᴛᴛ   ᴛᴛ

Plying the waters of Commencement Bay again brought nostalgia to the forefront of Bill's thoughts as he turned the wheel over to Jack. *'How can home seem so distant – in the past? Well, I guess the answer is that Tacoma isn't home anymore. I'm an Alaskan, and my home is Cottage Cove. Still, the City of Destiny looks great today.'*

As they approached Baker Dock, Bill could see a tugboat tied up to the north end, the chateau silhouette of his alma mater, Stadium High School, perched on the cliff above the boat. He asked the skipper, "Elmer, what outfit is that?"

"That's a Tacoma tug picking up freight, probably for the San Juans. I think that's Warren Larson's boat. He's a skipper now. Yes, there he is now – in the wheelhouse," Elmer pointed as a whistle sounded over the bay.

Ray called his name, and Bill hurried aft to help with mooring lines, both men keeping busy until the engines stilled.

Bill was crossing the deck of the barge toward their gangplank when Elmer called out, "Hey Warren, look who I brought home with me."

Larson laughed loudly and shouted from his tugboat, "Well, hello, Bill Pardue. Don't tell me you've given up on Alaska. Are you visiting or staying?"

"Just visiting, Warren. Are you going to be a tugboat skipper or a fisherman? Is your boat built yet?"

"No, but I've got a deal lined up with Day Island Marina for next year. Can I give you a lift to your grandma's place?"

Elmer nodded approval, and Bill left the barge and met his friend at the north end of the pier. He chatted with Warren about Tacoma, eliciting news about tugs and fishing boats, the subject changing to cars as Warren opened the door of his new Nash Rambler.

They drove into Old Town as Ole Olson's name was mentioned, requiring the two friends to visit several taverns in search of the fisherman. Warren had seen his boat at the dock, and neither man was surprised to find him drinking with friends in the fifth bar they entered. A round of beers marked their arrival, Bill thinking he had imbibed enough.

Moments later he escaped the gathering, slipping away from the seaman-fisherman raillery to walk up the hill to see his grandmother. Mae had written his family that he was coming, and Grandma had everyone over for dinner, his sister becoming the interrogator, asking a multitude of nosy questions about his fiancee. Bill was only too happy to talk about his love, managing to bring Pardue's Lodge into the conversation on a couple of occasions. All in all, he had a wonderful time, regretting only that he couldn't accept his father's invitation to go crabbing at Tokeland in the morning. He was on call until the skipper got new sailing orders.

Charley telephoned the next morning from his parents' home, offering to buy Bill lunch at the S.U.B. Quick to accept, Bill walked up Carr Street and crossed over the hill, eventually finding his way to North Fifteenth Street. He stopped at the fraternity house for a moment. There wasn't a single member at home, so he continued on to the Student Union Building.

Charley was waiting patiently in his usual manner, talking to two co-eds Bill couldn't recognize. Introductions didn't help since the girls were only sophomores, and he thought to himself, *I've been away a year, and I don't know anyone. I feel like an old man standing in front of the S.U.B. Maybe we can visit Doctor Thompson later,* and then queried aloud, "Is R. Franklin Thompson still President of C.P.S.?"

His inane question elicited laughter from his three companions, one of the girls replying with teasing tones, "Doctor Thompson will be here forever. When did you say you graduated?"

Later in the afternoon they drove along Sixth Avenue to the Blakely home overlooking the Narrows Bridge, and Bill commented, "I told you Doctor Thompson would know us. I bet he can name every student on campus, and some of us alumni, too."

"He does live up to his reputation, doesn't he? We'll hear more on that subject at dinner. Dad is an enthusiastic Loggers booster. He didn't miss a home game while I was playing basketball.

By the way, he tells your tame bear story frequently. He's really not much of a fisherman, but he's planning a fishing trip this fall with Uncle Blackjack. I hope you're ready for another dose of Blakelys."

Bill laughed in real pleasure, retorting, "You bet, paying customers are what I need. Are you coming with them?"

"I don't know, Bill," hesitating briefly, Charley continued, "I have a problem."

Pulling over to the curb, he looked at Bill in a sober and serious stare, so unusual for Charley that Bill wondered whether he was joking or really had a crisis. Moments passed as neither man said a word.

"Jeez! What do you think of abortion, Bill? I mean, it's terrible, I know but I'm in a bind," Charley's voice cracked emotionally.

Realizing his friend was asking for advice, something he'd never done before, Bill thought carefully before answering with a question, "Did you get some girl pregnant?" and when Charley nodded, Bill added, "And you want to marry Alexis?"

"Yes, she wants an abortion, but she seems willing. . ."

"Wait a moment! Alexis is the girl? Then why not get married and start your family early?" Bill puzzled aloud.

Charley shrugged his shoulders expressively, "She doesn't want a baby. She seems willing to marry me, but keeps talking about an abortion. And I thought I understood women, huh!" Hearing no advice forthcoming, he continued, "What should I do?"

Bill overcame his momentary loss of words with another question, "Do you really love Alexis? I mean for a lifetime commitment?"

At his friend's nod, love and misery equally present in his eyes, Bill spoke his mind, "I don't think Alexis is very mature – maybe even a bit flaky. You wish for her to bear your child, and you want to marry her. Fine, tell John Furrer he's to be a grandfather, and you'll have both wishes come true, plus you'll be heir apparent to a small fortune."

Charley's expression brightened at the advice, and Bill felt compelled to dampen his friend's sudden optimism, "Whoa! I doubt if

Alexis will like her father's knowing, nor your telling him. You may get a wife that doesn't love you."

Charley ignored the latter advice, beaming as he drove away from the curb, cheerfully averring, "I love Alexis, and she loves me. Thanks for the advice about enlisting John's support. I'll call him tomorrow."

π   π   π

Bill rushed up the gangplank with knapsack over his shoulder, puffing as he stood on deck and glad he didn't miss the MacDonald's sailing time. He had walked all the way from Old Town, actually trotting the last few blocks when he saw lights and activity on the tug, aware that midnight had passed. Charley had dropped him off at his grandmother's house while she was playing Bingo at the Eagles Lodge, and he didn't get Elmer's message until well after eleven o'clock.

Their sister ship, the *Dunedin,* had developed engine problems and was limping into Seattle for repairs. The *MacDonald* was directed to Dupont to pick up her munitions barge and take it north tonight.

Cookie staggered aboard, followed by his helper who appeared sober enough to manage the recalcitrant tippler. Bill threw his gear on the mess table and ran aft in answer to the first mate's call. On his command he cast off the stern line and then the spring line, asking the mate, "Where's Jack? I haven't seen him."

"He'll join the boat at Dupont. He took his family to a Tigers game tonight and couldn't make the midnight departure. Slim, will you straighten up our lines while I help the skipper?"

During the ensuing five days, the young man relived that fateful voyage of '49, towing explosives up the Inland Passage, visiting the site of the sinking of the *Amanda Jackson* in Grenville Channel and sailing on to Ketchikan. No untoward incident marred this trip, his night vigil in the narrow waterway and his sighting of his home on

Cottage Cove the next day assuaged his apprehension. He doubted that he could ever forget that fateful catastrophe.

Playing poker occupied much of his spare time, a run of luck lasting right up to the final hand dealt as Elmer sounded his horn in Tongass Narrows. Everyone folded his cards with various degrees of disgust as Bill laid down aces over eights. He collected the pot and went below to gather his gear, smiling at his good fortune of winning over a hundred dollars since leaving Dupont.

As he emerged on deck, a Coast Guard patrol boat drew parallel to the steadily moving *MacDonald,* and a youthful ensign spoke over the bullhorn, "Hello, *MacDonald,* my commander sends his regards. Thanks for notifying us about your cargo. We'll come along side and swap deckhands now."

Harry stood beside the officer, moving to the port rail as the boats touched fenders. He threw his gear to Ray and jumped over the narrow gap of open water, Bill laughingly following suit in the other direction. The two friends exchanged greetings as they passed, Harry adding congratulations from the tugboat's deck, "I like your girl, Slim. You're a lucky guy."

His final words were barely spoken when the patrol boat skewed sharply to starboard and thundered across the channel, everyone seemingly eager to get away from the cargo of explosives.

TT   TT   TT

Mae's slight form was identifiable on the Coast Guard pier from a half mile away, a fluttering hankie brandished in her extended hand. Bill waved cheerfully back, eager to set foot on shore and greet his fiancee.

"Miss Wilson has been waiting for you over two hours, ever since Captain Hairston radioed my commander for assistance. I hope my girl will be half as excited when I report for duty in Seattle next month," the youthful officer confided in his passenger, both men wearing broad smiles of anticipation.

The star-crossed lovers united in a close embrace as soon as Bill stepped onto the dock, oblivious to the gawking sailors lining the boat's rail. Hearing an awed comment, "Lucky guy!" from the gallery of spectators, Bill kissed Mae again, and giving her admirers a casual salute, he replied, "The luckiest guy in Ketchikan, fellas!"

Holding Mae in the crook of his right arm, he hefted his knapsack with his other and headed for the station gate, listening to his suddenly talkative sweetheart tell all about their wedding plans. He smiled and nodded during the walk to the Carlsons, an occasional squeeze of approval all that was necessary to hold up his end of the conversation.

Later they sat in Julia's kitchen and were served lunch, the "mother figure" unabashedly joining the continuing discussion with comments and advice. During a lull in the dialogue she asked, "Have you told Bill about Gene's wedding present, Mae?"

A bright, shiny tear appeared in the corner of her eye as she bubbled, "Daddy's wonderful to me. . .us. He really approves of our marriage. He chartered a local tug and barge to take our bedroom addition to Cottage Cove. Roy and Blackjack have gone ahead and spent our money on building materials and equipment for the lodge. The Blakely family is giving us a septic tank, and Olaf is going along to install it and to pipe fresh water into the house. I guess nobody wants to meet Brownie in the middle of the night. What else, Julia?"

"Well, John Furrer has ordered a kerosene refrigerator, and we're giving you a proper bed, Roy swears Bill's old one isn't fit for new-lyweds. Charley has volunteered to go along and work if he can come back for his wedding rehearsal," Julia said.

Mae broke in, "You and I are standing up for Alexis and Charley and vice-versa at our wedding. The rumor is that it's a shotgun wedding, and Alexis confided as much to me."

Bill glanced over to Julia, an avid listener to their gossip, and responded, "Yes, I talked to Charley. Ladies, we know more than necessary about this situation. We'd better keep it to ourselves."

TT TT TT

The small tugboat and its barge stood out to sea, its former cargo stacked on the beach where it had been delivered. Gene and Einar were in the skiff offshore, planning a blasting operation while Olaf and Aaron dug a pit for the septic tank east of the cabin. Charley and Bill carried perishable supplies up to the cabin where Mae stowed them inside. Olaf set up the kerosene refrigerator while the two friends relieved him in the pit, now four feet deep and into rocky soil. Gravel was great for a drainage field, but Bill just hoped they could dig deep enough to hold the tank.

By nightfall everyone was starved for his meal of chicken and dumplings, the volunteer crew loosely gathered around the table in the dim glow of the lantern – planning for the morrow. Bill finally shooed the gang out of the cabin so he could help Mae clean up before she went to bed, the guest tent crowded with sleeping bags as the six men retired for the night.

Shortly after breakfast the next morning, Einar lit his first fuse, rowing hastily to shore and scurrying behind the lumber pile. Everyone ducked behind something, waiting patiently for the eruption. They were all a bit disappointed when a muffled poof sounded and sea spray landed around them.

Einar laughed in relief, trying to appear nonchalant as he explained, "Ha! Ha! I only used a single stick of dynamite to break up the rocks near shore. I'll have to use a bundle for my next job – those three boulders out there."

He taped eight sticks together and rowed out to the second riffle showing in the ebb tide, the husky Scandinavian undeterred by the frigid water or the volatile explosives. Bill and his friends knew they should be working but were fascinated by the blasting operation.

Having reconnoitered the obstacle the previous afternoon, Einar entered the water and dove below the surface with dynamite in hand, emerging in thirty seconds with a fuse held in his hand. He scrambled aboard the skiff, lit the fuse with shaking fingers and rowed hell-bent-for-lection to shore. Bill waded out to seize the skiff's bow and beach it before both men dove for cover.

'None too soon,' was Bill's errant thought, as cacophonous thunder roared over the bay, shards of rock falling everywhere, evidence of three decimated boulders.

Mae wrapped a blanket around Einar's shoulders as Gene and Bill went out to inspect the remains, returning a half hour later with pleased expressions. The third obstruction, the one which had almost claimed Bill's boat during the storm last winter, would be blasted tomorrow.

Over the next two days work progressed on all the projects rapidly, Roy and Julia flying in with Ed Luden on Sunday to visit Aaron and the construction. Einar left with them after lunch, the float plane now able to moor safely at his slip. Charley asked the pilot to return the next day for the three members of the wedding party. The rehearsal was scheduled mid-week, and the expectant groom was eager to see his fiancee.

That evening Mae had running water in her kitchen sink, and the toilet bowl was flushing properly. Gene and Olaf worked in the uncertain light cast by lanterns, hanging the bathroom door before testing their system for real. Tomorrow they would finish sealing and insulating the addition, most outside work already completed.

Ed Hill arrived in the morning, surprised at the new look of Pardue's Lodge, and upon viewing their meager larder, offered his services as a hunter and fisherman.

In an aside to Bill, he reported, "Your friendly bear has been a recent visitor. I think he followed me over here – my salmon smell, you know."

During mid-morning Olaf fed their last chunk of smoked halibut to Brownie, with everyone gathered in the yard to greet "Bill's pet" from a distance. His absence had caused Bill to fear for the bear's well-being, and seeing him beg for fish had been a welcome relief. He was light-hearted and high-spirited as the airplane flew him away from Cottage Cove.

ᛟ   ᛟ   ᛟ

Charley was unhappy because Alexis spent all her energy on the wedding preparations and seemed to ignore him, and Bill was impatient to return home as soon as he'd purchased his list of hardware items. Only the three women seemed happy and cheerful, Roy consoling both young man with platitudes and unwanted advice.

But time passed and so did the wedding rehearsal and its related social events. As they prepared to return to Cottage Cove, Mae received a letter from Helen telling of her pregnancy and inviting her to visit Metlakatla.

"Why don't you stay with the Williams' while we finish our work   on Pardue's Lodge?" Bill suggested when he recognized her desire.

"Oh, could I, Bill? Helen says she can't come to our wedding because her baby's due in September. You could drop me off and stay for dinner. Maybe Ed could join us."

Their pilot agreed good-naturedly, informing the couple that he had a morning flight to the Stikine River gold camp before flying them to Metlakatla the next day. Dinner sounded good to him as long as they left an hour before dark so he could land at Bill's place in daylight. He planned to spend the night at the lodge and fish the next morning before flying Olaf and Gene back to Ketchikan.

The seaplane climbed into a clear and sunny sky, the brisk southwesterly breeze giving it buoyancy in the air. They admired the scenery as they headed straight for their destination, clearing Gravina Island and Blank Inlet before sighting the Tsimshian town. Ed landed the seaplane in the harbor like the veteran he was and taxied the craft into the float plane slip to secure it. All three walked ashore together, returning waves from Malcolm Angias and Jack Williams on the oil dock, a faint call carrying over the intervening fishing fleet, "See you later!"

Mae recognized and greeted everyone they encountered along the street leading to Helen's, Bill feeling pleased that he knew so many of the people also. The Tsimshians were good neighbors, and living isolated on Duke Island the Pardues would need friends. Helen appeared on the porch to greet her friends, her roly-poly appearance somehow not unattractive. She seemed healthy and cheerful in her role of a mother-to-be, which Bill figured would be short-lived. She looked awfully close to the end of her pregnancy.   "Welcome back, Mae," she hugged her friend warmly, adding, "And you too, Bill and Ed."

Bill replied, "Congratulations, Helen! When is Junior due?" He deposited a kiss on Helen's forehead, leery of hugging his old friend in her present condition.

"About the same time you two get married, which is why I can't be there. Congratulations to both of you on finding each other. Now come with me, Mae, and we'll gossip while I cook. You men go around back and keep Cousin Arthur company. He's back from the wars and is a full-fledged civilian again."

Bill nodded agreeably and led his pilot guest around the house, seeing the young man stoking the coals in an open grill. Intentionally keeping his tones cheerful, he greeted the wounded veteran, "Hi, Arthur. It's good to see you again. I hear you're an ex-Marine now."

Arthur offered a gnarled right hand to Bill, grinning as he quipped at his momentary hesitation, "Hi, Bill, go ahead and shake it, my arm won't fall off. Ha! Ha! Maybe I ought to learn to shake hands with my other hand."

The three men relaxed as they awaited the working stiffs, drinking beer and chatting about their friends. John, Malcolm and Jack would be along after five o'clock, and Tsimchuck and Gregori were working on Pardue's Lodge - a nice surprise to Bill.

Arthur talked freely of his experiences in Korea and subsequent recovery at the Presidio, explaining how doctors had saved his arm. He demonstrated his prescribed therapy by squeezing a small rubber ball in his fist, one of a dozen exercises the doctor had suggested to him.

"My right arm is never going to be normal, so I can't work on my father's boat. I'm going to follow Helen's advice and attend the College of Puget Sound on the G.I. Bill this fall. The Metlakatla schools need good teachers, and that's where my future will be."

Bill agreed enthusiastically on both points, "Hey, it'll be great to have another C.P.S. alum in the area, and I know you'll do well as a teacher - maybe even principal."

A little later Arthur asked Ed, "Whatever happened to that Marine who flew up to Juneau with us? That other wounded veteran, Amos Jones?"

Ed pondered the question for a moment, finally giving a nod of understanding as he replied, "You mean that big Negro fellow who said he was filing a claim at the territorial capital? Didn't you work with him at Furrer's, Bill?"

"Yes, for one shift anyway. Just long enough to infect him with homesteaditis. Don Wilson helped him get a veteran's homesite south of Fairbanks. I hope he makes a go of it. That country's mighty cold for a southern Negro."

Malcolm joined the party, followed shortly afterward by the two Williams men, John burying a soaked gunny sack of clams under the coals and placing two salmon on the grill over them.

Dinner was a lengthy affair, everyone moving inside to eat as the mosquitoes took over the yard. Ed finally announced it was departure time, and the two men broke away from the party reluctantly, Bill kissing Mae good–by as he hurried off after the pilot. Eight-thirty turned into nine o'clock as Ed double checked his aircraft, Bill casting off the mooring lines as the engine sputtered to life.

They were forced to taxi in a tight circle as a pair of fishing boats crossed the channel, Ed finally revving his engine and heading into the wind for a takeoff. Bill observed the scenery below with a practiced eye, spotting his friends standing in the Williams' yard watching their late departure and then looking southwesterly along the desolate stretch of Nichols Passage, finally checking the Warburton Island light over his right shoulder.

He shouted over the motor's noise, "It's the end of a beautiful day, Ed. When do we..."

The unnatural sound of a metallic ping cut his query short, the plane yawing to port as Ed cursed and fought the controls, going with the tight turn as a successive trickle of ticks and scratches followed the distressed craft toward the white-capped surface. Ed wrenched the controls with compelling force in a desperate effort to head for Metlakatla, a loud crack shattering the air behind Bill. A quick glance over his shoulder disclosed a disintegrating tail section, and suddenly the plane flipped completely over as all control was lost, and a tight spiral developed as the engine pulled them toward the water. Ed cut the motor a couple of seconds before the impact, yelling, "Hold your head in your arms, Bill, we're going in."

The float plane struck the surface nose-down still in its death-spiral, the left pontoon snapping loose in consonance with most of the left wing. Noise and pain blended in Bill's shuddering body, conscious but stunned and breathless as a sudden silence enveloped the wreck. Shaking his head slowly, and feeling his bruised and aching body carefully, he concluded nothing was broken. Releasing his seat belt, he fell awkwardly on his head and shoulders, the icy water covering his face.

Sputtering irritably as he scrambled to his knees, he worked his way forward as the plane slowly rolled over, water pouring into the cabin. He followed Ed's form through the starboard door and onto a pontoon. The two men struggled for balance as they straddled the float and the cabin sank beneath the surface, inspecting each other critically.

Ed spoke first, "This wreck's going to sink. I'm sitting on a hole in the pontoon. The port float broke loose when we crashed. Maybe it's okay. We're both bloody but in one piece. Think we can swim to the other pontoon?"

Bill's eyes followed Ed's pointing finger, seeing the object behind him, bobbing in the waves. No answer was necessary as the plane shuddered in a death throe, spilling Bill into the water. Ed followed, and both men swam away from the sinking debris toward their only hope, the silvery torpedo-form a hundred feet away.

Ed fell behind slowly, Bill treading water as he gauged the distance to their "life raft," calling encouragement to his partner, "Come on, Ed, it's only thirty feet away."

Together they paddled forward in the gathering darkness, neither a good enough swimmer to make shore. The two men silently congratulated each other with a warm hand clasp. They had survived the wreck and the sinking and now prayed that someone had seen the airplane fall from the sky.

Moments later Ed cried out, "Damn, it's cold! What I wouldn't give for a life vest, but they're in Davy Jones' Locker along with the rest of my plane."

"I've checked this pontoon and can't find any punctures. We just have to hang on until help arrives. Which way is the tide going?" Bill asked tentatively.

"I don't know. Seems the Warburton light and the town haven't moved any. Maybe we'll stay right here - be easy to find," Ed said optimistically.

The two men exchanged hopeful comments periodically during the ensuing hour, their morale needing reinforcement. Fishing boat lights emerged from the harbor, moving in a criss-cross pattern as they advanced toward the drifting pontoon with two men still clinging to it. The light on Warburton Island changed position slowly, both men now aware they were moving away from Metlakatla.

Ed's breathing grew shallow, and he coughed several times. Bill encouraged him, "Spotlights are just a mile behind us, Ed. They're looking for us. Hang tough, buddy."

The pilot's quiet nod was unseen in the darkness so Bill reached out and touched his friend's hand, saying, "We'll make it, Ed. Hang on."

Ed croaked out a reply, and the waiting to be rescued continued.

Their makeshift life raft drifted further to the southwest, staying just out of reach of the Tsimshian fishing fleet, its boats now strung out over a five mile path. Ed croaked a meaningless phrase as his hand slid past Bill's, the stronger man diving beneath the pontoon to grab a handful of coat. He wrestled the choking and incoherent pilot onto the pontoon, holding it steady by treading water.

Bill called out "Help!" a couple of times before realizing his voice was not carrying any distance. He thought, *'My cries can't be heard fifty feet away, let alone a half mile. That lead boat would find us if he'd just quit zigzagging. He's so close and yet so far. I hope Ed can hang on, I don't think I have enough strength to pull him back again. I wonder what time it is? Must be well after midnight.'*

Keeping his legs in motion and his mind active, albeit dreamily thinking of his lovely Mae, Bill maintained a hopeful watch on the boat lights. Several spotlights had dimmed, and boat lights were disappearing into the harbor when Ed moved and uttered a thin croak, "Boats are gone. They quit looking for us."

Bill countered with brave words backed by thin hope and little faith, "Look! The three boats nearest to us are still searching. They'll find us any minute."

Ed slipped into unconsciousness, Bill moving to support his body on the float, cold seeping into the hapless men. Mind drifting in consonance with the life raft, Bill caught himself dozing as the seemingly endless night progressed, one time awakening to find he was paddling a few feet from the pontoon. The three boats were now parallel to the survivors, searching between them and Annette Island. His mind screamed repetitiously, *'Over here, men, over here.'*

Suddenly coming awake with a sense of dread, Bill felt over the metal skin of the pontoon without avail. Ed had slipped quietly away into the depths of Nichols Passage, Bill saying a short prayer for his friend. His determination grew as the situation looked more hopeless than ever. He would hang on to his float for however long his rescue took.

Repeating that thought over and over and refusing to succumb to the cold tranquillity of the sea, he muttered aloud in a desperate and raspy voice, "I'm hanging on all night if necessary. Come on, fellas, where are you?"

A beam of light traced a search pattern a short distance away, a second boat doing likewise to the east. He turned his head to seek the third boat and beheld a minor miracle. A daylight glow permeated the horizon, outlining the fishing boat, less than a hundred feet to the west.

"Help! Help! Help!" Bill screamed in a voice hoarse from the cold and disuse, the boat's searching spotlight swiveling one hundred eighty degrees as a thin whistle sounded from her wheelhouse. A moment later the bright light blinded the feebly waving survivor.

Malcolm's familiar voice resonated over the water, "Catch this lifesaver, Bill. I'll give you a hand."

A round cork ring splashed near him, and as he failed to move toward it, his rescuer dove into the water and swam to him.

"Hang on, Bill. I'm right here. Slip this lifesaver over your head, and let's get you aboard my boat."

Lifted over the low rail by Arthur's strong left arm, Bill sank to the deck, leaning on the rail to watch Mal clamber onto the deck. Both men accepting the blankets which Arthur produced as he exclaimed, "How did you last all night? Until daylight? You're amazing, Daylight Bill Pardue!"

Malcolm asked a single anxious question, "Where's Ed? Did you see him after the crash?"

Bill shook his head despondently, explaining hoarsely, "Ed slipped away during the night. I never saw him go, but his death gave me the will to hang on. Thanks for not giving up on me."

The rescuers nodded with understanding, Arthur announcing, "I'll signal John and Jack, and we'll head for port. You two get into the cabin and put some dry clothes on."

π   π   π

Malcolm shook Bill awake, a difficult task with the survivor's body crying for rest. He said, "We're coming into the harbor. Let's get you up on deck where Mae can see you. She'll be waiting on the dock."

Sure enough, Bill could make out his sweetheart standing before the crowd near Malcolm's berth, an engulfing roar of welcome greeting him as he stepped into sight and waved. Mae's cousin held her erect when her knees buckled in relief and remained beside her even after she straightened up.

Malcolm showed off for his friends, his seaman's skills more than adequate as he took his boat into the berth without slowing her engine, slamming her propeller into full reverse while swinging her bow around, allowing Mae to leap aboard and run to her tottering fiance. Another cheer came from the well-wishers on the dock as the two lovers embraced, the girl's face wet with happy tears as the couple comforted each other.

ᛚ   ᛚ   ᛚ

"Hey, welcome back, Daylight Bill: You're one tough cookie," Max Gilloy greeted him on his return to the green chain crew, his friendliness in marked contrast to their normal relationship. The other men in the mill came over to say hello to the survivor of the Nichols Passage plane crash, cheerful small talk preceding the whine of the big blade. Everyone hustled back to the work stations as Bill began pulling lumber from the moving chain.

'A few weeks ago Max looked daggers at me, and now he's my buddy,' was Bill's echoing thought. 'I guess my sobriquet is here to stay, and I'll be famous for a little while longer. Why do I feel guilty that my luck was good and Ed's was bad?'

'And fortune was certainly with me when I avoided entanglement with Alexis. My Mae is more woman and has a sterling character, while Alexis is all show - shallow is the word. It's obvious that Charley loves her dearly, but she's going to break his heart. Well, John gave them a good start with a fantastic wedding, a honeymoon in Hawaii and a big raise. I wonder if Furrer can arrange a deferment from military service? Charley's Air Force R.O.T.C. training only makes him a better choice for Korea.'

"Hey, Daylight Bill, can I buy you a beer after work? I'd like to hear about your plane crash," Max called over the pile of lumber.

A chorus of muted shouts from his co-workers caused him to smile and agree good-naturedly, offering, "Okay, fellas, I'll buy everyone a round at Abner Hall's place right after work." Bill had told the story far too often for his own taste, but friends were curious, and there were always a few who hadn't heard the tale directly from the survivor.

Satisfied with his reply, the men went back to pulling lumber, and Bill returned to his reverie, recalling Gene's report on the lodge renovation before he left for Seattle on a Furrer errand. *'It is wonderful news that everything is shipshape, thanks in a large part to the arrival of Malcolm and his friends when Gene needed help the most. Our lodge will be waiting for us on our honeymoon. Alan Harkins will make his first flight on our new contract when we move into our home. There I go, feeling guilty again because I've got a replacement so soon after Ed's death. I have to get on with my life.'*

ᴛᴛ   ᴛᴛ   ᴛᴛ

Bill waved companionably to his co-workers as he left the lumber shed, calling out a reminder to those within earshot, "See you at Abner's for a beer."

"Bill Pardue, have you forgotten that we're going to the department store to buy curtains for our house?" Mae chided him from the office doorway.

"Ah, Honey, I forgot. Come on down to Abner's with me. We can have dinner after I buy the guys a beer and tell my story again. Besides which, didn't you accept a dinner invitation from Dolly? Maybe she and Curly are free this evening," the unchastened groom-to-be asked.

Grinning conspiratorially at her love, she playfully asked, "Am I old enough to visit Creek Street with all you grown-ups? Will Abner ever serve me spirits again?"

The couple walked out of the yard laughing, hands clasped in unison as several workers followed at a discreet distance, Max's singular twang making the comment, "Daylight Bill's a lucky guy!"

Still acting like lovers, Bill and Mae walked down Creek Street, entering Abner Hall's restaurant with a flourish. Spotting Curly at the bar, the young man greeted him warmly, "Curly, good to see you. Mae and I were just talking about you. Can I treat you and Dolly to dinner this evening?"

"Hi, Bill, Mae. Sounds good to me. I'll go tell Dolly we're dining out," Curly said as he left his stool.

"Well hurry back, my friend, I'm buying all these roughnecks behind me a beer. I'll save one for you," Bill offered as Curly hastened through the door.

"By golly, Bill, does that apply to the owner? I'd like to toast your health and well-being after that plane wreck and your good fortune in finding this young lady. How are you, Mae?" Abner greeted the couple with his biggest smile.

The door slammed noisily behind Bill, Mae's smile fading as she squeezed her fiancé's fingers in caution.

Rick Honeycutt's booming voice carried to the bar, "What's the occasion, gents? Where the hell is. . .er. . .Max?" The bruiser's rough voice faltered as he saw Mae and then recognized his old adversary turning to face him.

An intimidating suspense hovered over the room, eyes flitting from Rick to Bill and back to Rick like observers in a tennis match.

The big man's frown changed to a look of confusion as he studied the couple, aware of the onlookers, including his buddy Max, gathered around Bill. When he moved, he did so hastily, a rare look of contrition on his face.

Sweeping his cap from his brow, he nodded at Mae, exclaiming, "Miss Wilson, I apologize for. . uh. . ."

Mae's smile returned as she graciously saved the mumbling scoundrel from further embarrassment, "I accept, thank you, Mister Honeycutt."

Bill relieved any remaining tension when he invited Rick to his party, "Will you join us, Honeycutt? I'm buying a round for my friends here."

"Why, thanks, Bill, and I congratulate you and your lady. I hear a wedding is due. Oh yeah, Karl says hello. He's a good boss."

Mae looked questioningly at her fiance, as did most of the men in the room, Max inadvertently spilling the beans by asking, "Gee, Daylight Bill, do you think you could get me a job on the tender, too?"

Rick laughed at his sidekick's question, clarifying his old enemy's good deed from earlier in the summer while thanking Bill, "You're a fair man, Pardue. Vouching for me with Karl got me a good job. I appreciate your help."

"Well, you must be doing a good job if you're still working for Karl, he doesn't stand for any tomfoolery from his employees," Bill stated as he paid for the round being served to his friends, starting his narrative with a, "Now gentlemen, let me tell you about that long, cold, hard night I spent in the waters of Nichols Passage."

By the time he was being pulled out of the sea at daylight, Bill noted that Dolly and Curly had joined Mae and Abner at a table, and all four were drinking champagne. He raised his glass in a salute to his fiancee and finished his story. Max handed him another beer, questions galore requiring a sip or two to moisten a dry throat and slake his thirst. He watched as Mae turned her own glass over this time, winking at him for approval and beckoning him with a crooked finger. Their meal had arrived.

Chapter Seven

Bill tugged his tight collar with his index finger, the tuxedo about one size too small for his tall frame. A hand fell on his shoulder companionably, his father-in-law's voice carrying parental pride as he said, "Isn't my daughter lovely in her wedding gown? How'd I ever sire such a beautiful woman, Son?"

"Aye, that she is. Ha! Ha! You told me often enough that she favors her late mother. Don't try taking credit for her beauty at this late date."

Gene smiled nostalgically as he mused quietly, "I do see a lot of her mother in her, but Mae is her own person, and I'm proud of her."

Pausing beside his son-in-law as they watched the bride circulate among her guests in the Carlson home, the older man quipped with a happy grin, "Now that we're in complete agreement on how lucky you are to be my son-in-law, I'd better tell you that I deposited a hundred dollars in Mae's savings account yesterday - just for an emergency."

Bill smiled in appreciation, replying, "Thanks! My name's on that account now, and I put my folks' gift in it, too. Don Wilson advised us to carry the checking account for business purposes - taxes, I believe. Pardue's Lodge is a registered partnership by the way."

Mae approached her men and queried happily, "What are you two plotting? Darling, you're suppose to mingle with the wedding guests."

"I know, but Dad has been telling me stories about his beautiful daughter. Did you know he made a contribution to our emergency fund?" Bill retorted.

Mae leaned over and kissed her father's cheek, shooing her husband away imperiously, "Go visit our friends. I'll stay with Daddy."

Bill made a round of the Carlson house, finally escaping by following Malcolm onto the porch, kidding his buddy, "Oh no you don't! Members of the wedding party have to circulate. No fair sneaking out here, although it is peaceful, isn't it?"

"Yes, and it's fortunate our unpredictable weather was fair today since everyone had to walk up the hill from the Community Hall after the wedding ceremony," Malcolm commented. Pausing briefly to gather his thoughts, he continued, "I'm envious of your marriage, my friend. Grandpa is always telling me to find a girl and settle down, but this is the first time I feel like agreeing with him. In fact, I'm flying up to Hoonah tomorrow to visit a Tlingit family I met last spring in Juneau. Well . . .actually, it's John Moses' daughter Annie I'm going to see."

Bill cocked an eyebrow and quipped, "Why haven't I heard of Annie before, old buddy? Where. . . ?"

"Bill Pardue, I've been looking everywhere for you," Julia exclaimed in mock exasperation, "Your wife is ready to cut the cake, and your presence is required."

TT   TT   TT

The silvery float plane overflew their home as Bill directed the pilot on a sightseeing excursion, Alan buzzed Ed Hill's boat in Judd Harbor before circling back along the coast, passing beside Duke Hill before commencing their landing approach. Mae complimented their new friend on his touchdown as they taxied into shore, and Alan was quick to assist her in unloading the unopened wedding gifts and provisions.

Declining her offer of coffee with a conspiratorial smile on his lips, he bade them a happy honeymoon and flew away into the twilight sky.

Grabbing armfuls of packages, the newlyweds trod silently up to the lodge, Bill dropping his burden unceremoniously to carry his bride over the threshold.

Bestowing a regal peck on her husband's cheek, Mae proclaimed, "Home at last! Don't you just love it? Now, get to hopping, my darling, everything we brought here today has to be in the house before dark. I'll light a fire and make the bed."

᛭   ᛭   ᛭

Weeks passed joyfully in a solitude interrupted only by a brief visit from Ed Hill, presenting his best wishes and leaving behind a quarter of venison. Of course, their friend Brownie came by regularly, begging for a handout of salmon or halibut.

The weather grew cooler as the days grew shorter, rain an ever present companion of the wind and clouds. One day Alan flew over the lodge, dropping a small bundle of mail on their doorstep.

Julia's letter disturbed their idyllic feeling of well-being when she wrote that Alexis professed shame at having her baby in Ketchikan. The couple moved to Seattle amid hints of a troubled marriage.

Gene's letter announced the arrival of the first fishing party consigned to the new Pardue's Lodge, a group of three Furrer customers coming up from Seattle. Actually, in reading further, Bill discovered the lumbermen would arrive after the Carlsons visited - a trip paid for in provisions. Gene, Olaf and Aaron would arrive tomorrow morning, with Roy and Julia coming the next day to stay but a single night. Gene would remain at the lodge to meet John Furrer and his companions next week.

After reading short notes from his folks, Don Wilson and Helen Williams - Sue Ann's birth announcement, the hosts began preparations for their arriving guests. Mae did housecleaning while Bill took his boat around Duchess Island in search of king salmon. Both were anxious to have everything under control at the start of their tourist business.

TT   TT   TT

Nodding expectantly at each other as the sound of an airplane engine crossed the bay, the couple donned jackets and hurried down to the boat slip. They fidgeted with nervous energy as the Harkins' float plane taxied into shore to discharge passengers and supplies. Soon they were greeting their friends and unloading a dozen crates of food and four knapsacks. Alan waved his hello and good-by, staying in the pilot's seat until the cabin was empty. As Bill and Gene swung the tail into shore, he fired up the engine and taxied away, soon rising toward the northeast in a perfect takeoff.

Gene took Olaf fishing while Aaron helped Bill carry the supplies up to the house where Mae stowed them in cupboards and in the corner of the second bedroom. The two fishermen returned triumphant with five salmon, Olaf's small chum going to a friendly Brownie right after the smokehouse began smelling. As their entertainment for the day lumbered into the forest with his meal, the men entered the house to gather around the table and share the latest gossip from Ketchikan.

"Bill, I'm sure glad to see Brownie's still around and healthy. Thanks for letting me feed him," Olaf said, switching subjects after a brief moment. "Malcolm Angias came south with me from Juneau on my last run and showed me a picture of his girl - pretty young lady. He sounded kind of serious. What's going on, Bill?"

"I reckon he was returning from Hoonah where his girl's family lives. Could be that he is serious," Bill confided.

Mae piped in, "Oh! I bet he is, dear. You know, Helen married John, the Blakely - Furrer wedding was the talk throughout southeast Alaska, and then you and I became a couple. I think Malcolm's feeling his age, he's due."

"Hal Ha! Malcolm told me as much, what with Arthur courting a college co–ed in Tacoma," Olaf informed them, and then added, "But I heard Alexis and Charley are having marital problems. What do you hear, Gene?"

"Just what you said. Neither of those youngsters is very mature. Alexis doesn't want the child, and Charley's talking about accepting an Air Force Reserve commission. Dragging a reluctant wife along to Lackland for training doesn't bode well for their marriage."

"Dad, where's Lackland?" Mae asked curiously.

Gene replied, "Down in Texas, honey. Around San Antonio if I remember correctly. Of course, Charley can claim a draft exemption on fatherhood, but ROTC is voluntary. He may want a career with the military."

"And I thought my fraternity brother was a bit mercenary when he became Furrer's son-in-law. He may be more independent than I gave him credit for. The Air Force isn't a bad career option," Bill mused, adding with a laugh of self-derision, "Ha! I don't make much sense, do I?"

Everyone nodded in agreement, offering no further opinion on the Blakelys. Desultory conversation resulted in Mae's chasing the men out of her kitchen while she prepared dinner.

After the meal they listened to the evening news on the radio and then laid plans for tomorrow's fishing activities. "Early to bed, early to rise" was reiterated several times as the men retired to their tent.

ᴨ   ᴨ   ᴨ

Mae was the sole host meeting the airplane in the morning, guests fishing off Duke Point while Bill was fetching a quarter of venison from Ed Hill's place. Roy and a stranger climbed onto the pontoon and helped Julia climb from the aircraft cabin onto dry land.

A warm welcome ensued, Roy setting to work unloading the plane while Julia introduced their companion, "Mister Richards, our hostess is an old friend, Missus Pardue. Mae dear, Robert is one of Mister Furrer's party. He came up from Seattle early, and we offered him a seat on our flight."

"Welcome to Cottage Cove, Mister Richards. Why don't we go up to the house for coffee and cookies," Mae offered.

Roy was still busy and declined, "I'll take care of Harkins and the supplies. You folks go ahead."

Bob Richards agreed readily, "I need my coffee, Roy, but I'll come back and give you a hand in a few minutes."

The visitor followed the women across the yard, complimenting his hostess on the lodge, "You and your husband have a wonderful spot for a lodge, Missus Pardue. I'm acquainted with your father, and he described it very well. Where is Gene, anyway?"

Showing her guests into the house, Mae replied with a grin, "Dad's fishing, of course. He'll head back now that the plane is here. Has the weather in Seattle been as rainy as here?"

Mae quickly put her guest at ease, Julia nodding like a mother hen as she approved of her young friend's manner, finally commenting on the pristine beauty of Pardue's Lodge and asking about Brownie.

During the ensuing week the bear didn't disappoint the lodge guests, cooperating with the tourists as they came and went, quite content with a slab of fish on each visit.

When the last scheduled flight arrived, Blackjack and the elder Charley deplaned, unannounced but welcome guests. Wintry temperatures accompanied the Blakely brothers, and Mae invited them to sleep inside, Gene having vacated his bed that day. They endured four days of rugged Alaskan weather before Alan Harkins could land to pick them up, their fishing limited to the western shoreline of Ray Anchorage and the quieter waters of Morse Cove.

π   π   π

One gray and desolate morning Bill was trolling off Duke Point, his hands and feet numb from the damp coldness pervading the atmosphere. His attention was caught and held for a moment by the sound of rifle shots in the distance, a fishing boat visible in midchannel.

'Crazy fishermen,' he thought, 'Probably shooting sea lions. Those pests have been chasing salmon all fall, but why shoot them now? After the season is over? Wonder where they're going?'

As Bill secured his gear and cranked up the Johnson, the fishing boat emitted a thin, shrill whistle and turned toward him.

Meandering away from the rocky coast into the open waters of Ray Anchorage, Bill idled his motor as he waited for the oncoming boat to intercept him. The fishing boat's white hull was stained with a greasy mixture of blood, oil and seaweed, square black letters amidst the grime spelling out, Nooksack City.

"Hello the boat! Is that Pardue's Lodge up ahead?" shouted a bearded man dressed in oilskins. A second figure with rifle in hand, a look-alike for the talker, stood beside him on the bow, and two men were visible in the wheelhouse.

Bill waved casually, shouting back, "Yes, I'm Bill Pardue. What can I do for you?"

Closer up the two men looked as seedy as their vessel, the original greeter saying, "Fellow over at the Boca de Quadra cannery told us about your lodge. I'm Jed Simpson from Bellingham. My brothers and I could use a home-cooked meal - something other than fish. Is your restaurant open?"

Bill laughed derisively as he explained, "Ha! Ha! We're not exactly a restaurant, Jed, just a fishing lodge with a good cook. If you can furnish the spuds, my wife will feed us all roast venison with potatoes and gravy."

Jed's brother pushed forward to the rail and offered, "You got any pesky sea lions around? I'll shoot 'em for you. I hate sea lions!"

Bill shook his head and replied, "No thanks. I'd rather you didn't shoot that rifle in Cottage Cove. My wife and I like a quiet place."

Jed glared at his oafish brother, ordering him, "Put that gun away, Zeb, and haul that sack of potatoes on deck. I want to dicker with Bill for our meal."

Turning back toward the open boat, he offered, "We're short on cash, but long on potatoes. Would you consider a swap?"

"Sure, Jed. Like I said before, meat and potatoes will be our dinner today. Are you and your brothers heading back to Bellingham?" Bill asked conversationally.

"Yes, we're late this fall. Hit a deadhead, and our propeller went kaput. Had to wait for a new blade to be flown up from Seattle. You know, we can't stay long today. Got to eat and run if we're going to cross Dixon Entrance this afternoon," Jed informed him.

Bill raised an eyebrow in consternation, observing, "It's a long run down to Canada. I don't think you'll have enough daylight to reach the other side."

"Oh we'll manage as long as the seas are calm and we can see the beacon lights. Don't worry about us. We know our way around these waters," Jed averred with confidence.

Bill gave a gesture with his hand and shouted, "Okay, let's go to dinner then," gunning his motor and leading the way over calm waters to his slip.

ℼ   ℼ   ℼ

As the couple stood watching the *Nooksack City* motor along the coastline toward Revillagigedo Channel, Mae breathed a proverbial sigh of relief, commenting wryly, "Phew! What a family. I hope they don't come back. Brother Zeb is not only crude and foul-mouthed, but he just plain smells bad."

"They appear to be a rowdy bunch, don't they? But they behaved themselves while they were our guests - if you excuse Zeb's language," Bill reminded his wife.

Mae laughed without humor, asking, "Ho! Ho! And you are ready to air out the house. I know, I know, not all guests will be likeable."

Shots sounded from the departing vessel, and Bill pointed in its direction as he said, "What's Zeb shooting at now? Sea lions?"

"No, he's aiming at the trees. Do you think he shot a deer? Oh, I hate poachers who kill for fun. That's just like that crazy Zeb," Mae lamented.

Bill spun on his heels, muttering, "I'll check it out." He hastened to the lodge to don a jacket and take his rifle from the rack. He checked the 30.06 and pocketed a half-dozen shells as Mae followed suit, cautioning her husband, "Take it easy, Bill, there's no hurry. I'll take along bread and smoked salmon, and we'll need a pack if Zeb downed a deer."

A tight grin with a curt nod was Bill's only reply as he waited patiently while Mae packed a lunch. Hoisting their lightly filled knapsack over his shoulder, he led the way across the meadow and into the forest.

Both of the Pardues were puffing by the time they skirted the slopes of Duke Hill, Mae calling out excitedly, "Look dear! There's blood on that tree trunk."

Bill examined the fir bole, agreeing with his wife, "Yes, you're right, Zeb hit some critter. Hey, wait a moment. This spoor isn't from a deer. Damn! It's a bear's paw print."

Mae moaned at the suggestion that a bear had been shot, wailing, "Ohhh! Not our friend Brownie?"

"I don't know that any other bear is in the area, honey. Let's follow these tracks."

Together they trailed blood spatterings and paw marks up the hill, Bill finally commenting over his shoulder, "Less blood may be good news. Any bear that was critically wounded should have dropped by now. Maybe . . .I hope it's just a flesh wound."

The slope of Duke Hill began to look familiar to the trackers, Mae soon asking, "Isn't that deadfall over there where you first met Brownie?"

"Shhh! Did you hear that noise?" Bill queried in hushed tones.

After a moment in his listening pose, he answered her question, "Yes, and I think you've found our quarry. We're downwind of him, and he's distracted by his wound. Easy does it now."

Bill climbed higher on the hillside to reach a level with the upper side of the rotting old tree trunk, gesturing for Mae to stay behind him. He saw a black bear burrowing into the deadfall but couldn't identify the beast as his bear.

He filled his lungs with air and called out, "Brownie! Hey big boy, is that you?"

The startled animal spun about and raised high on his hind legs, emitting a shrieking roar as a challenge, Bill continuing in softer tones, "Hi there fella, are you hurt?"

Brownie dropped to all fours, sniffing the air and tossing his head at the familiar voice, the fur on his shoulder matted red. Neither withdrawing nor advancing, Brownie was yet threatening in his anguished state, and Bill considered what he should do.

Mae solved her husband's dilemma, reaching forward into his knapsack for their lunch, suggesting, "I'll feed Brownie this smoked salmon. That'll calm him down."

Bill agreed readily enough, but warned her, "Stay clear of my line of fire. If he attacks you, I'll have to shoot him."

Mae nodded as she edged forward, talking to the bear with a soothing voice, allowing him to hear and smell her as she approached. When she was twenty feet from the beast, he raised on hind legs and pawed the air, his low gravelly growl not hostile at all - only repining.

As Brownie returned to all fours, Mae stepped forward three paces and threw the fish at the bear's paws, retreating carefully to her husband's side. The animal seized the morsel in his jaws and sauntered away, stopping at the edge of the forest to eye his friends before disappearing into the greenery.

"His injury doesn't appear too serious, thank goodness, but that last look was most certainly a 'don't follow me' warning. I hope he'll be all right, dear," Mae concluded as she followed Bill down the slope toward home.

It would be months before they saw their ursine friend again, the young couple destined to the wintry seclusion of Cottage Cove - not at all a concern. They still considered themselves newlyweds and looked forward to exploring life together.

ᛏᛏ   ᛏᛏ   ᛏᛏ

The Pardues stood hand in hand watching the float plane rise over Ray Anchorage, returning to Ketchikan with Mae's father aboard. His arrival for a brief holiday visit had resulted in a cozy affair, seemingly becoming a crowd when Ed Hill joined them for Christmas dinner. Aside from a single mail drop the previous month, their solitude had been unbroken.

News from the outside was interesting, if somewhat remote, that is until Gene reported on the Blakelys. Alexis had returned home un-expectedly to have her baby, and Charley was undergoing pilot training at Lackland Air Force Base in Texas.

An unusually taciturn Charley had escorted his pregnant wife to her father's home wearing his reserve officer's uniform, and es-chewing any explanation to their friends, had flown out the next day. A Christmas card from the Blakelys had offered no explanation either to a marriage problem or his military status. The Korean War seemed close to home.

A welcome dietary relief ensued Gene's brief sojourn, fresh apples and oranges augmenting their usual cans of fruit, with potatoes and onions a nutritional replacement for beans and rice. They managed to stretch a bottle of wine over several meals, consuming its dregs in a toast to 1952.

ᛏᛏ   ᛏᛏ   ᛏᛏ

A rare spate of sunny weather in February brought Alan Harkins around on a mail drop, with tidings of the birth of Anne Blakely on January tenth. Charley had caught a hop to McChord Air Force Base in Tacoma from San Antonio and flew commercially to Ketchikan to visit mother and daughter for a weekend. Bill and Mae actually received a birth announcement signed by both parents.

"Maybe they've patched up their differences," Mae said optimistically.

"Or maybe not, honey. It'll be a while before we know. All we can do is wish them well."

π   π   π

A gray shroud enveloped the lonely boat in mid-channel, the oil-skinned figures fighting off boredom as well as the chilly drizzle. Cottage Cove was barely visible through the mist on this first day of spring. A series of rain squalls had prolonged wintry weather throughout southeast Alaska.

A slight figure in the bow dug into a soggy cardboard box and pulled out a sandwich wrapped in wax paper, offering it to the frustrated and fidgeting man in the stern. Mae spoke in forced but cheerful optimism, "Relax, dear. You caught a halibut on the way out here."

Bill sighed with impatience and then chuckled in wry humor, "Ha! Ha! Thanks, Mae, for the sandwich and the reminder that my fishing is merely a pretext to keep busy. I just hope the *MacDonald* didn't pass south during the night. It's due back any time now, and we could use some potatoes and beef."

"I thought I saw a ship, or maybe a barge, north of here when you were filling the Johnson with gasoline. But it faded into the mist like a ghost. Hee! Hee! Can the *MacDonald* be a ghost ship?" Mae teased.

Her husband grinned good-naturedly, responding in kind, "It may become one if these clouds get any lower. We'll have to head home if it gets any foggier. Where did you see our ghost?"

Mae pointed due north at a curtain of rain blocking the channel, and both searched the gloom intensely, Bill finally muttering, "I think that's Mary Island to the left. I don't see. . ."

"There! Coming out of that rain shower east of Mary Island. Isn't that a tug and barge?" Mae interjected with excitement in her manner.

Bill smiled in agreement, averring, "Your eyesight is certainly better than mine, dear. Yes, now I can see the tandem headed our way. Let's go meet that boat. *MacDonald* or not, we'll do a little horse trading."

A half hour later the Pardue's open boat bobbed alongside the *MacDonald*, the tugboat slowing, but not circling. Ray helped Mae aboard as Bill grabbed the halibut and scrambled over the low rail. The deckhand explained, "Skipper says we're running late. There's another storm due in Dixon Entrance tonight. Elmer figures to be in Grenville Channel by then. Cookie's got hot food for you folks in the mess. Nice seeing you. I have to get back to the wheelhouse."

"Thanks, Ray" Bill shouted to the hustling deckhand, adding quietly to his wife, "Come along, Mae. We'll dicker with Cookie."

The cook's wide grin revealed several gaps as he swung the door open with a flourish, bowing to Mae as he gallantly offered, "At your service, Missus Pardue. Come in and have a hot meal. You too, Slim."

A youthful cook's helper hastily laid out two bowls of stew on the table, its aroma mixing pleasantly with the ever present smell of coffee. Bill handed the young helper the halibut, addressing his old friend, "Cookie, is fish a fair trade for potatoes and beef?"

"Sure, Slim. Go ahead and eat while I fill a gunny sack for you. Captain Hairston will be down in a minute," the cook replied, pausing to add, "Did you know Harry's serving in the U.S. Navy? He's a bos'n mate aboard a supply ship in Korea. Damn war! I miss him."

Talking as he worked, Cookie traded gossip with the young couple, albeit allowing them but a brief word or two.

"Well, has our old friend here filled you in on all our news, Slim?" Elmer queried, and with a charming smile addressed the young lady, "Cottage Cove seems to agree with you, Missus Pardue."

"Please call me Mae, Captain Hairston. Thank you and Cookie for your hospitality."

The skipper responded, "You're welcome, Mae, and my name's Elmer. I'm sorry we can't stop for a visit. We've managed to spend a little time with Slim in the past, but we're overdue in Tacoma. The *MacDonald* won't be plying these waters for a few months. We're scheduled to tow mothballed ships from Vallejo to Bremerton - tin cans, I believe."

"I'll miss seeing you guys sailing past our home. I wish you fair seas, but I expect a visit next time you're in Alaskan waters," Bill said as he rose to his feet.

Mae followed suit, stepping to the mess door as she smiled a farewell, "Thanks Elmer, and you too, Cookie."

Bill shook hands warmly and took the supply sack from the cook with a brief, "Thanks!" Moving with haste, the pair boarded their boat as Ray ran aft to loosen their lines, their trusty Johnson catching on the first pull of the starter rope.

Running crosswind to the advancing weather front, Bill guessed they were ten miles from home with visibility diminishing. He thought to himself, *'Plenty of daylight left, but the rain is getting heavier.'* The bow crashed through a frothy crest, spraying him back to alertness.

Mae grimaced as the seawater splashed into the boat, crouching on her knees to bail with an old coffee can.

Between her unstable stance while bailing water and the rocking motion of the small craft in turbulent seas, Bill was not surprised that his wife appeared pale and uncomfortable when she resumed her seat. His stomach was becoming queasy, and he felt the advent of seasickness approaching.

Exchanging wan smiles, the two sailors braved the tempestuous wind and rain, Duke Island soon providing a rough shield from the advancing weather front. They were weary, wet and chilled when they landed at their boat slip, both wondering aloud if their venture had been worth the trials of the trip.

Bill summarized the day's events in a laconical prophecy, "Today will be a day to tell our grandchildren about."

π   π   π

Mae visited their neighbor's primitive cabin for the first time when she accompanied her husband to Ed's Judd Harbor hermitage to share their largesse of potatoes and an onion. Ed inveigled her to cook up a batch of fish and chips for their midday repast and, in turn, listened to her gossip interminably as she stood over the cast iron range.

Bill remained as quiet, if not as attentive as his neighbor, realizing for the first time just how lonely life in the wilderness must be for his non-complaining wife. At Ed's place she was letting off steam, prattling to a friendly face other than his own being a rare opportunity.

On the return trek he suggested they fly to Ketchikan for a visit, "Maybe we should go see the Carlsons -and your father."

"Ha! Ha! You think I'm going stir-crazy at Cottage Cove, don't you? Well, maybe a little bit anyway. But talking at Ed Hill was a welcome relief. Hee! Hee! He didn't interrupt, did he?" Mae replied good-naturedly, and without a break pointed out their financial status, "We can't afford a vacation. Every dime we make is needed to build our guest cabin. I doubt that old tent can last another season."

Bill held out his hand to assist Mae as she jumped over the narrow rivulet, both hikers startled to find a mangy brown bear standing ten feet away. Brownie was back, no sign of a wound in his shaggy fur, but looking thin and hungry.

Bill whistled through his teeth as he gathered a breath of air, calmly talking to their animal friend, "Pshew! Hello, old fella. How are you? You look like hell, but I don't see any scars. Just hungry, huh? Well, follow Mae and me to the cabin."

"Nice Brownie. Are we still friends?" Mae added with a hint of uncertainty in her tone, hurrying to keep pace with her long-legged husband and noting that the lumbering bear crossed the field right behind them.

She moved ahead to open the smokehouse and take out a fifteen pound fresh halibut, lamenting in a wee voice, "I guess we eat rock cod tonight, dear."

꠸   ꠸   ꠸

"Gin!" Mae called out excitedly, a roguish smile on her lips.

Bill groaned loudly, lamenting his frustrations, "Four games in a row isn't fair, Mae Pardue. Where did you learn to play rummy - Creek Street?"

Their play was abruptly interrupted by a thumping sound on the east wall, a rare disturbance in the aftermath of a forty-eight hour storm. Bill stood up and seized his rifle, and picking up their big flashlight, hurried out the door with a warning to his wife, "Stay inside, dear."

Circling the cabin he heard coughing sounds emanating from around the corner, turning it to find the doubled-over figure of a man, indistinguishable as he lay hunched in his oilskins.

Kneeling down, Bill queried in curiosity as well as concern, "How did you get here, friend?"

A bedraggled Tsimchuck raised his face into the rain and coughingly pleaded, "Bill. . .cough. . .Gregori is hurt and sick. . . cough. . .over there. . . cough. . . "

Bill leaned his rifle against the wall and literally picked up the old man, plodding resolutely around the house and calling loudly to his waiting wife, "Mae, fix the spare bed. Tsimchuck's here, and he's ill."

Together they removed the coughing man's wet garments, and then Bill toweled his wrinkled body dry while Mae put stew on the stove to warm. He covered the exhausted Tsimchuck with thick wool blankets, and Mae handed the old man a steaming cup of coffee.

The venerable Tsimshian elder appreciated the warmth to his hands as much as stomach and said so, "Hmm, good! I'm so. . . cough. . .cold. You must help Gregori. He's very sick."

"Where is he? What happened?" Bill queried impatiently, eager to help his friend.

"Our outboard motor ran out of gas a mile east of here, and the waves smashed us into the rocks. Gregori pulled me . . .cough. . . out of the water to safety and then just dropped. I carried . . .cough . . . him a few hundred feet, but I'm too old. . .cough. . .not strong like I used to be."

Bill interrupted, asking another question, "Is he straight east? Near the shore?"

When Tsimchuck nodded and coughed, the young man left his care to Mae, and donning a coat, he marched east in the glow of his flashlight. He'd retrieve his rifle later.

As he stumbled along the rocky shoreline, he called Gregori's name repeatedly, a response hoped for but not expected. Ten minutes later he climbed atop a large boulder to flash his light over the area, searching for some sign of his friend. Swinging the beam along his back trail, he spotted Gregori's huddled form not ten feet from where Bill has passed just moments ago.

He took but a moment to verify Tsimchuck's diagnosis of the seriousness of Gregori's condition. He was gravely ill but still alive. Cradling him gently in his arms, Bill trod home talking to the unconscious man all the way to the cabin.

π   π   π

The weight of a gnarled hand on his shoulder snapped Bill back to awareness, Tsimchuck coughing whenever he spoke, "It's light out. . .cough. . .how is Gregori?"

Mae answered from her bedroom where their still unconscious friend lay, "He's no better, Tsimchuck. His face is white as a sheet. I think he's had a heart attack. He needs a doctor immediately."

Bill nodded agreement readily, vouchsafing, "We can make Metlakatla. The weather has calmed considerably during the night," and turning to the old Indian, added, "You'd better stay here in bed Tsimchuck."

"No! I go. . . cough. . .stay with Gregori . . .cough. . .only a little sick," the Tsimshian stalwartly insisted.

Mae concurred, "Tsimchuck needs a doctor, too. We'll all go."

"Okay, dear. I'll get the boat ready. You two can dress Gregori. Wrap him in a warm blanket," Bill suggested as he hurried out the door.

A half hour later they were prepared to travel, Bill lowering the comatose form of their friend onto a cot stretched over two seats, Mae sitting on a padded life preserver on the deck near his head, and Tsimchuck slouched in the bow seat as a lookout.

Mae's voice carried a sense of urgency as she offered, "I have a thermos of hot coffee for our patients, a canteen of water for us and a bag full of bread and smoked fish. Quit worrying, dear, and let's get to the doctor."

A brief grin creased Bill's otherwise serious countenance as he replied, "Yes, Ma'am," and poled away from the slip.

"I figure we should reach Metlakatla before dark if we manage to avoid weather delays. Tsimchuck is going to guide us through Cat Passage into Felice Strait. I've never been in those perilous waters, but it will save time," Bill explained to Mae as he cranked his Johnson to life.

Mae shouted over the clamor of the fifteen horsepower motor, "Are we going around the north end of the island?"

"Yes, we should be okay until we near Point Davison and enter more open waters. Clarence Strait into Nicholson Passage could be rough seas."

Mae nodded wordlessly, watching the worried expression on her husband's face become more intense as he planned the day's trip in his mind. The boat ran smoothly before the trailing sea breeze, and she settled back to savor the quiet morning air.

∏   ∏   ∏

The Warburton light was visible ahead and Annette Island was to starboard as the open boat sped through choppy seas toward Metlakatla. It had been a long and tedious day for its passengers as Mae nursed both of the old men. Gregori was still unconscious but alive, while Tsimchuck sprawled in the bow in a coughing torpor.

Suddenly the rays of the setting sun shot through a slit in the overcast sky, Gregori's senses reacting to the stimulus of bright light by opening his eyes to view the sunset and muttering Tsimchuck's name.   The old Indian reacted to the mumbled call with a frantic awareness, summoning his strength to exchange places with Mae, both his cough and stupor somehow forgotten in his friend's moment of need.

A dozen hybrid Chinook phrases passed between the old partners, Gregori's voice rising in a thin pitch as they embraced one last time.   As the last ray of light flicked off and twilight enveloped them, Tsimchuck commenced a low chant.   Gregori Zohkov had died quietly in the arms of his companion of many years, and tears filled all three pairs of eyes while his death song carried across the harbor to Malcolm's dock.   Bill thought the last of a breed had died, the American son of a Sitka Russian.

On the shore a small gathering collected about the waiting Malcolm, recognizing the sound of Tsimchuck's lament and surmising that Gregori was dead.   Bill hand-signaled Mal that a doctor was needed, his buddy puzzled by the gesture until the chanting was broken by a paroxysm of coughing, and Tsimchuck's heaving body slid to the bottom of the boat.

Ready hands were available to assist them as Bill nosed into the dock, Mae accompanying friends and two stretchers to the doctor's office.   Jack Williams directed Bill around the dock to his gas pump, finally helping the young man lift his boat above the high tide mark.

"You and Mae must be tired," the elder Williams sympathized as he offered, "After we visit the doctor to see how Tsimchuck is doing, you two must go to my son's house to rest.   John is in Ketchikan, but Helen will welcome you, and I'm sure the tribal elders will drop in to thank you for rescuing Tsimchuck, one of the few original Tsimshian settlers left in Metlakatla."

꒞   ꒞   ꒞

At a late breakfast the next morning, Jack brought news that Tsimchuck had pneumonia.   He had coughed up phlegm once during the night but otherwise had slept well. The doctor had called Tsimchuck, "a tough old Tsimshian," and then ordered him to stay in bed until his lungs cleared.

Relieved that the old man had survived the trip in better condition than he expected, Bill asked, "What did the doctor say about Gregori? And when are the funeral services?"

"He said Gregori's heart gave out," Jack replied.

Helen inserted, "The funeral is scheduled for tomorrow afternoon. What are your plans afterward?"

Glancing at his wife for approval, Bill suddenly grinned as he answered, "Mae's going to Ketchikan, and I'm taking the boat back to Cottage Cove."

Their two friends looked at each other and then Mae in puzzlement, and Mae blushed prettily as she announced, "I think I'm pregnant, and I want to see my own doctor to confirm it. Besides, Daddy will be flabbergasted at being a grandparent."

She paused for a sobering moment before concluding, "Isn't life strange? And yet quite predictable, I guess. One life is gone, and another is arriving. Darling, if our child is a boy, can we name him Gregori?"

Chapter Eight

Bill stared glassy-eyed across Tongass Narrows from the living room window of Gene's apartment in Ketchikan, waiting patiently for Mae to finish dressing for their ten o'clock meeting with the banker. He practiced applying for a loan in his mind, anxiety with this new experience needing some preparation. Roy Carlson had insisted on helping the Pardues obtain a building loan to construct their guest cabin before the summer sports fishing season commenced. Bill had said hello to the stern old gentleman in their bank a couple of times, but he really didn't know Mister Thompson.

"Why do I need to go with you, dear? You could meet with the banker by yourself more easily," his wife inquired from the other room.

"Because we're partners. I want you to see what we're getting ourselves into, and I want Mister Thompson to meet both of us.

Haven't you finished yet? Come along, Mae, before you're too beautiful for that banker."

Mae walked into the room, smiling coquettishly as she turned gracefully for his inspection, and retorted, "Thank you, dear. Didn't you say we should try to impress the banker?"

He chuckled as he took her hand and walked with her out the door, his nervousness gone and his mood cheerful. His wife had a knack for vesting him with great self-confidence, another reason Bill wanted her at his side for the ten o'clock conference.

Laughing joyfully in each other's company and at their proposed venture, they entered the bank on the heels of the lady cashier who unlocked the doors. Mae whispered conspiratorially, "Are we being too eager? Being the first customer, I mean."

Bill nodded and answered cheerfully, "Ha! Ha! We are certainly punctual, aren't we, dear?"

"I appreciate that, Mister and Missus Pardue. It's good to see you again. Please come into my office," the gentlemanly banker welcomed them with a wide smile, at odds with Bill's previous picture of a stern and foreboding figure.

"Thank you, Mister Thompson. Roy Carlson sends his regards," Bill stated a bit formally as he escorted Mae to a chair.

"Yes, I know. And I've heard from Missus Pardue's father, John Furrer, Don Wilson and Blackjack Blakely. Even Dolly Arthur stopped by to sing your praises. As if I needed anyone to vouch for Daylight Bill Pardue, a man everyone in Ketchikan knows as reliable, trustworthy and fortunate. How did you survive that plane crash anyway?" the banker asked in real curiosity.

After Bill told his story one more time, and Mae charmed Mister Thompson with a tale of Brownie, their "pet" bear, the banker put aside his smile and turned to money affairs.

"I've reviewed your loan request for one thousand dollars, and then I talked to a friend in the construction business. Pardue's Lodge is a far piece away, and a guest cabin will cost you dearly," Mister Thompson opined.

Bill interrupted politely, "Yes, sir. But my wife and I have a growing clientele, and we can repay the bank in three or four seasons."

"Of course, Bill. May I call you Bill?" the banker asked and at his visitor's nod he continued, "And call me John. Bill, I'd like to offer you and your wife full bank services, including an open-ended account to build guest facilities. I suggest a three-room, twelve-bunk cabin instead of a single room. You should have accommodations for women and families which offer some privacy, and a bigger facility won't cost much more once the contractor is on site. I agree that your venture is sound, and I offer you folks my financial advice as well as the bank services. In fact, I plan to be one of your customers myself. Blackjack has invited me to join his party this summer."

Ⱦ   Ⱦ   Ⱦ

The following days passed swiftly, details occupying their talks with the contractor, and planning for the upcoming sports season requiring Bill and Roy to utilize another roll of butcher paper for their list. Mae visited with Alexis and her baby during the mornings the two men charted the lodge's destiny on the store counter.

One noon Bill stopped by the Furrer home to pick up Mae, and Alexis insisted he stay for lunch. She let him read Charley's last letter from Texas, his old friend relating amusing stories from his training as a fighter pilot at Lackland. His correspondence to his wife was newsy and sociable, but lacked any personal touch - not a spousal letter in Bill's mind.

Alexis commented, "Charley's a lousy writer. He called over the weekend with news that he's going to Korea after he gets his wings next month. We disagreed again, I don't think he needed to volunteer. We would have accompanied him to Germany if he had accepted flying duty in Frankfurt. I just don't understand why he likes the idea of fighting in Korea."

With a rare display of tact, Bill held his tongue and let Alexis do the talking. John Furrer's entry on a midday visit to his granddaughter provided the Pardues with the opportunity to exit without further comment.

Walking along the street, he breathed a heavy sigh of relief and muttered, "Whew! Your friend Alexis is such a shallow character."

Mae quickly retorted, "Your buddy Charley is a lousy father. He's only seen his daughter twice and never asks about her."

'No rebuttal to that criticism,' he thought to himself, dropping the subject as he tacitly agreed with his wife.

π   π   π

It had been raining steadily all week, and Bill was glad that Mae had remained in Ketchikan with her father. He had accompanied the construction crew to Cottage Cove, swapping dry quarters and his cooking to the contractor for freight transportation - half a ton of food supplied for the summer operation of Pardue's Lodge.

One of the carpenters framing his guest cabin was a cousin of Amos Jones, the Fairbanks homesteader. Polite conversation soon turned into a friendly relationship, Amos often serving as a subject of mutual interest. Besides, the older man was working with Don Wilson to get his own homesite up north, irascibly utilizing the third person in their banter, "Ozzie Jones, he can be a successful rancher. He's got Amos to look after him."

Subsequent conversations demonstrated Ozzie's pride in his cousin's accomplishments, as well as giving Bill a vivid, if depressing, insight into life for a Negro in the deep South. The two cousins were from east Texas where their kin had been tenant farmers for four generations. The war and Amos' ambition and courage combined to place the two men in Alaska on their own. Almost a hundred years had passed since the Civil War, but few Negroes had become landowners.

Fortunately, Ozzie was not only industrious but a journeyman at his trade, earning him respect and acceptance from the crew. However, Bill was the only person with whom he conversed in more than a word or a phrase, the other men's approval not including social-ability.

The Negro did sit in the evening poker game when Bill was playing, and he always lost a dollar or two. During one hand of stud poker, the foreman raised bullishly, overly proud of a pair of jacks against Ozzie's pair of queens. Ozzie cogitated deliberately, and when his boss grew irritated at his slowness, he folded his cards. Bill was the only player who caught the flash of his whole card - a third queen. He said nothing, figuring correctly that Ozzie couldn't bring himself to win from his emotional foreman and spoil the fun. Sitting in the game with his coworkers was satisfying enough for a Negro in this day and age.

Their friendship resulted in Ozzie's making occasional suggestions for improvements to Pardue's Lodge, always when he and Bill were alone. A couple of his ideas saved time and money when the foreman implemented Bill's "ideas." He was grateful to his friend when the job was completed before Mae's return from Ketchikan.

Standing on the boat slip admiring the view of a partial sunset, Ozzie advised, "If I were you, Bill, I'd build a real dock here. The boss has plenty of lumber left over, and I bet he'd sell it to you cheap."

Bill ruminated for a spell, finger stroking his chin as he considered the possibility. "How about staying here and building it for me? I like several of your suggestions, but I wouldn't know where to start. I can afford three dollars an hour with board and room, plus an airplane ride to Ketchikan when Don Wilson sends for you. What do you say?"

π   π   π

The construction tug and barge had just disappeared up Revillagigedo Channel when Malcolm Angias motored into Cottage Cove, bursting with personal news. "Annie and I are getting married in July - up in Hoonah. Will you be an usher? Arthur's going to be my best man."

"Yes, of course, I wouldn't miss it for the world, It's about time you settled down," Bill replied and then directed Mal to his mooring stump, "Tie up over here. Here he comes now - Amos Jones' cousin."

The Indian and the Negro eyed each other with curiosity, Malcolm extending his hand cordially as he inquired, "Glad to meet you, Ozzie. Are you another homesteader like Amos and this galoot?"

Ozzie flashed his white-toothed smile and nodded, saying, "As soon as Don Wilson finishes my paperwork, I'm leaving for Fairbanks. But doesn't the Territory call this land a homesite?"

"Homesite or homestead, it doesn't matter, we Tsimshians call it a land grab. Say, do you guys want to go fishing with me? The dock can wait until tomorrow," Malcolm responded.

Bill declined, "No, but thanks. I haven't seen Brownie since I returned home. I'm going over to Ed Hill's with a sack of potatoes and ask about the bear. Ozzie will go along with you though. He deserves a break."

ᛌ   ᛌ   ᛌ

The three men stood shoulder-to-shoulder on the half-finished dock and watched Alan Harkins' silver float plane taxi toward them. Mae leaned out the window, waving enthusiastically as soon as the propeller jerked to a halt. Bill responded with a grin and wave before leaning forward to guide the starboard pontoon alongside the dock. The aircraft was secured against four bumpers of the quartered automobile tire which served as a cushion for the plane. Ozzie had scrounged the rubber tire from his old boss and promptly nailed the pieces in place. The carpenter had certainly earned his keep the past couple of days.

Mae climbed out of the cockpit and fell into her husband's waiting arms, obviously happy to be home. She smiled as she greeted her dear friend, "Hello, Malcolm. Congratulations on your engagement. The news is all over Ketchikan that your bachelor days are all but over."

"Yes, I'm finally getting hitched, 'Little Sister.' I just had to follow your example," Malcolm teased gaily.

Mae laughed outright at his jibe and at his good humor, and glancing at the stranger beside him, introduced herself, "Hi, I'm Mae. You must be Ozzie Jones. Don Wilson sent word for you to come see him. Are you going to take up a homesite, too?"

"Yes, Ma'am! Up north near my cousin Amos, I hope. Did Mister Wilson say where it's located?" Ozzie asked expectantly.

"No, but you'll hear tomorrow. You can fly out with Alan in the morning."

Alan piped in, "No, in the afternoon. I'm taking Bill up on his offer of fishing. I haven't had a lazy day off since I took over Ed Luden's business."

Bill chuckled at Ozzie's frustrated expression, chiding him, "Ha! Ha! Quit worrying, my friend, Don will be there all day. Besides, you have to finish the dock before you leave Cottage Cove."

After dinner the five friends sat around the table exchanging news. Mae belatedly remembered that Charley Blakely had crashed his airplane in Texas. He was injured but not seriously, according to Alexis.

Malcolm asked her about her baby, which resulted in stories about her visit to the doctor and Julia Carlson's grandmotherly attitude.

Everyone insisted on Malcolm's relating details of his courtship and engagement, and then Ozzie inveigled a re-enactment of the Daylight Bill tale from the principal character.

When Bill fell silent for the last time, Alan and Ozzie exchanged glances meaning, "Who's next?" Ozzie volunteered an amusing incident in North Africa, poking fun of himself continuously.

"Well, there we were - in the middle of nowhere. Two hundred some Negro soldiers, the only white man being Captain Avery, our company commander who got us lost. We heard gunfire to the east of our position so Captain Avery ordered us to mount up. I was the oldest volunteer so I was a platoon sergeant, and Amos was one of my squad leaders - a corporal. Anyway, I was the last to climb into the back of that six-ply, and off we roared to be heroes in a live battle."

Ozzie paused, reliving events in his memory before sharing them with his friends, "Some of the men were scared white, but not one of them would admit it. I was surprised that I was eager for combat. We so wanted our Negro company, 'Buffalo Soldiers,' to look good. Since we couldn't live with the white army, maybe we could still help win the war. Well, we crossed a barren pass of rocks and sand, ending up in the next valley where Patton's army had won the field. And to make matters worse, I leaned out of our truck to wave at our heroic leader, ivory-handled six-gun and all, just as our driver dodged a tank. I tumbled askew beside the General's jeep and broke my leg in the process. Well, Patton stopped to have me loaded into the seat behind him. He offered to drop me off at the field hospital which I thought was a good idea."

He laughed uncontrollably for a moment before concluding, "Ho! Ho! Ho! Everyone along the route hailed the Negro hero who was wounded with the 'Great Man' in North Africa. I believe I may be the only colored soldier photographed at the front with George Patton. Anyway, I spent the rest of the war in Oklahoma counting supplies. But I'm a bona-fide veteran, which makes me eligible for my land claim."

"What a wonderful story, Ozzie," Mae praised the grinning home-steader as she led a round of applause for his effort.

Bill turned to Alan and teased, "Can you top that tall tale, my friend?"

"Well now, I can tell you all about my career as a gold miner although I can't throw a name like George Patton into my yarn. About the closest I came to brushing elbows with a famous man was in Wrangell in 1939 when I sailed up the Stikine River with Jack Norris," Alan drawled as he paused dramatically, waiting patiently for the inevitable question.

"Who is Jack Norris?" chorused the gathering.

"I'm glad you asked, folks. Jack was a fine sawyer and a self-proclaimed independent thinker from Peshtigo, Wisconsin. Deciding

Alaska was about to become a state...no, don't laugh, folks! He was ahead of his time, I know, but we can agree with his idea. Anyway, Jack packed his wife and three kids in his trusty old Ford and headed west, ending up with friends in Ruston, Washington. And then fate intervened, producing a once-in-a-lifetime deal for the Alaska-bound adventurer. Jack discovered his means of transportation north when he saw the *Puyallup Queen* for sale at the Tacoma Yacht Club. He fell in love with a majestic cruiser with a clean white hull and polished mahogany wheelhouse, and its roomy cabin could sleep six people. The fact that it was tall, top-heavy and shallow-drafted didn't faze him. He was quickly the owner - captain of the vessel."

A titter of laughter escaped through the screen of Mae's fingers.

Alan acknowledged the interruption, "It's not nice to poke fun at landlocked sailors, Mae. The *Tacoma News Tribune* had only praise for his stalwart determination in its news coverage. Well, maybe the reporter did question the old tub's seaworthiness - I forget the details. Anyway, the Norris family set out that summer through the Inland Passageway to Ketchikan, tooting the boat's horn at every gill-netter, troller, tug, ferry and packet on the sound. Everyone blew their horns and waved in recognition, making Jack feel like a real captain and person of note. They were clearing Point–No–Point as a Japanese freighter passed them, ignoring Jack's toot and leaving a wake which almost capsized his boat. Like a true sailor, Jack shook his fist at the ship and shouted a salty phrase or two questioning its skipper's ancestry, but no amount of attention-getting behavior could change the ship's course. After that incident, Jack wisely avoided large ships and any kind of waves, staying in Port Hardy for two days until Queen Charlotte Strait calmed down."

As Alan sipped a bit of coffee, curiosity overcame Bill who urged, "Come on, Alan, what happened next?"

"The *Puyallup Queen* reached Ketchikan without a hitch in sixteen days. After the fanfare of his arrival wore off, Jack inquired about gold mining, and some fellow sold him a worthless claim on the Stikine River. I know it was worthless because I bought the one next to it. Anyway, we met in Wrangell and wasted the rest of the summer in the gold fields. The only color either of us saw was when we worked for wages in other mines. Jack was a determined cuss, still working that pile of gravel when I caught a ride on a fishing boat going south to Ballard."

Malcolm shook his head in puzzlement, "I've never heard of Norris. What happened to him?"

"Oh, he sold his claim for gas money and sailed back to Tacoma. Even found a buyer for his boat, so he could return to Peshtigo with money in his pocket. End of story," Alan concluded.

"Wait a minute! You said you were going to tell us about your gold-mining career," Bill complained teasingly.

"And that I did. A few words was all my experience in gold-mining was worth," Alan retorted, and answering Mae's questioning look with a, "Yes, Jack Norris is real, and my tale is kind of factual. Truth is more interesting than fiction - sometimes."

Bill laughed jovially as he entered a word of doubt, "I read that story when I was a kid delivering the *News Tribune*, and I didn't recognize it until you were through. You ought to join my friend, Warren Larson, as an entry in the Tall Tale Contest. He almost won last year, and your yarn would be a challenge to him."

"I'm turning in. Your job is to give me material for another tale. How big are the fish in Cottage Cove?" Alan joshed as the story session broke up.

π   π   π

The Pardues and their out-of-the-way lodge had attained a favorable repute during the previous sports fishing season, with party after party passing through Cottage Cove. An occasional stopover by commercial fishermen added revenue to Mae's baby fund, a hoard of coins and one-dollar bills filling the old coffee can in the cupboard.

For the Fourth of July dinner, there were fifteen men staying in the guest cabin, an older couple using their second bedroom, nine crewmen from two fishing boats tied up to the dock and Ed Hill. Bill began steaming clams and potatoes in his Indian-style pit just as Alan arrived with a keg of beer and a twenty-eight pound turkey. Ed's smoked salmon and Mae's barrel of crackers were consumed with much of the beer while everyone laid out blankets and tables in a picnic setting near the steaming pit.

The clams went just as quickly, and thin halibut steaks were grilled on the hot rocks while the big bird roasted in the oven. Still, full plates of turkey dinner were eaten by those present until not a scrap of cooked food was left. When the keg ran dry, the Gig Harbor crew produced a case of Olympia quarts, both boats and the float plane destined to remain overnight at the dock, another feast of bacon, eggs and pancakes being consumed by the crowd in the morning.

Bill fretted about Mae's working too hard cooking for guests, particularly as her pregnancy began to show or when there was a large number of people - like on the Fourth. His wife laughed off his concerns as her health and strength were sound. Mae felt good and said so repeatedly as she reassured him.

Brownie returned to entertain guests, most of whom insisted on throwing one of their catches to the begging bruin. Sportsmen visiting the lodge expressed disappointment if the bear failed to show during their stay. Brownie's reputation had produced an expectancy in visitors, enhanced no doubt by Alan's fanciful narrative on their inbound flight.

During the Pardues' absence to attend the ceremonial wedding of Annie Moses and Malcolm Angias, Ed Hill forsook his hermitage to tend the lodge and its visitors. Upon their return, he professed having a wonderful time as caretaker and host, but he was soon on the forest trail home to his own place - and solitude.

Ŵ   Ŵ   Ŵ

Malcolm and Annie Angias deplaned one rainy day in September, arriving at Cottage Cove to manage the lodge for a couple of weeks. They had honeymooned in Seattle and established a home in Metlakatla during the summer, and were filling in for the Pardues while Bill took Mae to Ketchikan to deliver their baby.

Bill was fidgety, and Mae was cheerful when they arrived at her father's apartment to await the addition to their family. Gene was excited enough at the prospect of being a grandfather that he worked in town for the duration of Mae's pregnancy. He was first to inform them of Charley's return to Ketchikan, sans uniform, and his appointment as assistant manager of the mill. They were all invited to the Furrers for an impromptu welcoming party that evening.

Gene had walked over to the Furrers' place early, volunteering to help John with the "surprise" party, and Bill had borrowed his Chevy to drive Mae to the affair. Leaving Gene's apartment a bit later, Mae had her first pang of labor. Bill drove straight to the hospital, and Gregori Eugene Pardue arrived in the wee hours of 11 October, 1952.

Bill enjoyed a hectic but happy first week of fatherhood, mixing family responsibilities with social obligations while preparing for the coming winter. Banker John Thompson informed the young innkeeper that their loan had been all but repaid, whereupon the bank had granted the Pardues a new line of credit for 1953.

Charley and Bill visited Creek Street one evening, consuming smoked salmon and beer while comparing notes on their perilous adventures - and unique survivals. The normally loquacious extrovert said little about his family life, although he expressed continuing interest in Bill's son.

One evening the two families got together for a social visit, everyone being on good behavior with the children getting a lot of attention.

Mae commented afterward that everything seemed fine in the Blakely household, but Bill's nod of assent was with tongue-in-cheek. He hoped for the best but had serious doubts that their goody-goody behavior was reality. However, Charley deserved credit for working at his marriage and at his job of assistant manager. The title was neither nominal nor taken for granted by Charley, who quickly accepted any task and learned the business from the ground up. John Furrer praised his son-in-law regularly, assigning him more and more responsibilities. Bill was sure he would take over as manager next year and let John fulfill his desire to travel around the world.

Bill was happy for the Blakelys, not the least envious of their wealth and position in Ketchikan. He and Mae had their own dreams and a wonderful marriage, and when Gregori was a week old, the Pardues returned to Cottage Cove to close the fishing season.

π   π   π

The Pardues had settled into their winter mode, guests long since departed, when the islands were struck by a violent storm spinning out of the Gulf of Alaska. Winds increased steadily to gale force over the lodge, rain squalls obscuring the landmarks along the inland passage.

Wrapped in oil-skins, Bill staggered through wind gusts to his slip and battened down his fishing equipment.   Ducking his head to escape a swirling squall of rain, his gaze swept over Revillagigedo Channel briefly. Movement brought his eyes back to a gray wall beyond the entrance to Ray Anchorage, and he sighted a boat struggling in the heavy seas. A clear glimpse of Karl's cannery tender showed it was on a southeasterly heading.

'Why, I think Karl's trying for Cottage Cove, but something's wrong,' Bill thought as the boat weaved through one rain squall after another. 'The tender is crossway to the wind and is taking a lot of water over her gunwale. Say, maybe it's that magnetic disturbance af - fecting his compass. I've run into that problem a time or two myself. I bet Karl is running blind, using a faulty heading to reach Ray Anchorage.'

He ran to the house for his signal light and to tell Mae his intentions of helping the tender. Minutes later he was underway toward the last position of the tender, worried that Karl might end up on the rocks by Duke Point.

Bill hugged the shoreline, relying on his familiarity with its hazards to reach the vicinity of the tender. Suddenly a gust of wind caught its rising bow like a sail and spun the light craft askew, a wave crashing unceremoniously over Bill and his sputtering Johnson. Reversing course to the southwest, the beleaguered sailor faced the storm while he held the outboard steady with one hand and bailed seawater with the other.

The wind's force abated a bit as he ended up a few feet offshore amidst several rock formations. Inadvertently he had found a half-mile long stretch of fairly calm water, but right in the middle of the rocky shoreline that had claimed Tsimchuck's boat. He didn't breathe easily again until he exited the hazardous patch and bounced through rough seas again.

The squall had blown away from the island, and the cannery tender was in plain sight less than five hundred yards away. Bill swung his light overhead, rotating its beam until a blinking light responded. He thought he heard the tender's horn sound, but the howling wind was too overpowering to be sure.

Karl swung his vessel northwesterly, waves once again crashing over her port rail as he paralleled Bill's course, lights signaling a silent message. Soon both craft were smothered by another torrent of rain, yet they emerged five minutes later on the same heading, albeit now but a hundred feet apart. Pardue's Lodge and dock were visible ahead, and Bill waved Karl forward as he took the smaller craft next to the beach and leeward of the wind. He was able to reach his dock and pull his rig high and dry before the tender nosed into the landing.

Bill seized the thrown bow line, Karl shouting into the wind, "Thanks, Bill. My compass was all mixed up, and the channel acted like Dixon Entrance."

"Come up to the house. Mae will have hot coffee ready for us," Bill yelled back.

Four crew members traipsed up the muddy trail following their host, their perilous adventure finally becoming just another day in the life of an Alaskan fisherman.

Mae met them at the door with a pot of steaming java and a half-dozen porcelain mugs, pouring quaffs of the warming liquid into each cup as the men introduced themselves.

"Howdy, Missus Pardue. This coffee is a godsend," Karl said, adding, "Didn't I hear that you have a son now?"

"Yes, Karl, and please call me Mae. You're all welcome to our home, and you can meet Gregori at dinner. In the meantime, I started a fire in the guest cabin, and you can all dry out for an hour or so."

A baby's cry of hunger came from the bedroom, interrupting Mae, who responded hastily to the call. Over her shoulder she smiled with a murmur, "The baby's always hungry."

"Thank you, Mae. We'll get out of your way," Karl replied, ordering one of his men, "Tad, take a cup of coffee down to Honeycutt and help him secure the tender. Come on men, we'll go next door and clean up for dinner."

ᵀᵀ ᵀᵀ ᵀᵀ

Rick Honeycutt was cradling the baby in his huge hands, two pairs of watchful eyes fastened on his grip as his "kitchee-coo" drew a happy gurgle from the tot. His interest in Gregori and his gentleness in playing with the baby soon dispelled any parental concerns, all remnants of hostility between them forgotten.

Gregori had been responding to "Greg" equally as well as his given name, and now learned he was "Little Gregori" to Rick, who declared proudly, "See, he knows his name already. He's a bright youngster."

"Ha! Ha!" Mae chortled, "He'll do anything for attention, including gurgling at strangers. But he is smart."

"Sure he is, and I'm not a stranger anymore, am I, Little Gregori," Rick chattered on, adding a kitchee-coo for good measure.

The baby gurgled and smiled beatifically, Rick's face turned into a frown as he yelped, "Oops!"

Mae laughed cheerily, commenting in a wry voice, "Come to Mama, Greg. "I'll change your diaper."

"Ha! Ha!" Bill laughed loudly, "Our son has shown everyone what his big smile means - a sigh of relief. Want to change Gregori, Rick?"

"Yeah, Rick, how about finishing what you started?" Karl teased.

Grinning cheerfully, Rick declined, "No, thanks! Mae is much more capable than me. Bill, how about joining us in the other cabin for a game of cards. I think your wife and son deserve a rest. Thanks for dinner, Mae."

᛭   ᛭   ᛭

Alan Harkins flew his float plane to Cottage Cove for an early Christmas celebration, Gene, Aaron, a pack of mail and gifts accompanying their friend. As Mae cooked a holiday-style feast, she and Bill opened the parcels. What the written messages failed to convey, the three visitors were quick to report.

The Korean War continued to plague the world, statehood was no closer to congressional action, and the price of lumber was holding steady. On a more personal level, the Carlsons were all well, Charley and Alexis had flown to San Francisco for a business vacation while Grandpa babysat Anne, and Tsimchuck was fishing with Malcolm.

All the wrapped packages contained clothing, mostly for Gregori - useful as he was growing so fast. Mae had been busy knitting, giving her husband and her father each a heavy sweater, with scarves for Alan and Aaron. Bill and Alan loaded the plane with outgoing mail and Christmas gifts, plus over a hundred pounds of smoked halibut which Blackjack Blakely had ordered.

The weather break lasted but a single day; by late afternoon Alan insisted on leaving, his judgment confirmed when rain fell upon the lodge just after dark. By morning, winter's gray pall had returned in full force, and the Pardues were isolated once again.

Ed Hill showed up for Christmas dinner with a trio of hand-carved toys for the baby and a wooden stool for the Pardues. He received his knitted scarf with a knowing smile and settled back to tell a story to Gregori.

"I saw a big fat brown-colored black bear on the trail coming down here. Brownie wouldn't talk to me and actually growled when I walked toward him. I wonder how big black bears get? He keeps growing," Ed paused, asking Bill, "Have you ever seen Brownie this late in the year?"

"No, he's always holed up in the winter months. In fact, I haven't seen him since before Thanksgiving. Are you sure the bear you spotted was Brownie?"

Ed nodded, answering, "Yes, but maybe he has to eat more as he grows bigger. Anyway, I waved a piece of halibut at him, and when he wouldn't approach me, I left it on the ground. Strange animal this year!"

Gregori gurgled in seeming agreement, his attention focused on their neighbor during the story. Ed did such a good job of spinning yarns to the baby, he talked him to sleep for his afternoon nap.

"Your son is growing a mile a minute, Mae, and he's a smart little guy. Pays attention when his elders talk and doesn't interrupt. I like that!"

"Ha! Ha!" Mae chuckled, agreeing in a teasing tone, "You're right, Ed, but what are you going to think when he's old enough to talk back?"

Ed smiled and retorted, "He'll always listen to his Uncle Ed. We understand each other like the old friends we're going to become."

π   π   π

Gregori squealed in delight, fisting his rag doll and pounding on Bill's stomach with abandon. Father and son were wasting a stormy afternoon, roughhousing on the kitchen floor. Although it was technically the third day of spring, rain and wind had dominated the weather all week.

The boy's hair was darkening as it grew, favoring his mother, but his father's blue eyes shone with mischief as he attacked his daddy with gleeful energy.

"Will you boys go into the bedroom and play. I've got to cook dinner," Mae repined teasingly, admonishing her husband, "And change Greg's diaper before you put him down for his nap."

Bill did as he was told, the baby fast asleep the moment his daddy tucked him in. Winter had been a wonderful opportunity for the father to spend time with his son, and now he wondered how he could maintain their closeness with business and guests in the offing. He decided that he would just have to find the time.

His reverie was interrupted as Mae exclaimed, "Is that a plane's engine I hear, dear? What would bring Alan out in this weather?"

Both threw oil-skins over their heads and rushed outdoors, the droning sound of a low-flying aircraft increasing in volume as it flew overhead, a parachute bundle drifting downward in the wind. Alan's plane wigwagged its wings as it climbed northeasterly, and Bill threw off his cape to run down the trail to the beach where he retrieved his soaking package in a foot of water.

"It was fortunate that you heard Alan's plane in time, or we never would have found our mail. As it is, your ham is doubly salted, and the waterproof bag containing our letters has failed. Let's dry everything before we read the latest news," Bill chattered as he unwrapped the damp mail.

Mae picked her father's letter off the floor, laughing as she admitted, "Hee! Hee! I can't wait for these to dry out. Let's read them carefully."

They shared the contents of the drop one letter at a time, his mother's newsy message containing one of Ed Garrison's clippings from the *Tacoma News Tribune.* Bill read it to himself, laughing as he paraphrased it for his wife, "Ha! Ha! My friend, Warren Larson, finally won that Tall Tale Contest in Seattle. He received the trophy for 1952 and a grand prize - a tugboat painting. Should I read the tall tale aloud? It's included in the article."

"Yes, let's hear it," Mae agreed readily, then added with a wry smile, "But don't embellish the story as you tell it. Just read what is written."

"NIGHTMARE DELUXE"

It all happened back in the good old days before the war, 1941, in fact. I was a junior deckhand on the *Foss 16.* I won't mention the skipper's name for security reasons; the mate was R.E., now running a boat in Shelton, and Elmer E., now skipper of the *Carl Foss*, was cook.

At the time of this story the *Foss 16* was on a steady tow from Shelton to Townsend. Everything went smoothly as long as we were home at least once a week, and the skipper didn't run out of things for the crew to do.

One cold, windy night we were storm bound in Still Harbor. We'd been there four days with 14 inches of ice and snow on the deck. The company was yelling "Townsend needs the logs!" and the crew had the worst case of "channel fever" I'd ever heard of. Elmer, doing his best to keep things in hand, made doughnuts that evening.

I had just laid down in my bunk when the skipper started the engine and hollered for the deckhand to get the *¢#%& anchor up. A half hour or so later I awakened to hear the skipper's tender voice screaming, "Run out all your wire and hook it to anything that'll hold our weight! Then get two 30 foot logs out of the tow and run them under the boat to use as axles."

Again that gentle voice: "Don't tell me what you think, just do what I tell you, or you'll shine the bilge for a week!! Now get eight of those doughnuts from the cook and inflate them to 150 pounds each. Don't just stand there and stare, you &?%*¢, you sick or something?"

When I looked out of my window, low and behold, we were passing Jason Lee School. What a spectacle we were making of ourselves; a tug was rolling on doughnuts with 24 sections of logs behind down the main street. I dropped back in bed. This was too much!

The dispatcher was saying, "Okay, if you're that far in, make it fast to Movie Star Island, and come on in."

Skipper replied: "*Foss 16* off and clear. Thank you, operator."

It so happens, as any towboatman knows, that Movie Star Island is located at 9th and Broadway. When I looked out the door, we were coming down St. Helen's Avenue, and we were really rolling. The deckhand was on the tail of the tow with a line in one hand and a pevy in the other. The voice from above threatened, "If he misses that fire plug, I'll skin him alive!"

The next thing I knew someone was shaking me saying, "We're in! Going home?"

That for the books, is how that fireplug was torn from its mooring and why that log was lying in front of the Roxy Theater the next day. I know, I was there!"

"Hee! Hee! It's kind of funny, but isn't it awfully dumb?" Mae asked, shaking her head in consternation.

"Tall tales are supposed to be fanciful to be truly appreciated. I told you my old buddy has a wild imagination. Now I wonder if I can believe Mom's postscript. Warren told her they lost his trophy and his grand prize. Another tall tale?"

Greg's awakening noises ended their impromptu holiday sojourn into the world of letters, Bill thinking ahead to their first guest reservations in just six weeks. Tomorrow he'd tackle that list of chores he'd been scribbling on an old piece of butcher paper.

Chapter
Nine

Consecutive sunny days in April were rare, and as Bill trolled off Duke Point, he bemoaned the lack of guests at Pardue's Lodge. He rambled on at the fish that weren't biting this morning, "Damned salmon! Won't bite on a nice day like today. Wonder if you'll be more cooperative when the Blakely party is here in two weeks."

He chuckled at his talking to himself, but continued in a pessimistic yet cheerful tone, "Probably won't be able to fish out here because the weather will be lousy."

His one-sided conversation with the local fish population was disrupted by the drone of an approaching outboard from the south. At first Bill believed that Ed Hill was coming over by boat, but then he remembered his neighbor had been to play with Greg on Sunday, the frequency of his visits negating their classification as an event. Ed claimed "Dutch Uncle" privileges, enthralling the lad with story after story. Ed's behavior was reminiscent of their stay at the Boca de Quadra cannery, minus the beer incentive.

Besides, the oncoming craft carried two men, soon identifiable as Tsimchuck and Malcolm, both waving comfortably as the distance closed. Malcolm idled his motor as his boat circled the fisherman, calling out, "Hi Bill! Grandpa guarantees the sunshine will last two more days, until Thursday at least. He insisted on fishing at his old haunt by Duke Island, and, of course, he wants to meet Gregori's namesake."

Bill nodded enthusiastically as he pulled in his line and replied, "Sure, you're welcome to stay as long as you like. Our cabin is ready, but our first customers won't be here for awhile. How have you two been?"

"Ho! Ho! My grandson has been very busy this winter. I'll have another great-grandson by fall," Tsimchuck joked, a lively spirit showing through his aged features. He held himself straight with head high and chin set, posing for Bill to show his dominant control of a withered body.

"Is that a fact or another of your Grandpa's predictions, Mal?"

Malcolm smiled broadly, announcing, "Annie is expecting in September, but Grandpa knew before I did - probably just a good guess."

"It was no guess - I knew. Now let's quit jabbering and go see Gregori," Tsimchuck retorted.

Mae was surprised and happy when she met her visitors at the landing, doubly so when they produced gifts for Gregori and fresh fruit and vegetables for their board. She kissed each friend on the cheek and led them up to the house to see her napping son. Their admiring comments soon woke Gregori, who entertained everyone while Mae cooked dinner.

Bill opened the gift which the men had brought to the Pardues and held up a rather large blue sleeper.

Malcolm explained, "Annie sent something for Gregori to grow into. She's knitting a smaller version for ours."

Mae teased from across the room, "Is it pink or blue, Malcolm?"
"Blue, of course. Annie is very determined to present me with a son. Indians prefer boy children, doesn't everyone? But I like girls, too," Malcolm ruminated.

A Tsimshian scarf slid out of the wrapping paper, Tsimchuck quick to say, "That's my family talisman, like the one Helen gave Bill that time. Father and son will share good fortune in their life together."

ᵀ ᵀ ᵀ

As Malcolm shoved his boat into the bay in preparation for departure, he remarked on Brownie's absence during the past two days, "A visit to Cottage Cove doesn't seem complete without an appearance by your pet bear. Where do you suppose he is, Bill?"

"I'd say he's hibernating in his den, except we saw him a couple of weeks ago. Of course he was skinny and sort of crotchety. He came and went in a moment - as usual with a chunk of halibut in his jaws," Bill answered, and with a bemused expression, he added, "Ed Hill told me that Brownie growled at him one day on the trail."

Malcolm shrugged and suggested, "Next time Grandpa and I will catch a salmon for Brownie. He'll show up for that feast. Well, so long, we'll see you in June." He cast off his line and cranked up the outboard, the two men waving as they motored out of the bay, heading for home.

ᵀ ᵀ ᵀ

As a twilight glow shimmered on the rippling waters of Ray Anchorage, an airplane engine could be heard over Revillagigedo Channel, the Pardues eyeing each other with anticipation as the sound penetrated the cabin walls.

"I believe that's Alan Harkins delivering our supply order," Mae said hopefully.

Bill nodded happily and wondered, "The plane is on a landing approach, I reckon. Why is he arriving so late in the day? Come with me to meet the plane, honey, Greg's still napping."

The silvery float plane splashed down in a practiced manner, taxiing toward the dock with hands waving out the cabin windows.

"Isn't that Daddy beside Alan? And who's that in the back seat?" Mae questioned excitedly, a surprise visit by her father most welcome.

Bill muttered a puzzled answer, "I'm not sure, dear. Is that Olaf behind Gene? Come on, Mae, you claim the best eyesight around here."

"Ha! Ha! Except when I get excited. Yes, I believe you're right, Olaf is behind Daddy. And maybe that's Aaron beside his uncle."

As the propeller jerked to a stop, Bill ran out on the dock to help Gene secure the plane, a hasty handshake their only greeting. To all four men, he shouted, "Welcome guys! You're kind of late. Are you fishing with me in the morning?"

Alan called back from his seat, "You bet, Bill. It was the only day Big Swede and I could make it. We're both due back in Ketchikan tomorrow noon."

"But I get to stay for a whole week, and Uncle Olaf talked Julia into letting the kid miss school," Gene added with a grin.

Aaron stuck his head out of the rear of the cabin as he passed along supply bundles, "Hi, Bill, Mae. Where's Gregori? And Brownie?"

"Greg's napping and Brownie's absent, but I reckon we're all fine," Bill replied, suggesting to his wife, "You'd better get back to Greg. Take Grandpa with you. The rest of us can handle these supplies."

π π π

Gene cradled his cooing grandson in his arms as Mae cleared the table, fresh vegetables and Julia's apple pie having made dinner seem a feast. Alan had been loquacious as he reported items of late news, including his sighting of the *MacDonald* and barge passing through Tongass Narrows on its northerly run to Valdez.

"Went through during a torrential rainstorm just five or six days ago. I guess its California towing work is over." Alan paused as he changed the subject, "Say, did you hear that Alaska Territory has a new governor? Ike appointed B. Frank Heintzleman earlier this month. The Republicans are filling a lot of offices although Bartlett is still our delegate to the U.S. Congress."

Bill was quick to ask, "Is Eisenhower for Alaskan statehood? I haven't heard his position yet."

Alan shrugged, giving a mixed answer, "Yes and no, politics being what they are. He's reportedly pro-statehood for both Alaska and Hawaii, but members of his cabinet keep talking about a commonwealth status, like Puerto Rico was given last year. Ike's okay, but Estes Kefauver is Alaska's true friend. His support a couple of years ago almost got us statehood. I keep worrying that politics will be Alaska's downfall."

Those gathered around the table nodded in silent agreement, Gene finally speaking, passing along a surprise announcement, "Bill, Charley said to tell you that he and Alexis are expecting in the fall. Something about San Francisco and its Golden Gate being a romantic vacation spot. Anyway, all appears well with the Blakelys. As a matter of fact, John Furrer is planning a trip to Tahiti after the baby is born, which means Charley will be managing the mill before year's end."

"That is good news, Gene. I guess the lumber business is booming," Bill replied.

"Yes, it is, and I expect our economy to remain healthy as long as there is war in Korea. The Furrer Mill is a Ketchikan mainstay, with Charley lining up customers in the lower forty-eight states while I keep finding new stands of timber to harvest," Gene explained, and looking at his grandson, he added, "But tell me about the resort business. Are you ready for sportsmen? How about plain tourists?"

"We've got lots of guests through the Fourth of July holiday. The Blakelys are bringing Banker Thompson and Lawyer Wilson next month to open the season, and the Carlson family has reserved the entire lodge for the first week in July. Who's all coming, Aaron?"

The teenager was pleased to be included in the conversation, announcing, "Mom, Dad, Uncle Olaf, Mister Furrer and I are coming for sure. And Dad's invited Mister Blakely, he likes your place, and Einar, the dynamiter, to be our guests."

"And I'm coming, too," Gene inserted, adding with a grin, "You'll have a full house, Daughter."

Aaron continued with hardly a pause, "Good news, folks, I've been helping Dad with reservations, and Pardue's Lodge is full through July. Letters of inquiry keep coming in to the store. I bet August is full by the time we get back to Ketchikan. Dad says your business is a 'going concern.' Isn't that neat?"

"Yes, it certainly is. Maybe I can afford a diesel generator for electricity next season. Will your mother let you work for me this summer, Aaron?" Bill queried.

Grinning with anticipation, the young man confirmed his employment, "Sure, after school is out, but I have to be home by August the twenty-first. We're going down to Seattle for a Carlson-Nelson family reunion."

"Fair enough, Aaron. I bet your Grandpa and Grandma Nelson are hosting the gathering in Ballard, aren't they? You'll relish their Scandinavian smorgasbord. I wish we could visit my family in Tacoma this year," Bill mused wishfully, looking over at Mae.

She responded affirmatively, "The three of us can fly south at the end of the season if Roy and Aaron keep booking customers. Gregori needs to meet his grandparents - and vice versa."

Olaf interrupted the Pardues with a proposition, "Say, don't spend all your profits before I tell you about the twenty-one foot cruiser I've found for Pardue's Lodge. A fellow in Juneau owes me a favor and offered me first crack at buying his boat - he's moving to Fairbanks. It's powered by a hundred-and-fifty horse marine engine, has a single cabin which sleeps four and deck space for five or six fishermen. Roy's checked with your banker, and he's cleared its purchase, but we have to close the deal before next Wednesday. Are you in a buying mood?"

Gene urged acceptance of Olaf's offer, "Sounds like a good deal. Olaf knows boats, and his endorsement convinced me. I can stay over with Mae and Gregori for a few days while you look the boat over."

"What's your friend's price? Mae and I don't mind a little debt, but this deal may overextend our credit. We'll have to install a fuel tank for that big an outfit," Bill replied with consideration and a glance at his wife.

Happily pushing his friend toward a bigger and better business, Olaf chuckled a retort, "Ha! Ha! Not so much, only six thousand dollars. And you'll need two fuel tanks, gasoline for the boat motors and diesel oil for your generator-to-be. Are you ready to fly up to Juneau with me tomorrow?"

"Let me sleep on it, Olaf. Mae and I need a little thinking time. Besides, early to bed goes well with early to rise. See you all at six o'clock in the morning," Bill said as the guests filed out the door headed for their bunks.

π   π   π

Bill should have been weary after his busy day, fishing in the morning and then flying to Ketchikan, but he felt full of energy. While Alan and Olaf refueled the plane and Aaron hurried home, the prospective boat purchaser telephoned John Thompson, receiving more encouragement to expand his business.

As he hung up, a waving figure walked onto the pier, Roy Carlson calling out in a teasing tone, "Hi Bill! Has that nosy Big Swede convinced you to buy that boat?"

Bill grinned at the jibe, answering in kind, "Ho! Ho! And what's Little Swede been up to? John Thompson tells me you've been talking to him."

"True! Quite true! I'm a busybody, too, but you'll love the deal I've found for a generator. Just what you're looking for, and the banker agrees, doesn't he?"

"Yes, as you well know, you and Olaf are. . ."

"Don't look a gift horse in the mouth, Bill Pardue," Olaf interrupted with a slap on the back, "With my brother and me lending a hand, and the bank manager agreeing with our business acumen, you'll be a famous innkeeper in no time."

Roy chuckled and piped in, "Ha! Ha! He's right for a change, except we all know Daylight Bill is already famous." All three friends laughed companionably, Bill just shaking his head in wonder, silently accepting his friends' good offers. He'd find a way to thank them later.

Abruptly, Roy snapped his fingers, recalling aloud, "Don Wilson says to wait for him. He'll handle your paperwork in exchange for a free ride to the territorial capital.

π   π   π

Roy's figure diminished in size as the plane roared over the choppy waters of Tongass Narrows, climbing steadily on a northerly heading. Noise again moderated, and Don Wilson returned to his patter of light jokes, Alan ignoring the big man since he'd heard the comedy routine many times. However, Bill and Olaf provided laughter enough to fuel the lawyer's performing ego, and Don didn't slow down until Alan stood the plane on a wing tip, showing them a dramatic view of Mendenhall Glacier glistening in the bright sunlight.

The pilot declared, "I've seen that glacier a dozen times and never seen it so beautiful."

He banked one more time and flew down the face of the majestic ice mass, silence in the cabin testifying to its magnificence.

Don finally broke the spell by shuffling papers in his briefcase, handing Bill a document entitled "Bill of Sale."

Reading its print carefully, Bill soon frowned in confusion, querying, "If I'm buying a generator from the Hard Luck Mine on the Stikine River, how do I get it to Cottage Cove?"

Don smiled benevolently, handing his client a contract form and proclaiming, "Your contractor will transport it and two fuel tanks to the lodge when he goes south to build the generator housing and lay the fuel lines. It's all one big deal. You need to sign both copies; Mae's signature isn't needed."

Bill threw up his hands in mock frustration but signed on both dotted lines. As he returned the papers to Don, he accepted another form, the lawyer instructing him, "This title document for the boat will need Mae's signature as well as yours. Send it to my office after your wife signs it. In the meantime here's a bill of sale which will suffice tomorrow."

Bill accepted the last paper with distaste, muttering *sotto voce*, "All this mumbo-jumbo! Can't we just buy the damned boat? And generator?"

"Hee! Hee! Lawyers have to make a living, too, Bill," Don retorted in good humor, reminding his friend, "You're a businessman in Alaska, not a chechako."

Olaf laughed outright, pointing to the bill of sale and teasing, "You're a chechako unless you rename the boat. See, it's called *'Chechako Dream.'* The owner has lived up here for about as long as you have, Bill. Are you going to change her name?"

"Ha! Ha! No, I like the name. You guys are always calling me a chechako, and I have my dream of Pardue's Lodge riding on this boat's financing. *Chechako Dream* is apropos. That is, if I decide to buy it."

Everyone laughed at his feeble last-ditch attempt at independence, himself included. Bill was committed to the course of action, and both he and his friends knew it.

π   π   π

"Where has the sun gone?" Bill lamented aloud as he navigated the gray pall of Frederick Sound in the *Chechako Dream*, still hoping to reach Wrangell before the visibility was gone. "I need gas and a good night's rest before I tackle any more rain and fog."

In his mind he reviewed his grandiose scheme to sail night and day south to Cottage Cove, recalling Olaf's suggestion that he take it slow and easy. The ferry skipper reminded him that he would be alone on his voyage through waterways strange to him, saying, "Don't bite off more than you can chew, Bill. You're not an experienced pilot even with those fine nautical charts you purchased. Safety first is a good motto."

The following hour seemed interminable, one twinkle, then two, soon turning into an irregular pattern of lights which could only be Wrangell. Bill steered a course for the bright orange Union 76 sign, and a teenager wordlessly tied the *Chechako Dream* to the pier as an older man stood ready at the gas pump.

"Want me to fill her up, stranger? Say, is that a Norberg 150 power plant?" the gasoline dealer asked.

"Yes, to both questions. Is there a place around here where I can moor for the night? I need a little sleep," Bill replied as he sat on the edge of the pier.

"Stay right here if you like. I'm closing up after I finish fueling your boat. How do you like the Norberg? A lot of boats use it, I know," the man queried conversationally, changing tone abruptly to call out to the lad, "Bobby, run home and tell your mother I'll be home in fifteen minutes."

Bill waited until the boy was on his way before offering, "My wife likes to know the dinner hour ahead of time also. About the Norberg, it's been running well today, but I just bought this rig up in Juneau and haven't had much experience with inboard engines. What do you know about it?"

"Well, I hear it's got plenty of get-up-and-go, but fairly guzzles gas when you use all that power. There we are, tank's full up. That'll be twenty-three fifty. Not too bad for the run down from Juneau."

Bill handed the correct change to the dealer and bid him a goodnight, belatedly remembering to thank him for the overnight berth. "Anytime" was the mumbled reply as the man turned off the lights and walked away.

Laughing wryly to himself, he thought, *'I should have asked if there's a cafe nearby. All I've got aboard is a day-old sandwich, can of red kidney beans and warmed-over coffee. Oh well, I'll make do with beans tonight and bologna in the morning. Sleep is what I really need.'*

ᵀᵀ   ᵀᵀ   ᵀᵀ

Bill cast off his spring line and maneuvered the *Chechako Dream* through a flotilla of fishing boats leaving the harbor. Daylight was but an hour old when he opened the throttle slowly and ran into the clear waters of Stikine Strait, finally increasing his speed until he was fairly flying over the white caps. After a few minutes of racing, he slowed to normal speed, his gasoline gauge showing the effects of fuel consumption during full power usage. He guessed he could travel at twenty-five knots if he needed to, but half-speed was much more economical.

By noon he was well into Clarence Strait and the sun had made its appearance for the day, clouds now obscuring its rays entirely, In the distance he could make out a tug and barge traveling south before him, and with wishful thinking, assumed it was the *MacDonald.*

Once again increasing the Norberg's revolutions, his boat soon overtook the slower vessel, his hopes fulfilled when he identified his old towboat. He passed the trailing barge and tooted his horn, its automobile sound carrying to the tug. He eased alongside the stern, where Ray appeared to secure two ropes to the tug's starboard cleats. Bill cut his engine and scampered over the bow onto the *MacDonald.*

"Hey, Slim, that's some cruiser you're sporting there. How come you're so far from home?" Ray asked curiously as Cookie and Dick called greetings from the mess doorway.

Bill shook hands and said hello to his former shipmates, meeting a few new men as he asked and answered questions for half an hour. Cookie fed him a meal of leftovers which tasted like a gourmet meal - he was hungry, and Elmer talked him into a game of poker when Jack went on watch. By the time they entered Tongass Narrows, Bill was thirteen dollars poorer, about the same amount as his gasoline savings for hitching a ride.

The skipper walked aft with Bill, happy to be sailing in Alaska, but lamenting the Korean War, "Slim, we had a fine trip north and almost stopped to say hello at Cottage Cove. I think my port captain may send us to Pearl Harbor next week. It's got a damaged destroyer destined for the Bremerton Naval Yard. That war is pure hell, we heard that Harry was killed in action a couple of months ago. Not like World War Two when we fought to win."

"I'm sorry about Harry. He was a good man. It brings the war closer to home. We are sort of provincial up here," Bill replied.

"If you mean you like your peace and quiet, I agree. That's why I like the Tacoma - Valdez run," Elmer concluded, seizing one of the *Chechako Dream's* ropes and pulling the boat close enough for Bill to leap onto her bow decking. Their conversation ceased as the boats separated, Bill hurrying to his cockpit to start the Norberg before the barge overtook his craft. He still had another half hour before he would dock in Ketchikan, the gateway city barely visible to the south.

ᴫ   ᴫ   ᴫ

Overnight at the Carlsons provided Bill an opportunity to hear Julia's news at dinner and compare it with Alexis' gossip later in the evening. Charley didn't say much, appearing happy to let his wife carry the conversation during their short visit.

Bill and Roy were up at the crack of dawn, going over their butcher paper lists. By ten o'clock, Bill and Aaron had loaded the boat with over a ton of supplies.

"See you in a couple of weeks, Aaron," Bill called as he cast off a mooring line and swung his wheel over, turning his bow into the Narrows and speeding up. He was on his way home.

Bill mentally compared his first trip to Cottage Cove in a badly over-loaded open boat with the *Chechako Dream*. He thought, *'No doubt about it, I was lucky to make it to my homestead without an ac - cident or an incident, either was a possibility. Now that I'm well-equipped, I'd better not run afoul of bad weather or a lurking shoal. I've got my next three years income tied up in this boat and its cargo.'

After the previous two days' travel, the third day seemed routine, Bill passing familiar landmarks, comfortable in his progress down the middle of Revillagigedo Channel. Arriving home early enough to take his family for a joy ride, he demonstrated the boat's power in a speed run across Ray Anchorage to Pardue's Lodge. It was his moment of festive play before he settled down to a summer of all work.

π   π   π

The next morning Bill lit a fire in his smokehouse, soon mixing green alder in the crackling blaze. Gene handed him salmon fillets from his morning catch, and Bill quickly spread the morsels on the screened trays inside the roughhewn structure, billowing smoke bringing tears to his eyes.

Gene smiled at his son-in-law's efforts and advised in a teasing manner, "I usually fill the fish trays before throwing alder on the fire."

"Ha! Ha! Me too, but I'm in a hurry. It looks like Alan won't pick you up today. If he comes late enough tomorrow, you guys will have a load of smoked salmon to take to Blackjack. Besides, this chechako is hungry for a piece himself," Bill kidded back.

He now inveigled Gene into helping him with a series of heavy chores where two strong backs accomplished a lot of work. When Mae called them for lunch, Bill was feeding alder to the smokehouse firepot and responded quickly. Gene was cleaning silt out of their water tank by the creek and called out, "Give me five minutes, Daughter."

Time passed without Gene appearing, causing Mae to suggest, "Maybe you should go help Dad. The meat is getting. . .oh darn! Gregori's awake. Will you change his diaper while I warm the stew up?"

Both were engaged in their separate tasks when Gene yelled something from behind the house, his voice drowned out by a bear's challenging scream.

"Here, take Greg," Bill said as he handed his son to Mae and dashed out the door.

Gene was backing slowly around the smokehouse, speaking conversationally to the bear hidden from Bill's view, "Good old Brownie, easy does it fella. I'm a friend, easy old friend."

Stepping forward to side with Gene, Bill was greeted by a like roar from Brownie, who rose on hind legs and pawed the air threateningly.

"Look behind him, Bill, he's got. . .er. . .she's got two little black cubs with her. Brownie's a girl, and a mighty cantankerous mother with us men."

A half roar sounded as Mae and Gregori joined them, Brownie dropping to all fours and twitching her nose at a strange scent. She lumbered forward a dozen steps, black cubs playfully following, not at all disturbed by humans as long as their mother was with them. Another series of sniffs brought forth what Bill thought to be a friendly grunt.

"Well, old girl, your family must be hungry. Do you want some almost-smoked salmon?" Bill asked in a calm voice.

Brownie roared another complaint, not really threatening, but unsociable nevertheless. Mae answered with authority, "Be quiet, Brownie. Gregori and I will give you a hunk of salmon."

Brownie shook her head, Bill thought in agreement, and waited patiently for her handout. Mae walked slowly to the smokehouse door and opened it wide, letting the accumulated smoke escape skyward. With a set of tongs she grasped a large piece of fish and carried it toward the three bears until Brownie fidgeted by shuffling her forepaws.

Mae threw the salmon halfway to the bruin mother, who cocked her head aslant and studied Gregori with her inherently poor eyesight for several moments. The boy waved his arms and squealed playfully, Brownie listening and sniffing as Mae walked backward to the men.

Through comparing their young, the bear picked up the salmon and led her brood across the field into the forest toward Duke Hill.

"She's likely going to her den. I expect we know where she's been these past months," Bill stated as he shook his head in amazement and then addressing Mae, "You two females got along fine looking over each other's younguns, but Gene and I were warned to stay clear of those cubs. Cute rascals, weren't they, even if they were twenty-five pounds or so?"

π π π

Alan arrived twenty-four hours later, bringing supplies, mail and a message that the contractor was on his way, and then taking away Gene, a batch of smoked salmon and signed title papers for the *Chechako Dream* to be given to Don Wilson.

Gene shouted from the plane's float before he climbed into the cabin, "I'll tell Alan here and everyone I see, about the Pardue family and the bear family living side by side on Cottage Cove. It'll be great for business!"

Harkins plane was a distant spot in the sky when the couple heard a familiar rumble from the smokehouse, followed by Greg's answering squeal of laughter from his crib. Bill went inside to pick up his son, and together they joined Mae in the field where she threw salmon chunks to their three bruin friends. Both families were enjoying the good life of Alaska.

Epilogue

A chechako is commonly defined as a newcomer to Alaska, a greenhorn or a rookie being reasonable synonyms for the term. World War Two veterans settling on territorial homesteads often fit this category; men seeking their fortunes in the Klondike Gold Rush at the turn of the century were chechakos until they had wintered a season or two up north. Many men and women worked summers and carried their earnings back to the lower forty-eight states to spend and were classified as outsiders.

Tribal objections to Alaska's land policy received scant attention from their territorial government until after the Second World War. Statehood in 1959, national forestry boundaries and the Native Village Corporation Act of 1974 were a few milestones in the recognition of their claims.

Descriptions of Duke Island, Ray Anchorage and their surroundings are portrayed with reasonable accuracy, Cottage Cove and Pardue's Lodge being fictional personifications of post-war Alaska.

Black bears inhabit the islands of southeastern Alaska, adults weighing up to three hundred pounds and having brown or black coats of heavy fur. Brownie shouldn't be confused with the brown or Kodiak bears located further north. This grizzly variety can weigh two or three thousand pounds of grit, bone and muscle, standing on its hind legs to a height of eight feet. The southernly black bear is rarely ferocious, except in defense of its young and is seldom a threat to humans.

Father William Duncan and the Tsimshian people migrated to Annette Island in 1887. Ernest Gruening, B. Frank Heintzleman and E. L. Bartlett were actual government officials of the era, and Big Dolly and Curly were colorful characters of Ketchikan's famous Creek Street. Doctor R. Franklin Thompson was President of the College of Puget Sound (later to become a university) for two or three generations of students. Warren Larson is an Old Tacoma fisherman and tugboat captain well-known throughout the Puget Sound and North Pacific waters. His tall tale first appeared in *Piling Busters*, a publication of the northwest tugboaters in 1952.

All individual Indians join Bill Pardue, his family, his friends and assorted characters in the fictionalized version of the period.

Historical
Perspective

Across the prehistoric and legendary land bridge between two great continents came early man to Alaska millennia ago. Slowly the seeds of primitive civilizations grew throughout the vast expanse of the region: Eskimo villages along the northern shores on the Bering Sea and the Arctic Ocean, the Aleuts in the island chain stretching westward, the Athabascan Indians of the interior plains and valleys and the Tlingit Indians in the coastal islands to the south. Each group of people adapted to the exigencies of their home environment, accommodating their lifestyles to the sea, land and climate of their territory during the thousands of years prior to the arrival of European explorers.

Spanish ships touched along the north Pacific shoreline but briefly during the 1700's, preferring the warmer climates of Mexico and California. The more curious English explored the region in greater detail, but it was the Tsar's Danish captain, Vitus Bering, who chartered the hazardous reaches of the frozen north and claimed North America for Russia. Eventually the Russian Fur Company spread its tentacles along the coastline from the Eskimo villages of the Bering Sea to the rain forest of southeast Alaska, Sitka becoming its headquarters in America. A single attempt to expand south resulted in a fur and agriculture venture at Fort Ross, north of San Francisco Bay. Its distance from Sitka and lack of support from the company managers resulted in its failure after a few years.

During the early nineteenth century, the overlapping claims of Spain and Russia were disputed by England's Hudson's Bay Company and an influx of upstart Yankees. When the United States obtained the Louisiana Purchase from France, Americans took a more active interest in the area west of the Mississippi, including the Pacific coast.

Explorers Meriweather Lewis and William Clark, fur trader John Jacob Astor and Christian missionaries Marcus Whitman and Jason Lee were samples of the vanguard of American interests in the far west. With the Oregon Trail and the California gold rush, Americans soon became the dominant populace from San Francisco Bay to the Puget Sound.

Spanish-Mexican control waned before the American Civil War, with the Russians losing interest in Alaska during the same period. Times were changing for colonialism in North America, and in 1867 the Tsar sold his claims in Alaska for seven million dollars to the United States in a sale most Americans dubbed "Seward's Folly," or "Seward's Icebox."

Perhaps because such an indignant designation represented popular opinion of the time, an anomaly of government for the newly acquired land resulted over the next forty years. Alaska was neither "fish nor fowl," subsisting as an enigma in United States expansionist policy.

Into this no man's land of southeastern Alaska in 1887, Tsimshian Indians migrated from British Columbia to Annette Island, locating north of the newly created boundary line between Canada and the United States. Led by the Anglican minister, Father William Duncan, and his missionary family, the tribe settled on land held by its Tlingit and Haida cousins. Around the newly built town of Metlakatla, the Tsimshians continued their fishing culture and soon developed a fledgling lumber industry.

A decade later hardy souls seeking gold struck it rich in the small streams of Alaska's southeastern coast, the Klondike, and the Yukon. Change came quickly to the territory as tens of thousands of adventurers left Seattle and San Francisco to prospect for the elusive yellow treasure. Most travelers sailed the Inland Passage to Skagway or Dyer to begin the overland trek to Dawson, requiring transit through British Columbia waters and Yukon wilderness. Canadians' patience was put to the test as fortune hunters of all nationalities swarmed north to gold fields where American territorial governance was almost nil.

Recognition of Alaska as a treasure house brought the territory a new form of government, a voteless delegate in Congress authorized in 1906, and the territorial legislature formed in 1912. Natives still outnumbered white settlers during the first half of the twentieth century, although stateside interests invested in the territory's development and subsequently controlled its resources.

World War Two brought military defense to the forefront, the federal government pouring vast sums of money and materials into its northern front. It provided financial spur for the ensuing decade and gave rise to a cry for statehood.

The villages and towns of the Alaskan Panhandle were centers for the mining, timber and fishing industries, becoming destinations as well as ports of call. Juneau served as the government seat as well as the site of a major gold mining operation, Sitka continued its role as a lumber and fishing port of Baranov Island, and Ketchikan produced lumber and canned king salmon. Since it was the first United States port on the Inland Passage, Ketchikan was given the sobriquet, "Gateway to Alaska."

This gateway city was built on the western hillside of rugged Revillagigedo Island, and its main street ran along the waterfront with houses clustered on the hillside behind it.

Tongass Narrows separates the city from Gravina Island and Pennock Island, opening into Revillagigedo Channel which winds southeast past Annette Island toward Canada, a myriad of smaller islands dotting the seascape around Dixon Entrance and its more tempestuous waters.

During the late forties, veterans moved into this area and other sections of Alaska, seeking jobs, homes and open land, with the vast wilderness appearing to be available for settlement. Many people worked in the summer and went "down below" in the winter. The territorial legislature enacted a tax law for resident and non-resident workers alike, payment in deductions on wages equal to ten percent of their federal income tax. Alaska needed resources to develop programs which would convince the United States Congress that it was ready for statehood.

The territorial government responded to the young veterans, its new breed of citizens, by granting homesite claims. Indian objections to such land sales quickly arose to stymie the homesteading dreams of most chechakos, although intermittent sales of Alaskan land continued until 1982.

Proponents for statehood gained the ear of Congress, which proposed bills in 1948, 1950 and 1955, the last effort including Hawaii. Both were considered for a commonwealth status similar to that granted Puerto Rico in 1952, but statehood forces maintained their goal and were successful when President Dwight D. Eisenhower signed the Alaska bill on July 7, 1958. After fall elections to fill government offices, Alaska officially became a state on January 3, 1959.